The Times Calendar Cookbook

Katie Stewart was born in Scotland. After taking a domestic science course in Aberdeen, she moved to London to study for a diploma in catering and home management. She took a job with a family in France to perfect her French and then went to the Cordon Bleu school in Paris to take the Cordon Bleu diploma. Back in England she worked as a test supervisor for Nestlé and soon had the opportunity of going to New York, where she learnt about food photography and American foods and methods of cooking, later touring the United States to study regional cookery. On her return to England, Katie Stewart began a career in journalism. She became cookery editor of *Woman's Mirror*, then joined *Woman's Journal*, and for several years now has been food correspondent of *The Times*. Her writing and her television programmes – practical, funny and refreshingly free of gimmickry – provide her with a very busy working life. She lives in Sussex and has a son.

Other cookery books available in Pan

Batia Asher and Carole Robson	**Canny Cooking**
Kathy Barnes	**The Infra-red Cook Book**
Mrs Beeton	**All About Cookery**
Carol Bowen	**The Microwave Cook Book**
Kathleen Broughton	**Pressure Cooking Day by Day**
Lousene Rousseau Brunner	**New Casserole Treasury**
Savitri Chowdhary	**Indian Cooking**
Gail Duff	**Fresh all the Year** **Gail Duff's Vegetarian Cookbook**
Gay Firth and Jane Donald	**What's for Lunch, Mum?**
Theodora Fitzgibbon	**A Taste of Ireland A Taste of London** **A Taste of Scotland A Taste of Wales** **A Taste of the West Country A Taste of Paris** **A Taste of Rome A Taste of Yorkshire** **A Taste of the Lake District Crockery Pot Cooking**
Michel Guérard	**Michel Guérard's Cuisine Minceur**
Antony and Araminta Hippisley Coxe	**The Book of the Sausage**
Robin Howe	**Soups**
Rosemary Hume and Muriel Downes	**The Cordon Bleu Book of Jams, Preserves and Pickles**
Patricia Jacobs	**The Best Bread Book**
Enrica and Vernon Jarratt	**The Complete Book of Pasta**
George Lassalle	**The Adventurous Fish Cook**
Kenneth Lo	**Cheap Chow**
Claire Loewenfeld and Philippa Back	**Herbs for Health and Cookery**
edited by R. J. Minney	**The George Bernard Shaw Vegetarian Cook Book**
edited by Bee Nilson	**The WI Diamond Jubilee Cookbook**
Marguerite Patten	**Learning to Cook**
Jennie Reekie	**Traditional French Cooking**
Evelyn Rose	**The Complete International Jewish Cookbook**
Rita G. Springer	**Caribbean Cookbook**
Constance Spry and Rosemary Hume	**The Constance Spry Cookery Book**
Katie Stewart	**The Times Cookery Book**
Marika Hanbury-Tenison	**Deep-Freeze Sense** **Deep-Freeze Cookery**

Katie Stewart

The Times
Calendar Cookbook

Pan Books London and Sydney

First published 1975 by The Hamlyn Publishing Group Ltd
in association with Times Books
This edition published 1977 by Pan Books Ltd,
Cavaye Place, London SW10 9PG
3rd printing 1980
© Times Newspapers Ltd 1975
ISBN 0 330 25200 3
Set, printed and bound in Great Britain by
Cox & Wyman Ltd, Reading

Contents

Introduction

Fruit, vegetables, meat, fish and game mature according to the seasons and over the year offer us a wide variety of fresh foods to use in recipes. To use food 'in season' means buying the best quality at the most reasonable price, and this is what enables us to add variety to our menus and ring the changes in the meals we eat throughout the year.

Readers who used and enjoyed *The Times* Cook's Calendars will find some of the most popular recipes from them included here. Like the calendars, this book is built round the twelve months of the year, each month containing recipes suited to the climate of the season and making use of the fresh ingredients available and of good quality at the moment.

Gardeners who grow their own fruit and vegetables appreciate their marvellous fresh flavours – tender young leeks in early spring, the first new potatoes and sweet young carrots of summer. It's mainly around the seasons for home-grown produce that the chapters in this book have been planned, and each month I have given recipes for the fruit and vegetables which should be at their peak then. Cooks who don't grow their own produce should find the same home-grown foods available in the shops.

Nowadays of course fresh foods are imported from all over the world during our winters, so that most things are available all year round, although they may be expensive. This means that we can have almost any food out of its season, and it would be true to say that all the recipes in the book can be made at any time of the year. On the other hand, many foods are most suited to a particular season, and no-one feels like heavy puddings and casseroles in a heatwave or cold soups in the middle of January.

There has been another most important development in recent years, and this is of course the boom in home freezing. The ability to store surplus fruit and vegetables from the garden to brighten up winter menus, to stock up with meat when the price is reasonable, to set aside a spring chicken or some game for a dinner party, or to cook ahead for Christmas or another occasion are just some of the advantages of owning a freezer. At the end of each month are notes on making the best use of the freezer at that time of the year. I have concentrated mainly on the preparation and storage of fresh foods rather than on recipes, though these do get a mention. This is because prepared recipes have a limited keeping life, determined by the type of recipe and the ingredients. Fresh foods on the other hand have a longer storage life, in many cases until the next season starts. A supply of fresh foods in the freezer gives the cook the freedom to plan menus spontaneously, and it's a wise cook who stocks the freezer in summer with new vegetables and soft fruits so that she can add freshness and flavour to winter menus.

Freshness and quality should be top priority for recipe ingredients, and you should cook and serve foods using methods that enhance textures and flavours. Summer vegetables are often best served simply to show off their delicate flavours. Many are delicious served as first courses in oil and vinegar dressings. Main-crop root vegetables are good buys in winter months and are marvellous for baking or roasting; they need a little more dressing up but make lovely casseroles and soups.

Summer soft fruits have a short season; they can be eaten fresh or cooked to make the most delicious compotes, mousses and ice creams. They can be preserved in the form of jams and jellies, or frozen for later in the year. Cold weather means hot puddings and pies, and nothing can beat our lovely autumn apples, blackberries, plums and pears for flavour.

Green vegetables also vary with the seasons, and one variety or another is available all year round. Make use of spring greens early in the year, with spring cabbages, purple sprouting broccoli and spinach up to early summer. Then come beans, peas and courgettes, and autumn brings Brussels sprouts and winter cabbages. Although salads are traditionally associated with summer months, they are just as important in winter and are no more difficult to make. Crisp shredded cabbage, raw leeks, Brussels sprouts and watercress are all excellent, and chicory and celery can be used to give texture, with citrus fruits, apples and nuts added for flavour. I have included several recipes for winter salads to give you new ideas for them. Fruits can also be used in summer salads and they have a lovely fresh taste. Melons, oranges, grapes and bananas combine particularly well with oil and vinegar dressings, soured cream or mayonnaise. Garden herbs, the majority of which are only available in summer, can be used to flavour salads. Use them also in sauces for delicately flavoured chicken and veal dishes when fresh cool flavours will tempt hot weather appetites.

One of the most enjoyable things about summer is having meals out of doors. I have given plenty of ideas for quiches and savoury tarts which carry well for picnics as well as making excellent party food. Cold soups are lovely in summer, and you can round off the menu for a patio party with hot herb breads, cool wine cups and summer fruits and ice creams. In the autumn and winter our thoughts turn to steaming casseroles rich with flavour and colour from tomatoes, aubergines and green peppers, hot broths and winter soups served in mugs to warm your hands round. Scones, teabreads and home-made bread come into their own at this time of year, and now is the time to open your summer jams, jellies and chutneys. Recipes like these are wonderfully satisfying to make. They don't break the family budget for entertaining or everyday meals, but they show imagination and originality which are the art of good cooking.

When you are cooking every day for a family it is all too easy to just rely on the same old favourites and not try to vary the menus according to season. Knowing how to make the best use of foods that are available is a quality which makes a good cook even better and it takes real skill and imagination to make interesting dishes from everyday ingredients. But a new recipe is only new the first time and it is well worth experimenting to find out which dishes the family enjoy. Everyone likes good home cooking best of all and the appreciation of your family and friends will be ample reward for your efforts. This book is designed to make it easy for you to get the best out of seasonal foods right through the year and I hope you will enjoy using it.

Katie Stewart

Useful facts and figures

Note on metrication

In this book quantities have been given in both metric and Imperial measures. Exact conversion from Imperial to metric measures does not usually give very convenient working quantities and so for greater convenience we have rounded off metric measures into units of 25 grammes. The table below shows recommended equivalents.

oz/ fluid oz	approx. g and ml	recommended conversion
1	28	25
2	57	50
3	85	75
4	113	100
5 (¼ pint)	142	150
6	170	175
7	198	200
8 (¼ lb)	226	225
9	255	250
10 (½ pint)	283	275
11	311	300
12	340	350
13	368	375
14	396	400
15 (¾ pint)	428	425
16 (1 lb)	456	450
17	484	475
18	512	500
19	541	550
20 (1 pint)	569	575

Note When converting quantities over 20 oz first add the appropriate figures in the centre column, *then* adjust to the nearest unit of 25. As a general guide, 1 kg (1000 g) equals 2.2 lb or about 2 lb 3 oz; 1 litre (1000 ml) equals 1.76 pints or almost exactly 1¾ pints.

Liquid measures

The millilitre is a very small unit of measurement and we felt that to use decilitres (units of 100 ml) would be less cumbersome. In most cases it is perfectly satisfactory to round off the exact millilitre conversion to the nearest decilitre, except for ¼ pint; thus ¼ pint (142 ml) is 1½ dl, ½ pint (283 ml) is 3 dl, ¾ pint (428 ml) is 4 dl and 1 pint (596 ml) is 6 dl. For quantities over 1 pint we have used litres and fractions of a litre.

Can sizes

Because at present cans are marked with the exact (usually to the nearest whole number) metric equivalent of the Imperial weight of the contents, we have followed this practice when giving can sizes. Thus the equivalent of a 14-oz can of tomatoes would be a 396-g can.

Notes for Australian users

Quantities in the recipes in this book are given in metric and Imperial measures. The old Australian standard measuring cup is the same as the American standard 8-fluid ounce cup; the new Australian cup is bigger and holds 250 ml. Note also that the Australian standard tablespoon holds 20 ml and is therefore bigger than either the American (14.2 ml) or the Imperial (17.7 ml). The table below gives a comparison.

American	British	Australian
1 teaspoon	1 teaspoon	1 teaspoon
1 tablespoon	1 tablespoon	1 tablespoon
3 tablespoons	2 tablespoons	2 tablespoons
4 tablespoons	3½ tablespoons	3 tablespoons
5 tablespoons	4 tablespoons	3½ tablespoons

Notes for American users

The quantities in this book are given in Imperial and metric measures. The following information and list of equivalents or alternatives for some terms and ingredients used in the book should enable American readers to use the recipes successfully.

Liquids

Imperial	American
2 tablespoons	3 tablespoons
3 tablespoons	¼ cup
¼ pint	⅔ cup
½ pint	1¼ cups
¾ pint	scant 2 cups
1 pint	2½ cups

Note The Imperial pint is 20 fluid ounces whereas the American pint is 16 fluid ounces.

Solids

Imperial	American
8 oz butter or other fat	1 cup
4 oz flour	1 cup
8 oz granulated or castor sugar	1 cup
4½ oz icing (confectioners') sugar	1 cup
8 oz brown sugar	1 cup
12 oz golden syrup or treacle	1 cup
7 oz rice	1 cup
5 oz dried fruit	1 cup
2 oz fresh breadcrumbs	1 cup
4 oz chopped nuts	1 cup

January

Cold weather in *January* demands warm, nourishing foods. Weather permitting it is a good month for root vegetables, which is fortunate, for they make excellent soups and broths and combine with cheaper cuts of meat to make delicious casseroles. There are still supplies of game, both furred and feathered, and this is the month to make use of them before the season draws to a close.

Now is the time for spring greens, and Brussels sprouts are coming to their peak after the frosts. Good main-crop carrots, plenty of onions, parsnips, sweet crisp celery and imported chicory can all add variety to vegetables on the menu.

Home-grown apples and pears are available from store and this month early rhubarb makes a welcome appearance. Make good use of citrus fruits and towards the middle of the month look for the bitter Seville oranges which should be available for making marmalade.

Leek and carrot soup

Soups made from a purée of vegetables are the easiest of all to make. Serve this lovely soup with a bowl of grated Parmesan cheese handed round separately; a little cheese sprinkled over the hot soup tastes very good.

4 large leeks
450 g/1 lb carrots
50 g/2 oz butter
a generous litre/2 pints stock or
  water

salt and freshly milled pepper
1.5 dl/¼ pint single cream

Trim the base of the leeks and cut the green tops down to about 2.5 cm (1 in) from the white stem. Split each leek lengthways to the centre and wash well under running cold water to remove any dirt and grit.

Shred the leeks finely, peel the carrots and slice thinly.

Melt the butter in a large saucepan and add the prepared vegetables. Cover and cook gently for about 5 minutes, until the leeks are soft but not browned. Stir in the hot stock and season with salt and pepper. Bring up to the boil, cover with a lid and cook gently for about 1–1½ hours or until the carrots are quite tender.

Draw off the heat and pass the vegetables and liquid through a vegetable mill or purée in a blender. Return the soup to the pan.

Check seasoning and reheat. Stir in the cream and serve.
Serves 4-6

Kipper pâté

Serve this pâté as a first course with toast, or use as a spread on cocktail canapés. Either way remove from the refrigerator an hour before required so that the mixture softens slightly.

2 170- or 227-g/6- or 8-oz packets
  boil-in-the-bag kipper fillets
175 g/6 oz softened butter
salt and freshly milled pepper

squeeze of lemon juice
twist of lemon or finely chopped
  parsley

Simmer the kipper fillets in the bag as directed. When cool enough to handle, discard the skin from the fillets.

Mash or pound the kipper flesh along with the juices from the bag. Cream the butter until soft and beat in the kipper flesh.

Season to taste with just a little salt, plenty of pepper and a squeeze of lemon juice to sharpen the flavour. For a really smooth mixture combine the ingredients in a blender.

Spoon the pâté into a small serving dish, rough up the surface and chill for several hours. Garnish with a twist of lemon or a little chopped parsley and serve with hot toast.
Serves 6

Scotch broth

Broths make use of the cooking liquor from meat or poultry and much depends on the slow simmering to extract all the flavour. In many parts of Scotland broth is made all year round with peas or cabbage added according to the season.

450 g/1 lb neck of mutton or shin
  of beef
2.25 litres/4 pints water
3 level teaspoons salt
40 g/1½ oz pearl barley
2–3 carrots
1 onion

1 leek
1 small turnip
1 teacup shredded cabbage or fresh
  peas
1 tablespoon finely chopped
  parsley

Trim away any excess fat and place the meat in a large saucepan.

Add the water and salt. Place the pearl barley in a small basin and pour a little boiling water over to scald it. Stir and then drain. Add the barley to the soup pan. Bring to the boil, boil for 1 minute, then skim and lower the heat. Cover and simmer gently for 1 hour.

Peel and finely dice the carrots. Peel and finely chop the onion. Trim the leek and split it open, then wash under cold water and shred finely. Peel the turnip, then slice and dice neatly. Add the vegetables to the pan of broth, re-cover and simmer gently for a further 45 minutes. Add the shredded cabbage or fresh peas and cook without a lid for a final 15 minutes, or until the cabbage is cooked.

Draw the pan off the heat and lift out the pieces of meat. Strip any scraps of meat off the bone, shred finely and return to the broth. Check the seasoning and reheat.

Sprinkle in the chopped parsley just before serving.
Serves 6

Split pea soup

Split peas take a little longer to cook than lentils. In spring, colour the soup a delicate green and serve with freshly chopped mint scattered over.

100 g/4 oz split peas	a generous litre/2 pints liquor from
1 small carrot	boiled gammon or bacon
2 leeks	freshly milled pepper
1 stalk celery	bouquet garni
25 g/1 oz butter or bacon fat	25 g/1 oz flour
	1.5 dl/¼ pint milk

Soak the peas overnight in cold water to cover. Drain well. Peel and finely chop the carrot. Wash and shred the leeks and shred the celery. Melt the butter or bacon fat in a saucepan and add the vegetables. Sauté gently for about 5 minutes or until the vegetables are tender but not brown. Add the split peas and cook for a further few moments. Then stir in the stock, add a seasoning of pepper and the bouquet garni.

Cover with a lid and simmer gently for about 1 hour, or until the split peas are quite soft.

Draw the pan off the heat and remove the bouquet garni. Pass the soup through a vegetable mill or purée in a blender. Return the soup to the pan. Pour the milk into a basin and sift the flour over the surface; whisk until smooth and add to the soup. Bring up to the boil, stirring all the time until the soup has thickened. Taste and correct seasoning if necessary.

Serve with dice of crisply fried bread or with Italian *grissini* (bread sticks).
Serves 4-6

Chicken liver pâté with anchovy

Home-made pâté will keep for up to a week in the refrigerator and is a good choice to make ahead for a busy weekend.

225 g/8 oz streaky bacon rashers
450 g/1 lb chicken livers
5 anchovy fillets or 1 teaspoon
  anchovy essence
3 dl/½ pint milk
bay leaf

1 onion, peeled and halved
few peppercorns
25 g/1 oz butter
25 g/1 oz flour
salt and freshly milled pepper

Trim the bacon rashers. Stretch about six of the rashers with a table knife and use to line a 0.5-kg (1-lb) loaf tin. Slice the chicken livers and snip away the core. Chop the remaining bacon rashers. Pass the livers, bacon and anchovy fillets through the coarse blade of a mincer into a mixing basin – add the anchovy essence at this stage if used.

Measure the milk into a saucepan and add the bay leaf, onion and peppercorns. Bring slowly to the boil, then draw off the heat and leave to infuse for 15 minutes.

Melt the butter in a saucepan and stir in the flour. Cook for a few moments, then gradually stir in the strained milk beating well all the time to get a smooth sauce. Bring to the boil and season with salt and pepper. Draw off the heat and beat into the minced ingredients.

Pour this mixture into the lined loaf tin. Cover with a buttered paper and a square of foil. Set in a roasting tin with 2.5 cm (1 in) cold water. Place in the centre of a very moderate oven (160°C., 325°F., Gas Mark 3) and bake for 1½ hours. Remove from the oven and leave overnight with a weight on top. Remove the weight and the foil, turn the pâté out and cut in slices. Serve with hot toast and butter.

Serves 6

Haddock with butter sauce

Haddock is plentiful all year round but at its best during the cold winter months. Haddock has a delicate flavour and a firm white flesh, more expensive to buy than cod but excellent to use in recipes.

675 g/1½ lb haddock fillet	3–4 tablespoons milk
salt	15 g/½ oz butter

for the sauce:

75 g/3 oz butter	salt and freshly milled pepper
25 g/1 oz flour	chopped fresh parsley
3 dl/½ pint milk	

Skin the haddock fillet, remove any bones and cut the fish into four pieces. Season with salt and place in a buttered baking dish.

Add the milk and the butter in small pieces, then cover with a buttered paper. Place in the centre of a moderately hot oven (200°C., 400°F., Gas Mark 6) and bake for 20 minutes or until the fish flakes.

Towards the end of the cooking time prepare the sauce. Melt half the butter in a saucepan over low heat. Stir in the flour and cook gently for a few moments. Gradually stir in the milk, beating well all the time to get a smooth sauce. Bring up to the boil, stirring all the time. Season with salt and pepper and allow to simmer gently for about 3–4 minutes.

When the fish is cooked, lift the pieces out on to a hot serving dish and strain the juices from the baking dish into the sauce.

Draw the pan of sauce off the heat and beat in the remaining butter.

The sauce should be smooth and shiny. Pour over the fish, sprinkle with chopped parsley and serve.
Serves 4

Toad in the hole

A filling and easy-to-make lunch dish that's popular with children. Make it for them during the school holidays: it's the kind of recipe that satisfies hungry young appetites.

450 g/1 lb beef or pork sausages
15 g/½ oz lard, dripping or white vegetable fat

for the batter:

100 g/4 oz plain flour
¼ level teaspoon salt

1 egg
2.5 dl/½ pint milk

Place the sausages in a medium-sized roasting tin and add the fat. Set aside while preparing the batter.

Sieve the flour and salt into a mixing basin and hollow out the centre. Crack the egg into the flour and add about one-third of the milk. Using a wooden spoon, stir gently starting in the centre and gradually draw in the flour from around the sides of the bowl. Add the remaining milk gradually, stirring all the time. Beat well for 1 minute to aerate the batter.

Place the sausages in a moderately hot oven (200°C., 400°F., Gas Mark 6) for about 10 minutes until the fat is very hot. Pour in the batter and replace the tin in the oven, near the top. Bake for 25–30 minutes, or until the batter is well risen and crisp. Cut in portions and serve at once.
Serves 4

Cod with parsley stuffing

Cod is a good buy in winter and the meaty flesh suits January appetites. Cod cutlets are slices taken from across the whole fish and lend themselves to a variety of recipes. Cutlets cut from the tail end of the fish are the best to use for stuffing, because they are smaller and neater in shape.

4 tail-end cutlets of cod
few toasted breadcrumbs
lemon wedges

for the stuffing:

50 g/2 oz fresh white breadcrumbs
25 g/1 oz shredded suet
1 heaped tablespoon chopped
  parsley
salt and freshly milled pepper
1 small egg
1 teaspoon lemon juice
1 teaspoon anchovy essence

Rinse the fish cutlets and trim away the fins with a pair of scissors. Still using the scissors, snip out the centre bone from each cutlet to leave a space for the stuffing. Place the cutlets in a well-buttered baking dish and set aside while preparing the stuffing.

Combine the breadcrumbs, suet and parsley in a small basin. Add a seasoning of salt and pepper. Lightly beat the egg and then mix about 2 tablespoons of it with the lemon juice and anchovy essence, keeping the rest of the egg for glazing. Using a fork stir this mixture into the crumbs. Mix lightly and divide into four portions. Pack portions of stuffing into the centre cavity of each fish cutlet.

Brush the remaining egg over the fish and sprinkle with a few toasted breadcrumbs.

Cover with a buttered paper or foil and bake in a moderate oven (180°C., 350°F., Gas Mark 4) for 20–25 minutes. Garnish with wedges of lemon and serve.

Serves 4

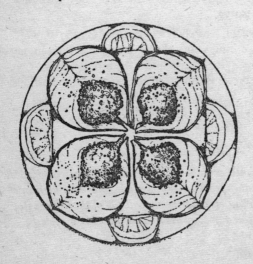

Celery and bacon au gratin

After the first frosts home-grown celery is extra crisp and full of flavour.
Use celery in the same way as cauliflower, leeks and chicory, to make a
tasty supper dish.

1 head celery
6–8 rashers bacon
40 g/1½ oz butter
25 g/1 oz flour
1.5 dl/¼ pint milk

100 g/4 oz grated cheese
seasoning to taste
pinch mustard
few fresh breadcrumbs

Trim and scrub the celery. Remove the 'strings' from coarser stalks
and cut the celery in 2.5-cm (1-in) slices. Cook in about 3 dl (½ pint)
lightly salted water until tender – about 20 minutes. Drain and
reserve the liquor for the sauce. Trim and fry the bacon rashers and
arrange in layers with the celery in a greased baking dish.

Melt 25 g (1 oz) of the butter in a saucepan, stir in the flour and
cook for a moment. Stir in 1.5 dl (¼ pint) celery liquor, beating to get
a smooth sauce, then add the milk. Stir until boiling, then add 75 g
(3 oz) of the grated cheese, seasoning to taste and a pinch of mustard.
Pour over the celery and bacon. Scatter a few breadcrumbs and the
remaining cheese on top. Dot the remaining butter over the top and
brown near the top of a moderately hot oven (190°C., 375°F., Gas
Mark 5) for 15–20 minutes or under the grill.
Serves 4

Chicken pilaff

The tastiest way of preparing rice is to cook it gently in a measured
amount of stock. By the time the rice is tender the grains will have
absorbed all the liquid and the resulting dish will be moist and full of
flavour. This recipe makes a little meat go a long way; add a handful of
sultanas and a few toasted almonds to the cooked chicken if you like.

3 chicken joints
50 g/2 oz butter
4 lean bacon rashers
1 onion

225 g/8 oz long-grain rice
bay leaf
6 dl/1 pint chicken stock
Parmesan cheese

Wipe the chicken joints and trim away any loose skin. Place in a
small baking or roasting tin with half the butter. Cover with buttered

papers and place in the centre of a moderate oven (180°C., 350°F., Gas Mark 4). Cook for 45 minutes–1 hour or until the chicken is tender. Remove from the oven and leave until cool enough to handle. Lift the chicken flesh away from the bones and separate into chunky pieces.

Meanwhile melt the remaining butter in a large saucepan and add the trimmed and chopped bacon rashers. Peel and finely chop the onion and add to the pan. Cover with a lid and fry gently until the bacon fat runs and the onion is tender but not brown. Stir in the rice, then the hot stock. Check the flavour of the stock and if necessary add extra seasoning. The rice absorbs the stock during cooking and if the stock is not seasoned enough the resulting pilaff will be insipid in flavour. Add the bay leaf and bring up to the boil. Cover with a lid and simmer very gently for about 20 minutes, or until the rice is tender and the liquid absorbed.

Remove the pan lid and cook for a further 5 minutes to dry the mixture a little. Gently fold in the cooked chicken flesh. Heat through and spoon into a hot serving dish.

Sprinkle with Parmesan cheese and serve.
Serves 4

Waterzooi of chicken

Vegetables give the flavour to the stock used for cooking the chicken in this recipe. The same flavoured broth is thickened and used to coat the sliced-up chicken flesh. Sometimes a few additional sautéed mushrooms can be stirred into the sauce just before serving. Extra stock and vegetables left over should be made into a soup – Waterzooi is very economical.

2–3 leeks	salt and freshly milled pepper
4 stalks celery	bouquet garni
2 carrots	juice of ½ lemon
1 onion	2 level tablespoons cornflour
25 g/1 oz butter	1 egg yolk
1 chicken, about 1 kg/2–2½ lb	2 tablespoons double cream
dressed weight	chopped parsley

Trim and wash the leeks and shred the white part. Scrub and slice the celery stalks, peel and chop the carrots and onion. Melt the butter in the base of a large pan. Add the prepared vegetables and cook gently until the vegetables are tender but not brown.

Place the chicken on top of the vegetables and add sufficient water to cover. Add a good seasoning of salt and pepper and a bouquet garni. Bring up to the boil, then cover and simmer gently for 45 minutes–1 hour or until the chicken is tender.

Lift the chicken out and allow to cool for a few moments. Peel away the skin and lift the flesh from the bones. Arrange the chicken flesh in a warm serving dish and keep hot while preparing the sauce.

Measure out 6 dl (1 pint) of the stock from the pan and strain into a saucepan. Check seasoning and add sufficient lemon juice to sharpen the flavour. Blend the cornflour with 2–3 tablespoons cold water and stir into the stock. Bring up to the boil stirring all the time until the mixture has thickened slightly. Draw off the heat and allow to cool for a few moments. Blend the egg yolk and the cream in a basin and stir in a little of the hot sauce. Mix well and return to the saucepan. Heat gently but do not allow to boil. Pour the hot sauce over the chicken, garnish with chopped parsley and serve.
Serves 4

Note Prepared in this way the chicken reheats very well. Cover the dish of chicken and sauce with foil and heat through in the oven.

Beef curry casserole

This recipe is particularly tasty because the raw meat is cooked in the curry sauce, taking in lots of flavour. Serve it with plain boiled rice.

675–900 g/1½–2 lb lean braising
  steak
25 g/1 oz butter
2 medium-sized onions
2–4 level tablespoons curry
  powder
1 level tablespoon flour

4 dl/¾ pint hot stock
1 rounded tablespoon apricot jam
  or sweet chutney
1 tablespoon soft brown sugar
juice of ½ lemon
½ level teaspoon salt
25 g/1 oz sultanas

Trim the meat and cut up into neat pieces. Place in a casserole and set aside while preparing the curry sauce.

Melt the butter in a saucepan. Peel and chop the onions, add to the butter and fry gently for a few minutes until the onions are soft but not brown. Stir in the curry powder and shake the pan over the heat for a few moments to extract the flavour from the curry. Stir in the flour and then the hot stock. Bring up to the boil. Add sweetness to the curry sauce in the form of apricot jam or chutney and the soft brown sugar. Then stir in the lemon juice, salt and sultanas.

Simmer for a few moments, then pour the contents of the pan over the beef in the casserole.

Cover the casserole and place in a very moderate oven (160°C., 325°F., Gas Mark 3) and cook for 2 hours or until the meat is quite tender.
Serves 4

Roast pheasant with oatmeal stuffing

As a rule game birds are not stuffed, the body cavity is too small to bother with. Pheasant can be an exception and in Scotland it is often served with an oatmeal stuffing. Oatmeal has a nutty flavour and a coarse texture that goes well with game.

1 brace pheasant	flour
6–8 streaky bacon rashers	watercress
50 g/2 oz butter	

for the oatmeal stuffing:

1 small onion	50 g/2 oz shredded beef suet
100 g/4 oz medium oatmeal	salt and freshly milled pepper

Have the pheasants prepared and ready for roasting. Trim the bacon rashers and set aside while preparing the stuffing.

Peel and finely chop the onion. Add to the mixed oatmeal and suet and season well with salt and pepper. Where possible add the mashed pheasant livers as well. Using a fork, stir in about 1 tablespoon water – just enough to moisten the mixture slightly.

Spoon the stuffing into the body cavity of the birds and press in lightly. Leave the ends of the birds open: the stuffing swells on cooking and takes in the moisture and juices from the flesh. Cover the breast of each bird with the bacon rashers and set them in a roasting tin.

Add about half the butter to the pan and spread the remainder over the pheasants. Place in the centre of a hot oven (220°C., 425°F., Gas Mark 7) and roast for 10 minutes. Lower the heat to moderately hot (200°C., 400°F., Gas Mark 6) and continue roasting for a further 40 minutes. Baste fairly often and about 10 minutes before the end of the cooking time remove the bacon rashers. Baste the birds and dredge the breasts with flour. Baste again and return to the oven to complete cooking time and brown. Serve with a garnish of watercress.

Serves 4-6

Sea pie

This old-fashioned meat stew with its unusual name has a delicious suet pastry top. Those who like dumplings will like this recipe – it makes a filling dish for cold days.

675 g/1½ lb stewing steak	2 onions
seasoned flour	1 small turnip
25 g/1 oz lard or dripping	4 dl/¾ pint stock
225 g/8 oz carrots	

for the suet topping:

175 g/6 oz self-raising flour	75 g/3 oz shredded beef suet
½ level teaspoon salt	cold water to mix

Wipe the meat and trim away any fat. Cut the meat into neat pieces and toss in seasoned flour. Melt the fat in a medium to large saucepan, add the meat and fry gently to brown on all sides. Meanwhile peel and slice the carrots and onions and peel and dice the turnip. Add the vegetables to the pan and stir in the stock. Bring up to the boil, then lower the heat to a simmer. Cover and cook gently for 2 hours.

Put together the ingredients for the suet pastry top. Sift the flour and salt into a mixing basin and add the suet. About 45 minutes before the end of the cooking time for the meat, make up the topping by stirring sufficient water into the dry ingredients to make a soft scone-like dough. On a lightly floured working surface pat out the dough to a circle slightly smaller than the diameter of the saucepan.

Remove the pan lid and place the suet pastry circle on top of the ingredients in the pan. Re-cover with the lid and continue to simmer gently for the remaining 30–40 minutes' cooking time. The suet pastry will rise and cook to form a delicious topping.

Cut the pastry top in wedges and serve along with the meat and
vegetables from underneath.
Serves 4

Hare in red wine

*For most of us it is usually more convenient to buy hare pieces and
about 900 g (2 lb) hare pieces would be sufficient for this recipe, but if
you start with a whole hare this is the way to cook it.*

1 hare, skinned and cut in joints	2–3 streaky bacon rashers
blood from the hare (see note)	1 large onion, finely chopped
bay leaf	1 clove garlic
few peppercorns	seasoned flour
few parsley stalks	450 g/1 lb small onions
½ bottle red wine	25 g/1 oz butter
2 tablespoons oil	225 g/8 oz button mushrooms,
15 g/1 oz cooking fat	trimmed

Place the hare pieces in a bowl along with the bay leaf, peppercorns,
parsley stalks, red wine and oil. Leave to marinate overnight,
turning the pieces occasionally. Drain the hare pieces and pat dry.
Reserve the marinade.

Melt the fat in a large saucepan, add the trimmed and chopped
bacon rashers and fry until the fat begins to run. Add the hare pieces
and fry to brown all over. It may be necessary to do these a few at a
time.

Remove the hare from the pan and keep warm.

Add the chopped onion to the hot fat remaining in the saucepan and
fry gently for a few moments to soften. Add the finely chopped
garlic and replace the hare pieces.

Sprinkle with a little seasoned flour and turn the hare joints in the
fat. Strain in the marinade and then add extra water almost to cover
the hare. Bring to the boil, cover with a lid and simmer gently for
3–4 hours, or until tender.

Towards the end of the cooking time, peel the small onions and
place in a saucepan. Cover with cold water and bring to the boil.
Simmer gently for 10–15 minutes or until just tender, then drain.
Melt the butter in a frying pan, add the mushrooms and fry for a
few moments. Lift the hare pieces from the pan and place in a
serving dish. Add the onions and cooked mushrooms.

Replace the pan of cooking liquor over the low heat and stir in the blood (see note).

Stir until the sauce has thickened but do not boil. Check seasoning, strain over the hare and serve.
Serves 6

Note An alternative thickening for the sauce could be a blend of butter and flour, using 25 g (1 oz) of each. Add to the hot liquid and stir until it comes up to the boil and thickens evenly.

Fried chicory

In this recipe the chicory can be boiled in advance and left to cool. Flour the heads and fry them to a crisp golden brown when ready to serve. The flavour is unusually good and they go well with pork chops, lamb cutlets and roast beef.

4–6 heads chicory	50 g/2 oz butter
seasoned flour	

Remove any outer damaged leaves of chicory and trim the base from each head. Add the chicory to a pan of boiling salted water and simmer until barely tender – about 15 minutes. Drain and cool.

When ready to serve, roll the heads of chicory lightly in seasoned flour to coat all over. Melt the butter in a frying pan. When hot add the chicory and fry gently for about 5 minutes, turning to brown them well on all sides and heat through. Serve at once with the browned butter from the pan.
Serves 4

Sweet and sour white cabbage

This unusual recipe is a good accompaniment for sausages, pork or duck. The mixture can be reheated and tastes even better the second time.

675 g/1½ lb (about ½ head) white cabbage	1 425-g/15-oz can tomatoes
1 medium-sized onion	salt and freshly milled pepper
25 g/1 oz white cooking fat	½ level teaspoon caraway seeds
1 level tablespoon granulated sugar	1.5 dl/¼ pint boiling water

for the sauce:

2 level teaspoons cornflour
1 level teaspoon sugar

1 teaspoon tarragon vinegar
4 tablespoons water

Remove any outer damaged leaves and cut the cabbage into quarters. Cut away the hard stalk and shred the cabbage finely. Peel and finely chop the onion.

Melt the fat in a heavy saucepan. Sprinkle in the sugar and heat steadily until the sugar melts and just begins to turn golden brown. Immediately add the roughly chopped tomatoes with the juice from the can and the onions and cook for a few moments.

Add the cabbage, a good seasoning of salt and pepper and the caraway seeds. Toss the ingredients and cook, stirring, for 3–4 minutes. Add the water, cover with a lid and cook gently for about 30 minutes or until the cabbage is tender, but still crisp and juicy.

Prepare the sauce by mixing the cornflour, sugar, vinegar and water together in a basin.

Stir into the cabbage and bring back to the boil. Cook for a further 3–5 minutes. Then dish up the whole contents of the pan. Scatter with chopped parsley and serve.

Serves 4

Creamed potato

Make creamed potato that looks appetizing and serve with any recipe that has a good gravy or sauce. Because of the egg added, this mixture browns well and makes an ideal topping for meat or fish dishes.

675 g/1½ lb potatoes
50 g/2 oz butter
salt and freshly milled pepper

1 egg yolk
about 1.5 dl/¼ pint hot milk

Scrub and peel the potatoes and cut up any large ones. Place in cold salted water and bring to the boil. Simmer for 15–20 minutes or until tender. Drain well and return to the pan for a few minutes to dry over the heat.

Press the potatoes through a sieve into a warm bowl. Add half the butter, a good seasoning of salt and pepper, the egg yolk and half the hot milk. Beat well with a wooden spoon, adding more milk as required to make a smooth creamy consistency.

Pile the potato mixture into a shallow serving dish, 'drizzle' over the remaining butter, melted, and put under a hot grill until crispy and brown.
Serves 4

Roast onions

Serve onions cooked like this with any roast, particularly beef or lamb, and remember that Jerusalem artichokes can also be treated in the same way.

4–8 onions, depending on size

25 g/1 oz dripping or vegetable fat

Peel the onions, leaving them whole. Where possible choose large onions and allow one per person. Place the onions in a saucepan, cover with cold water and bring to the boil. Simmer for 2–3 minutes, then drain well. Return the onions to the saucepan and place them over the heat for a moment to dry them well.

Heat the dripping in a roasting tin. Add the onions to the hot fat, baste well and place above the centre of a moderately hot oven (190°C., 375°F., Gas Mark 5) – the onions can be placed in the pan dripping around the roast joint. Roast for 45–50 minutes basting occasionally and turning when necessary for even browning.
Serves 4

Tomato-glazed onions

Larger onions are often used in a recipe for flavouring but the smaller-sized button onions are very good to serve as a vegetable. Spicy flavours like mustard or tomato ketchup can be used to glaze them and they make an excellent accompaniment for steaks or roast beef.

450 g/1 lb button onions
50 g/2 oz butter
2 tablespoons tomato ketchup

Peel the onions, leaving them whole. Cook in boiling salted water for 15–20 minutes until tender, then drain and keep warm. Add the butter to the hot saucepan and allow to melt. Add the tomato ketchup and bring to the boil. Replace the onions in the pan and toss well to coat with the glaze.
Serves 4

Pears and prunes in red wine

This is an attractive winter dessert using fruits. Cooking them separately keeps the pears a lighter colour and provides a good contrast to the dark prunes.

225 g/8 oz prunes	100 g/4 oz castor sugar
3 dl/½ pint water	juice of ½ lemon
1.5 dl/¼ pint red wine	450 g/1 lb pears

Soak the prunes overnight in 1.5 dl (¼ pint) of the water and the red wine. Place the prunes and liquid in a saucepan, add half the sugar and bring up to the boil. Simmer gently until the prunes are tender, then draw off the heat and allow to cool.

Meanwhile measure the remaining water and the sugar into a saucepan. Add the lemon juice and stir over low heat to make a sugar syrup. Peel, quarter and core the pears, adding them to the syrup as they are prepared to prevent discolouration. Bring up to the boil, cover and simmer gently until the pears are tender, about 15 minutes. Draw off the heat and allow to cool.

Remove the stones from the prunes and then combine the pears and the prunes and the liquid from both. Chill well before serving.
Serves 6

Orange chiffon

This light, frothy mixture is very quick to make. Serve it with cream and some thawed raspberries or strawberries from the freezer and it's like a taste of summer in wintertime.

2 oranges	15 g/½ oz powdered gelatine
½ lemon	3 large eggs
4 tablespoons cold water	75 g/3 oz castor sugar

Squeeze the juice from the oranges and lemon and set aside. Measure the cold water into a small saucepan, sprinkle on the gelatine and allow to soak for 5 minutes. Stir over low heat until the gelatine has dissolved and the liquid is clear. Draw off the heat.

Separate the eggs, cracking the whites into one basin and the yolks into a second basin. Add 50 g (2 oz) of the sugar to the yolks and whisk until pale in colour. Whisk in the squeezed fruit juice. Holding the pan of dissolved gelatine well above the basin, pour the contents slowly into the mixture. Whisk all the time so that the gelatine is immediately mixed through and well blended. Set the mixture aside until it begins to thicken and show signs of setting. Give an occasional whisk and leave the basin sitting on the kitchen table; it will only take about 20 minutes to reach setting point.

Whisk the egg whites until stiff, add the remaining sugar and whisk for a moment more until glossy. Using a metal spoon, fold the egg whites into the mixture gently but thoroughly. Pour into a serving bowl and leave in a cool place until set firm.

Serves 4

Rhubarb cake pudding

The slender stalks of early rhubarb have a pale pink colour and a delicious flavour. To use them in a hot rhubarb pudding seems a sensible idea for cold January days.

450 g/1 lb early rhubarb	little grated orange rind
100 g/4 oz castor or soft brown sugar	2 tablespoons water
	icing sugar

for the cake topping:

75 g/3 oz self-raising flour	50 g/2 oz castor sugar
pinch salt	1 egg
50 g/2 oz butter	

Wash and trim the rhubarb. Cut the stalks into 2.5-cm (1-in) lengths and put into a buttered 1-litre (1½- to 2-pint) pie or baking dish. Add the sugar, grated orange rind and water. Set aside while preparing the topping.

Sift the flour and salt. Cream the butter and sugar until light, then gradually beat in the lightly mixed egg. Add a little of the flour along with the last few additions of egg and then, using a metal spoon, fold in the remaining flour to make a medium-soft consistency. Spoon the mixture over the rhubarb and spread evenly.

Place in the centre of a moderately hot oven (190°C., 375°F., Gas Mark 5) and bake for 35–40 minutes or until the cake topping is well risen and golden brown. Sprinkle with a little icing sugar and serve hot with cream or custard.

Serves 4

Apple fritters

Dessert apples make the best fritters, they keep their shape and are not so moist as the more acid cooking apple. Use this batter to coat other fruits like bananas cut lengthways or well-drained canned fruit such as pineapple rings.

4 dessert apples	flour (see method)

for the batter:

75 g/3 oz plain flour	2 tablespoons water
pinch salt	2 tablespoons milk
1 egg	

Peel and core the apples, leaving them whole. Cut across into slices about 0·5 cm (¼ in) thick and place in a basin of cold salted water to prevent them from turning brown.

Sift the flour and salt for the batter into a mixing basin and make a well in the centre. Separate the egg, placing the yolk in the centre of the flour and the white in a mixing basin. Add the water and milk to the egg yolk. Mix them together and then gradually draw in the flour from around the sides of the basin to make a smooth batter. When ready to use beat the egg white until stiff and fold into the mixture.

Drain the apple slices, rinse in clear water and pat dry. Dust the slices with flour. This helps the batter to cling to the slices. Using a fork dip the apples into the batter. Allow excess batter to drain off and then lower the apple slices into about 2.5 cm (1 in) of hot oil – you can do this in a frying pan. Fry for 2–3 minutes, turning to brown them on both sides. Then lift from the pan on to a sugared paper. Keep fritters warm in the oven, uncovered so they remain crisp while you cook the remainder. Serve sprinkled with sugar and pass cream separately.

Serves 4

Zabaglione

Zabaglione can be made for fewer or more servings. As a rule, allow 1 egg yolk, 1 tablespoon sugar and 1–2 tablespoons wine per person.

4 egg yolks	4–6 tablespoons Marsala wine or
50 g/2 oz castor sugar	sweet sherry
	sponge fingers

Put the egg yolks in a medium-sized mixing basin. Add the sugar and Marsala wine or sweet sherry to the egg yolks. Place the bowl over a saucepan half filled with simmering water and whisk continuously over the heat until the mixture is thick and light – this takes about 5 minutes.

Remove from the heat and pour into four individual goblets. Serve with sponge fingers.

Serves 4

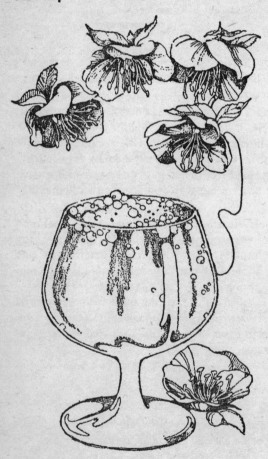

Quick fruit cake

Don't expect this cake to be as good as one made by the more lengthy creaming method. This is just a nice easy cake to make if time is short.

275 g/10 oz self-raising flour
2 level teaspoons ground mixed spice
1 level teaspoon salt
150 g/5 oz butter
150 g/5 oz soft brown sugar
2 large eggs

4 tablespoons milk
450 g/1 lb cleaned dried fruit, including currants, seedless raisins, sultanas, mixed peel, chopped nuts and chopped glacé cherries

Sift the flour, mixed spice and salt into a large mixing basin. Add the butter cut in pieces and rub into the mixture. Add the sugar, mix the ingredients and make a well in the centre. Lightly beat the eggs with the milk and add all at once. Using a wooden spoon stir first to blend the ingredients and then beat thoroughly to mix. Add the dried fruit and stir very thoroughly together.

Spoon into a well-buttered small roasting tin or shallow baking tin about 28 by 18 cm (11 by 7 in). Spread the mixture level. Place in the centre of a moderate oven (180°C., 350°F., Gas Mark 4) and bake for 1–1¼ hours, or until risen and golden brown.

Test by pushing a warmed skewer into the centre of the cake; if there is no uncooked cake mixture clinging to the skewer when drawn out, the cake is cooked.

Allow the cake to cool in the tin. Cut into fingers and store in a tightly lidded tin.
Cuts into 16 pieces

Wholemeal scones

How about opening one of those jars of jam you made during the summer months, then baking some hot scones and giving the family a treat for tea?

100 g/4 oz plain flour
pinch salt
1 level teaspoon bicarbonate of soda
2 level teaspoons cream of tartar

100 g/4 oz wholemeal flour
40 g/1½ oz butter
1 egg
milk to mix

Sift the plain flour, salt, bicarbonate of soda and cream of tartar into a basin. Add the wholemeal flour and mix well. Cut the butter in pieces, add to the flour mixture and rub in. Add sufficient milk to the egg to make the liquid up to 1.5 dl ($\frac{1}{4}$ pint). Measure this where possible, otherwise the amount required is usually about 4 tablespoons. Pour the egg and milk into the centre of the flour mixture and using a fork mix to a rough dough.

Turn the dough out on to a floured working surface and knead lightly. Pat or roll out to a thickness no less than 1 cm ($\frac{1}{2}$ in), then, using a 5-cm (2-in) round cutter, stamp out twelve scones. It will be necessary to use the trimmings of dough to make the last two or three scones.

Place the scones on a floured baking tray and dust with extra flour. Place above the centre in a hot oven (220°C., 425°F., Gas Mark 7) and bake for 10 minutes or until well risen.

Makes 12 scones

Chunky Seville marmalade

An abundance of citrus fruits means it's marmalade-making time. Sweet oranges, lemons and grapefruit are available all year round but the bitter Seville oranges which make the best marmalade have only a short season from about the middle of January to the end of February.

1.25 kg/3 lb Seville oranges
2.75 litres/5 pints water
2.75 kg/6 lb granulated or
  preserving sugar

2 tablespoons black treacle
  (optional)
juice of 2 large lemons

Scrub the oranges and pick off the small disc at the stalk end. Place in a large saucepan and cover with 2.25 litres (4 pints) of the water. It may be necessary to use two saucepans with half the oranges and a generous litre (2 pints) water in each. Cover with a lid and simmer gently for about 1½ hours, or until the oranges are quite soft – test with a sharp knife. Lift out the softened oranges, reserving the water they cooked in.

Cut each orange in half and, using a teaspoon, scoop out the pith and pips into a small saucepan. Add the remaining 0.5 litre (1 pint) of water, bring to the boil and simmer for 10 minutes – this extracts extra pectin from the pith and pips.

Cut up the soft peel, coarsely or finely according to how you like the marmalade. Return the peel to the original saucepan containing the water. Add the sugar, add the treacle if a dark marmalade is preferred, then add the lemon juice and the strained water from the pith and pips. Stir over low heat until the sugar has dissolved. Bring to the boil and boil rapidly for a set – about 15–20 minutes. Draw the pan off the heat, skim and pour into warm, dry jars. Cover with waxed paper discs while hot and seal when cold.

Makes 3.5-4.5 kg (8–10 lb)

Marmalade making
The principle of marmalade making is the same as for jam, the fruit peel must be simmered until quite tender before the sugar is added. When ready a piece of cooked peel squeezed between the fingers will feel quite soft. This initial cooking is very important for sugar has a hardening effect and once it is added the peel ceases to tenderize any more.

Any white sugar, other than icing sugar, is suitable. Granulated sugar or the special preserving sugar give the best results and produce less scum. A proportion of brown sugar can be used, but not more than a quarter of the total amount. Once the sugar is added, stir until every grain is dissolved before boiling for a set. Any sugar grains remaining will cause the marmalade to go sugary on storage.

Fast boiling is the secret of a good flavour and set. Large old-fashioned preserving pans are the best to use, the sheer size means you can boil the marmalade fast and allows the 'frothing up' of the mixture. Fast boiling means marmalade should reach setting point within about 15 minutes. In a saucepan, where boiling has to be more gentle for fear of boiling over, it can take up to 30 minutes.

Draw the pan off the heat when you test the mixture for a set. It will do no harm at all. In fact there is a very real possibility that your marmalade will boil past setting point if left cooking, especially if the result of the test shows that the mixture was ready. Have one or more cold saucers ready in the refrigerator. Spoon a little of the marmalade on to the cold surface and leave to cool for a few minutes. The sample should crinkle when pushed with the finger showing the start of a skin forming on the surface of the marmalade.

Don't pot the marmalade straightaway unless you like all the peel at the top of the jar. Allow it to cool for 20 minutes; a skin will form on the surface and when you stir the peel will hang suspended in the jelly. Pour into clean dry jars, cover with waxed discs immediately but leave until quite cold before sealing with cellophane covers. This reduces the risk of any condensation from the hot marmalade under the covers and therefore discourages the growth of mould during storage.

Seville orange marmalade

This recipe follows the more traditional method of making marmalade where the orange peel is shredded before cooking. A tablespoon of crushed coriander seed tied in a muslin bag and allowed to boil with the peel gives the marmalade a delicious flavour.

1.25 kg/3 lb Seville oranges	2.75 kg/6 lb granulated or
juice of 2 large lemons	preserving sugar
3.5 litres/5 pints water	

Scrub the oranges well and pick off the small disc at the stalk end. Cut the fruit in half and squeeze out the juice and pips. Quarter the peel and cut away any thick white pith. Shred the peel finely. Cut up the white pith coarsely and tie loosely in a large square of muslin along with the pips. The bag should be loose so that the water will circulate through the pith and pips and extract the pectin.

Place the peel, strained orange and lemon juice, the muslin bag of pith and pips and the water in a preserving pan. Bring to the boil and simmer gently for $1\frac{1}{2}$–2 hours or until the peel is quite tender.

Remove the bag of pith and pips and squeeze it well by pressing between two dinner plates. Add the sugar and stir over low heat to dissolve. Bring to the boil and boil rapidly for a set – about 15–20 minutes.

Draw the pan off the heat. Skim and cool for about 15 minutes. Pour into warm dry jars. Cover with waxed paper circles when hot. Seal when cold.

Makes 4.5 kg (10 lb)

Variation
Seville orange and ginger marmalade Tie 25 g (1 oz) bruised root ginger in the muslin bag with the pips and pith. When the marmalade is ready, draw off the heat and skim. Then add 50 g (2 oz) crystallized ginger, washed and finely chopped. Cool and pot as above.

Pressure-cooker marmalade

It takes less than half the time to make marmalade using the pressure cooker, but you can only make small quantities at a time.

900 g/2 lb Seville oranges
2 large lemons
1.75 litres/3 pints water

1.75 kg/4 lb granulated or
  preserving sugar

Scrub the fruit and pick off the small disc at the stalk end. Cut a slice off the top and bottom of each fruit and place the fruit in the pressure cooker, having removed the trivet at the base. Add 2 pints (generous litre) of the water, cover and bring up to pressure. Cook at 7-kg (15-lb) pressure for 15 minutes. Then reduce the pressure quickly under cold running water. Strain off the liquid from the pan and reserve.

When the fruit is cool enough to handle, halve the oranges and lemons and using a teaspoon scoop out the pips and pith from the centre of each. Boil these up with the remaining water for 20 minutes and then strain into the reserved liquid. Slice the peel evenly and measure the liquid and peel back into the open pan – this recipe should yield about 2.25 litres (4 pints).

For this second stage in the recipe the pressure cooker lid is not required; only the pan base is used. For each pint (generous 0.5 litre) of juice and peel add 450 g (1 lb) granulated or preserving sugar. Stir over low heat until the sugar has dissolved and then bring up to the boil. Cook briskly for a set – this takes 15–20 minutes. When setting point is reached, draw the pan off the heat, skim and leave to stand for 15–20 minutes. Ladle or pour into clean dry jars. Cover with waxed circles while hot and seal when cold.

Makes 2.5–2.75 kg (5–6 lb)

Using the freezer in January

If you have no time to make marmalade now, store Seville oranges in polythene bags in the freezer to use later. Freeze in quantities required for your marmalade recipe, adding an extra orange or so to allow for a slight loss of pectin content, the result of freezing. The oranges must be used frozen and therefore are only suitable for a recipe where the fruit is cooked whole. Follow the recipe for *chunky Seville marmalade* (see page 30) when using them at a later stage.

Freezing soups and stocks

Home-made soups are an excellent addition to your stock of ready-to-serve foods in the freezer. With a good supply ready made, the family can have a bowl of hot home-made soup every day. Replenish your stock with freshly made varieties as they run low.

On the whole potato-thickened or vegetable purée soups freeze best – recipes like this month's *leek and carrot soup* or *split pea soup* (see pages 8 and 10). *Scotch broth* (see page 9) also freezes well – a lovely warming broth to produce steaming hot for supper. Good stock makes all the difference to the flavour of soup. The kind most likely to be available at home is that made from a chicken or turkey carcass. Prepared stock is bulky to freeze unless reduced to a concentrated form and for the space it takes you might as well make up a soup and freeze that. Rapid boiling will reduce stock to a more concentrated form, and for other uses concentrated stock can be frozen first in an ice-cube tray and then tipped in a bag for storage. Add to casseroles or sauces.

Pour home-made soup into rigid containers and leave 1 cm ($\frac{1}{2}$ in) headspace at the top to allow for expansion. Seal and freeze. When required remove the soups from the freezer several hours beforehand. Chilled soups can be thawed in the refrigerator and served cold. For hot soups turn the contents of the carton into a saucepan when partly thawed and easy to remove from the container. Reheat gently and bring up to the boil, stirring to blend the ingredients, before serving.

Party garnishes for soups These can also be kept in the freezer. Keep toasted croûtons or plain ones ready for frying – they can be fried while still frozen. Parmesan cheese for sprinkling over soup is handy to have – but remember to take the quantity required out of the freezer in time for it to thaw and regain flavour.

February

In spite of occasional freak spring days, *February* is still predominantly a cold winter month. Prepare inexpensive but appetizing meals using offal meats like tongue, liver, kidneys, tripe and sweetbreads. Ring the changes with some of the excellent white fish this month offers, particularly cod, plaice and haddock, and also the seasonal mussels and scallops.

Buy fresh vegetables with a discriminating eye and make the most of leeks, spring greens and some of the fine cabbages – particularly red cabbage, soon to go out of season. February is a scanty month for home-produced fruit which makes it a good moment to cook some of the much loved traditional family puddings.

Florida cocktail

Choose medium-sized grapefruit and large juicy oranges. Use the empty grapefruit shells to make pretty serving cups for the fruit cocktail if you like.

2 grapefruit	50 g/2 oz castor sugar
2 oranges	1 teaspoon honey

Cut the grapefruit in half, loosen the segments and turn out into a basin, squeezing out all the juice from the fruit as well. Slice the oranges in half and prepare in the same manner as the grapefruit, adding the juice of the oranges to the basin.

Strain the fruit juice into a small saucepan, add the castor sugar and honey and stir over low heat until both sugar and honey have dissolved. Pour this syrup back over the fruit and chill thoroughly for several hours to emphasize the flavours.

Serve the fruit mixture spooned into four individual serving glasses – for a decorative effect frost the rims first. Run the cut edge of a lemon round the rim of each glass then dip the rim downwards into a saucer of castor sugar. As the rims dry they will turn frosty and white. Do not fill with the fruit mixture until ready to serve as contact with the moist fruit will make the sugary rims damp.
Serves 4

Brussels sprouts soup

Brussels sprouts that are a little too open for serving as a vegetable make an excellent soup. Even sprout tops can be used. The soup has a good green colour and a pleasant flavour.

25 g/1 oz butter	a scant litre/1½ pints chicken stock
1 medium-sized onion	225 g/8 oz Brussels sprouts or tops
225 g/8 oz (1 large) potato	salt and freshly milled pepper

Melt the butter in a saucepan. Peel and finely chop the onion and add to the pan. Fry gently for about 5 minutes until the onion is soft and tender but not brown. Peel and dice the potato and add to the pan along with the chicken stock. Bring up to the boil, lower the heat and simmer gently for about 15 minutes or until the potato is tender.

Meanwhile wash and trim the sprouts or tops. Add to the pan and bring back to the boil. Simmer for 10 minutes. Then draw the pan off the heat and pass the contents through a vegetable mill or blend to a purée in a blender. Return the soup to the pan. Season to taste with salt and pepper and reheat before serving.
Serves 6

Smoked haddock soup

If you take a fish like smoked haddock on the bone and use it to flavour a fish stock which makes up part of the recipe you can make a very tasty fish soup. This recipe has a part fish stock and part milk base and makes a fine start to a dinner party menu.

1 smoked haddock on the bone, about 675 g/1½ lb	25 g/1 oz cornflour
bay leaf	6 dl/1 pint milk
few parsley stalks	1 egg yolk
1 slice lemon	2–3 tablespoons cream
6 dl/1 pint water	lemon juice to taste
40 g/1½ oz butter	salt and freshly milled pepper
1 onion, finely chopped	pinch ground mace

Rinse the haddock, remove the fins and tail and cut up into large pieces. Place in a saucepan with the bay leaf, parsley stalks and slice of lemon. Add the water and bring up to the boil. Simmer gently, covered with a lid, for about 15 minutes, then strain off the liquor and reserve it. When the fish is cool enough to handle, remove the skin and bones and flake the flesh.

Melt the butter in the rinsed-out saucepan. Add the chopped onion and fry gently until soft but not brown. Stir in the reserved fish liquor and the cornflour blended with the milk. Bring up to the boil, stirring all the time. Reduce the heat and cook gently for 2–3 minutes. Stir in the flaked fish.

Blend together the egg yolk and cream. Draw the pan of soup off the heat and stir in the blend of egg and cream. Add lemon juice and freshly milled pepper to taste. Check seasoning for salt and add a pinch of ground mace. Serve with croûtons of toasted bread or garnish it with just a pinch of paprika.
Serves 6

Leeks in oil and vinegar dressing

Leeks served cold with a vinaigrette sauce, well flavoured with mustard and herbs, make an excellent first course.

8 small leeks	bay leaf
salt	2 hard-boiled eggs

for the dressing:

salt and freshly milled pepper	3–4 tablespoons olive oil
1 level teaspoon castor sugar	1 tablespoon chopped parsley or
2 tablespoons wine vinegar	chervil
¼ teaspoon French mustard	

Remove the outer damaged leaves from the leeks. Trim away the base and cut away the green tops leaving about 10 cm (4 in) of the stem of the leek. Slice through to the centre lengthways, open carefully and wash well under running cold water to remove all earth and grit. Tie in bundles of four, place together in a saucepan and cover with boiling water. Add a seasoning of salt and the bay leaf. Bring back up to the boil, then lower the heat to just simmering. Cover with a lid and cook very gently for 20 minutes until the leeks are quite tender. Take care not to cook too quickly, otherwise the leeks will break up. Lift from the water and allow to cool.

When cold arrange in a serving dish and prepare the dressing. Place a seasoning of salt and freshly milled pepper into a mixing basin. Add the sugar, vinegar and mustard. Stir to blend then add the oil

and mix well. Taste the dressing for sharpness – add a little more vinegar if required. Add the chopped parsley or chervil and spoon over the leeks. Marinate until ready to serve. Then garnish with the sliced hard-boiled eggs.
Serves 4

Moules poulette

Serve mussels prepared this way in individual gratin dishes to hold the sauce. To eat them, guests will require a dessertspoon and fork.

2.25 litres/2 quarts mussels
1 onion, finely chopped
3 dl/½ pint water
3 dl/½ pint dry white wine
25 g/1 oz butter
25 g/1 oz flour

1 egg yolk
2–3 tablespoons cream
juice of ½ lemon
freshly milled pepper
chopped parsley

Wash and scrub the mussels in several changes of cold water. Discard any with broken shells or ones that are not tightly closed. Pull away the beard from each one.

Rub the inside of a large saucepan with a buttered paper and sprinkle with the chopped onion. Put the clean mussels in the pan and add the water and wine. Cover the pan with a lid and place over high heat. Shake the pan occasionally and cook for 2–3 minutes or until the mussels have opened up. Remove from the heat, lift out the mussels and retain the liquid in the pan. Discard any mussels that

have not opened up, then remove remaining mussels from the shells. Place in gratin dishes and keep hot while you make the sauce.

Carefully strain the liquid from the pan. Melt the butter in a saucepan over low heat and stir in the flour. Cook gently for 1 minute then gradually stir in the hot mussel stock. Bring up to the boil stirring well to get a smooth sauce. Cook gently for a few moments then draw off the heat. Stir in the mixed egg yolk and cream and lemon juice to taste. Check seasoning with pepper and reheat. Pour the hot sauce over the mussels. Sprinkle with parsley and serve.
Serves 4

Haddock fish cakes

Fish cakes have one real advantage in that they can be prepared in advance ready for cooking. When well made they provide a very tasty meal that can be quickly set on the table.

450 g/1 lb cooked haddock fillet	1 egg
450 g/1 lb cooked mashed potato	toasted breadcrumbs
salt and freshly milled pepper	50 g/2 oz white cooking fat for
1 tablespoon chopped parsley	frying
squeeze of lemon juice	

Flake the fish taking care to discard all skin and bones. Place the flesh in a mixing basin with the mashed potato. Add a good seasoning of salt and pepper, the parsley and a squeeze of lemon juice. Separate the egg and add the yolk to the mixture. Blend the ingredients with a fork and then turn out on to a clean pastry board. With floured hands, shape the mixture into a thick roll. Set aside in a cool place to firm up.

Place the egg white in a shallow plate and whisk with a fork to break it up. Put plenty of toasted breadcrumbs on a square of greaseproof paper. Divide the fish-cake mixture into six or eight portions, depending on the size required. Round up each piece to a neat flat cake. Turn the fish cakes first in the beaten egg white, then in the toasted breadcrumbs. Pat the coating in and shake off any loose crumbs.

Melt the fat in a pan and allow to become fairly hot before putting in the fish cakes. Fry to brown on both sides and serve hot.
Serves 4

Old-fashioned fish pie

*Many of our traditional fish recipes are much improved if a mixture of
smoked and fresh fish is used. Chopped parsley, hard-boiled egg,
cheese or anchovy essence can be added and a little butter on the potato
topping makes the surface crisp and brown.*

450 g/1 lb cod fillet
225 g/8 oz smoked haddock fillet
1.5 dl/¼ pint milk

1.5 dl/¼ pint water
1 slice lemon
small bay leaf

for the sauce:

25 g/1 oz butter
25 g/1 oz flour
3 dl/½ pint fish cooking liquor
seasonings and flavouring (see
  method)

450 g/1 lb creamed potato
15–25 g/½–1 oz butter

Rinse the fish and cut into pieces. Place in a saucepan and add the
milk, water, lemon slice and bay leaf. Cover and simmer gently
until tender – about 15 minutes. Strain off the liquor and reserve
3 dl (½ pint) of it for the sauce. Discard the skin and any bones from
the fish, break the flesh into loose flakes and set aside.

Melt the butter in a saucepan and stir in the flour. Cook gently for a
moment, then gradually stir in the reserved fish liquor. Beat well all
the time to get a smooth sauce and bring up to the boil. Simmer
gently for 2–3 minutes, then draw off the heat. Fold in the flaked
fish and then add any one of the following flavourings: 2 heaped
tablespoons finely chopped parsley; 2 chopped hard-boiled eggs;
50 g (2 oz) grated cheese; 2 teaspoons anchovy essence. Taste the
mixture and add a little lemon juice and freshly milled pepper as
required.

Turn the mixture into a greased pie dish. Cover with the well-
seasoned creamed potato. Fork up the top and dot with butter.
When ready to serve, place near the top of a moderately hot oven
(190°C., 375°F., Gas Mark 5) for about 20 minutes. Brown under
the grill for a few seconds and serve.

Serves 4

Grilled halibut

Grilling is perhaps the simplest way to cook fish to perfection but it does require care. The secret is gentle heat and plenty of butter.

salt
4 halibut steaks, about
  100–175 g/4–6 oz each

50–75 g/2–3 oz butter
seasoned flour
squeeze of lemon juice

Wash and salt the fish and leave to drain. Take a heatproof dish or grill pan – remove the grid – and put in a generous 50 g (2 oz) butter. Turn on the grill with the dish or grill pan underneath and let the butter melt. Before it changes colour lay in the fish steaks, then immediately turn them over. Cook for 2 minutes, then turn and sprinkle the second side with flour. Cook gently for 10 minutes, adding another sprinkling of flour just before the fish is cooked, and baste with butter two or three times. When the fish is golden and the bones are loose remove to a warm serving platter. Add a squeeze of lemon to the hot butter, pour over and serve.
Serves 4

Scrambled egg with smoked haddock

In Scotland the flesh from smokies – small haddock smoked closed and unfilleted – is often added to scrambled egg. Smoked haddock fillet can also be used. Make scrambled egg for several servings in a frying pan; it's much easier to control the degree of cooking.

225 g/8 oz smoked haddock fillet
8 eggs
salt and freshly milled pepper

1.5 dl/¼ pint milk
50 g/2 oz butter
4 slices buttered toast for serving

Poach the smoked haddock in milk for about 10 minutes, then drain and flake the flesh. Keep the fish warm.

Whisk the eggs, a seasoning of salt and pepper and the milk together. Use the milk from poaching the smoked haddock if you wish, it gives a lovely flavour to the mixture but go easy on the seasoning added.

Melt the butter in a frying pan and pour in the scrambled egg mixture. Cook over low heat, drawing a spoon across the pan to lift up the egg mixture as it sets. Add the flaked haddock. Draw the pan off the heat when the mixture is thickened but still moist. Serve on slices of buttered toast.

Serves 4

Sauce-making

A smooth, glossy well-flavoured sauce makes all the difference to a simple fish or vegetable dish. Remember that if milk for making a sauce is infused and warmed first, it not only has extra flavour but is much easier to mix in. In a recipe using part hot stock and part cold milk, add the hot liquid to the roux first and stir in the cold liquid afterwards. The addition of a hot or warm liquid keeps the roux soft and makes it a lot easier for mixing. Beat a sauce well as it is coming up to the boil; beating not only makes it smooth but gives the sauce a gloss.

Preparing the roux can be the most time-consuming part of sauce-making and a considerable amount of effort can be saved by making it up in quantity and storing it in the refrigerator. The mix keeps for several months and will prove very useful.

To make the roux mix Melt 225 g (8 oz) butter in a large saucepan. Stir in 225 g (8 oz) plain flour and blend well. Allow the mixture to cook over a very gentle heat for about 15 minutes. As the roux cooks it will become lighter in colour and rather sandy in texture. Stir occasionally to check that the mixture is not scorching on the base of the pan. Draw off the heat and leave until cold, giving it an occasional stir. The mixture will now be quite hard. Using a wooden spoon, rub the mixture through a coarse sieve so that it becomes crumbly and granular in texture. This makes it easier to measure out. Tip into a polythene bag, tie closed and keep in the refrigerator.

When a sauce is needed you simply heat up the required quantity of liquid. To make 3 dl ($\frac{1}{2}$ pint) white sauce, warm up 3 dl ($\frac{1}{2}$ pint) milk in a saucepan. Sprinkle in 2 rounded tablespoons of the roux mix, stir to blend it in with the milk and then bring up to the boil, stirring all the time to get a smooth sauce. Season with salt and pepper and the sauce is ready. Because the milk is warm and the roux is already cooked, the ingredients blend very quickly and very smoothly. If the sauce is not thick enough sprinkle in a little more 'mix' and if it's too thick thin it down with milk. You can't go wrong. Think how useful and quick this can be for a sauce base to a cheese soufflé, to blend ingredients for a pancake filling, or to make a veal or chicken blanquette.

Scallops in the shell

Make the most of scallops, in season now, and their pretty shells which are ideal for serving. Ask the fishmonger for the deep-sided or concave half of each shell. Scrub them clean and rub the insides with oil before using. Otherwise, serve this recipe in individual gratin dishes.

6 scallops
100 g/4 oz button mushrooms
3 dl/½ pint water
1.5 dl/¼ pint dry white wine

bay leaf
lemon slice
salt and freshly milled pepper

for the sauce:

50 g/2 oz butter
50 g/2 oz flour
  cooking liquor (see method)
1.5 dl/¼ pint milk

2–3 tablespoons cream
25–50 g/1–2 oz grated Parmesan
  cheese

Cut each scallop into thick slices. Trim and slice the mushrooms. Place the scallops and mushrooms in a saucepan and add the water, wine, bay leaf, lemon slice and a seasoning of salt and pepper. Simmer gently for 15 minutes, then strain off the liquor and reserve for making the sauce. Keep the scallops and mushrooms warm.

Melt the butter in a saucepan and stir in the flour. Gradually beat in the reserved cooking liquor to make a fairly thick white sauce. Stir in sufficient of the milk to bring the sauce to a coating consistency. Add the scallops and mushrooms and heat through.

Draw off the heat and stir in the cream. Spoon the mixture into the six scallop shells and sprinkle with grated cheese. Reheat near the top of a moderate oven (180°C., 350°F., Gas Mark 4) for about 15 minutes, or until brown. Serve hot.
Serves 6

Casserole of beef with whole onions

When whole peeled onions are used in a casserole, they give a delicious flavour to the gravy while retaining their neat shape. They can then easily be removed, or not served to anyone who dislikes them.

675–900 g/1½–2 lb stewing steak
seasoned flour
25 g/1 oz dripping or white cooking
  fat
450 g/1 lb medium-sized or small
  onions

450 g/1 lb carrots
bouquet garni
4 dl/¾ pint stock
salt and freshly milled pepper
chopped fresh parsley

Trim away any fat and cut the meat into neat pieces. Roll in seasoned flour. Heat the dripping in a frying pan, add the meat and brown evenly on all sides. Lift the meat from the pan and place in a casserole.

Peel the onions, leaving them whole, and scrape and slice the carrots. Place the onions in a saucepan, cover with cold water and bring up to the boil. Drain and add to the casserole along with the carrots and the bouquet garni.

Add about 1 tablespoon of the seasoned flour to the fat remaining in the frying pan. If little or no fat remains, then add an extra 15 g ($\frac{1}{2}$ oz) dripping to absorb the flour. Cook over moderate heat, stirring well, until the mixture is well browned. Gradually stir in the hot stock and bring up to the boil. Add a seasoning of salt and pepper to taste and if necessary a little gravy browning to get a good rich colour. Draw off the heat and strain over the contents of the casserole. Cover with a lid and place in the centre of a slow oven (150°C., 300°F., Gas Mark 2) and cook for $2\frac{1}{2}$–3 hours or until the meat is quite tender. Remove the bouquet garni, sprinkle with chopped parsley and serve.

Serves 4

Chicken-liver pancakes

Stuffed savoury pancakes can be made ahead ready for reheating and as such make an excellent choice for a buffet lunch or supper. Serve them with a seasonal salad and there's no need to cook any vegetables at all.

12 prepared pancakes (see page 53)

for the filling:

65 g/$2\frac{1}{2}$ oz butter
450 g/1 lb chicken livers
4 tablespoons chicken stock or red wine
pinch mixed herbs

1 onion
40 g/$1\frac{1}{2}$ oz flour
4 dl/$\frac{3}{4}$ pint mixed milk and onion stock (see method)
salt and freshly milled pepper

Have the pancakes prepared and hot. Melt 25 g (1 oz) of the butter in a saucepan, add the trimmed chicken livers, the chicken stock or wine and the herbs. Cover and simmer for about 10 minutes or until the livers are cooked. Draw off the heat and pass the livers and liquid from the pan through a vegetable mill into a mixing basin, or chop very finely.

Peel and finely chop the onion. Place in a saucepan and generously cover with salt water. Bring to a simmer and cook gently in a covered pan for 10 minutes. Drain and reserve both onion and cooking liquor.

Melt the remaining butter in a saucepan and stir in the flour. Cook gently for a few moments and then gradually stir in about 1.5 dl ($\frac{1}{4}$ pint) of the onion stock and then 2.5 dl ($\frac{1}{2}$ pint) milk. Bring up to the boil, stirring well to make a smooth sauce. Season with salt and pepper and check flavour – it should have a mild onion flavour. Add about 3 dl ($\frac{1}{2}$ pint) of this sauce and the cooked onion to the chicken-liver mixture and blend well. Fill the pancakes with the liver mixture, roll up and place in a buttered baking or serving dish.

Thin down the rest of the sauce if necessary to make a coating sauce. Pour over the pancakes and put to heat through in a moderately hot oven (190°C., 375°F., Gas Mark 5) for 10 minutes. Cover with foil and extend the time to 30 minutes if reheating from cold.
Serves 4-6

Kidneys in mustard cream sauce

Kidneys, if they are to have a good flavour, must be eaten quickly and should not be kept longer than 24 hours in the refrigerator. Served in this way they make an excellent lunch or supper dish.

6–8 lambs' kidneys
1 teaspoon vinegar
50 g/2 oz butter
salt and pepper

1 rounded teaspoon flour
1.5 dl/$\frac{1}{4}$ pint fresh double cream
1–2 teaspoons prepared mild
 English mustard

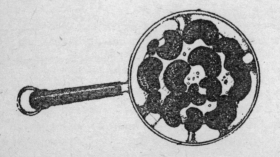

Remove any fat from around the kidneys. Snip out the core using a pair of scissors and remove the skin. Place in a basin, cover with cold water and add the vinegar. Leave to soak for 10–15 minutes.

Drain, pat dry and slice thickly. Add to the hot butter in a frying pan and fry gently for 5 minutes; do not overcook. Then add a good seasoning of salt and pepper and sprinkle over the flour. Stir to blend, then add the cream and mustard to taste. Bring up to the boil, stirring until thickened, then draw the pan off the heat. Serve with slices of hot buttered toast.

Serves 4

Lambs' liver with onions in wine sauce

Put the lambs' liver to soak in milk until required for cooking; milk has a tenderizing effect and makes it taste almost like calves' liver which, if it were not so expensive, would be the one to choose for this recipe.

2 medium-sized onions	seasoned flour
75 g/3 oz butter	3 dl/½ pint dry white wine or wine
450 g/1 lb lambs' liver, cut in slices	and stock

Peel and finely chop the onions. Add to the hot butter in a frying pan and cook gently for about 5 minutes until the onion is tender.

Meanwhile trim the liver and cut each slice across into thin strips rather as you would cut steak for beef stroganoff. Toss the strips of liver in seasoned flour and add to the pan of onions. Fry both together over fairly high heat, tossing the ingredients to seal the liver on all sides. Allow to cook for about 4–5 minutes, then with a perforated spoon lift the liver and onions out on to a hot serving dish.

Add the wine to the hot pan and allow it to boil up fairly fast. Stir to pick up all the flavouring bits in the pan and let the wine reduce by about half to concentrate the flavour. Pour over the liver and serve.

Serves 4

Grilled chicken

Choose the tiny poussins which can be split in half to make two portions, or chicken quarters for grilling. Remember that liquid spooned over foods during grilling prevents dryness and adds flavour. This can be pan drippings, flavoured butters, lemon and oil or a special sauce as below.

4 chicken quarters	salt and freshly milled pepper
2–3 tablespoons oil	1 tablespoon lemon juice

for the barbecue baste (optional):

2 tablespoons made mustard
½ level teaspoon salt
pepper
1 tablespoon soft brown sugar

2 tablespoons wine vinegar or
  lemon juice
3 tablespoons tomato ketchup

Trim the chicken pieces and place in a shallow dish. Mix the oil, a seasoning of salt and pepper and the lemon juice. Pour over the chicken and leave to marinate for an hour or until ready to cook.

Place the chicken pieces in a grill pan with the grill rack removed. Arrange the pieces flesh side down and baste with the oil and lemon marinade. Place under a moderately hot grill – the chicken should be about 7 cm (3 in) from the heat. Grill for about 10 minutes on the wrong side, then turn the pieces over, baste and grill right side up for 15 minutes. Test the joints by piercing a thick part of the joint with a sharp knife. The juices that run should be clear with no tinges of pink. Serve hot.

To give extra flavour brush the barbecue baste, made by blending all the ingredients, over the chicken pieces before cooking and when turning.
Serves 4

Cauliflower cheese

Gruyère cheese is expensive to use for cooking but it really does go crisp and brown under the grill and you can use less of it to get a good flavour. Hot cauliflower cheese is particularly good served with cold chicken.

1 medium-sized cauliflower

for the cheese sauce:
25 g/1 oz butter
25 g/1 oz flour
3 dl/½ pint part milk and part
  cauliflower water (see method)

salt and freshly milled pepper
75–100 g/3–4 oz Gruyère or other
  hard cheese, grated

Trim the cauliflower and break into medium-sized sprigs. Cook in boiling salted water until tender – about 8–10 minutes.

Drain and reserve 1.5 dl (¼ pint) cooking liquor for the sauce. Arrange the cauliflower sprigs in a buttered serving dish and keep warm. Melt the butter for the sauce and stir in the flour. Cook gently for 1 minute, then gradually stir in the hot reserved cauliflower liquor and then the milk. Bring up to the boil, stirring all the time to make a smooth sauce. Allow to simmer for 1–2 minutes, then season to taste. Add all but 25 g (1 oz) of the grated cheese and stir over low heat until the cheese has melted.

Pour the sauce over the cauliflower. Sprinkle with the remaining cheese and put under a hot grill until the top is crisp and brown.

Serves 4

Sweet and sour red cabbage

Success with red cabbage means getting the correct balance of sweet and sour flavours. Well cooked it makes a marvellous accompaniment for roast pork or duck.

1 small red cabbage (about 675 g/ 1½ lb)
50 g/2 oz butter
40–50 g/1½–2 oz granulated sugar

4 tablespoons wine vinegar
1 good tablespoon redcurrant jelly
salt to taste

Remove outer damaged leaves and cut the cabbage in quarters. Cut away the hard core and then shred the cabbage finely across the leaves.

Melt the butter in a heavy saucepan and add the sugar. Stir just to blend and then add the wine vinegar. Add the shredded cabbage and toss well to mix the ingredients. Cover with a lid and leave to cook over very gentle heat. The slower the cabbage cooks the better it will taste and it can easily be left to cook for 2 hours. Stir or shake the pan occasionally.

When ready the cabbage should be slightly moist without any liquid being visible. Add the redcurrant jelly and toss to glaze the cabbage. Season to taste with salt before serving.
Serves 4-6

Baked onions in white sauce

Onions in a white sauce are always a popular accompaniment to a roast joint, particularly lamb. They can be baked and served in the same dish. Place them below the roast in the lower part of the oven if they are cooked together.

450 g/1 lb medium-sized onions	1 tablespoon water
15 g/½ oz butter	

for the sauce:

25 g/1 oz butter	3 dl/½ pint milk
25 g/1 oz flour	salt and pepper

Peel the onions leaving them whole. Place in a saucepan, cover with cold water and bring to the boil. Simmer for 1 minute, then drain and place in a casserole. Add the butter and water. Cover with a lid, place in the centre of a moderate oven (180°C., 350°F., Gas Mark 4) and bake for 1 hour.

About 10 minutes before serving melt the butter for the sauce in a pan. Stir in the flour and cook gently for 1 minute. Gradually beat in the milk stirring well to get a smooth sauce. Season with salt and pepper and simmer gently for a few minutes. When the onions are ready, remove the lid from the casserole and pour over the sauce before serving.
Serves 4

Fried leeks with bacon

Leeks can be fried and served as a vegetable, but they must be cooked gently. With bacon added, they taste very good and can be served along with sausages, fried eggs or chops, or used as a filling for an omelette.

450 g/1 lb leeks	50 g/2 oz butter
100 g/4 oz bacon rashers	freshly milled pepper

Trim away the root and the green part of the leeks down to about 2.5 cm (1 in) from the white stem. Split open and wash well, then shred coarsely. Trim and chop the bacon rashers.

Melt the butter in a frying pan and add the leeks and bacon. Season well with freshly milled pepper. Stir, then cover with a lid and cook over gentle heat for about 20 minutes to soften. Serve hot from the pan.

Serves 4

Glazed cabbage

Cabbage is a difficult vegetable to present appetizingly and all too often it is just badly cooked and watery. Try cooking it using the conservative method, with a small amount of water in a covered pan.

450 g/1 lb (½ head) cabbage	salt and freshly milled pepper
1.5 dl/¼ pint water	15 g/½ oz butter

Quarter the cabbage and remove any stalks. Turn each piece head down on the working surface and using a sharp knife shred across the leaves finely. Wash in plenty of cold water and drain well.

Bring the water to the boil in a good-sized saucepan, add salt and then the cabbage. Cover with a lid and simmer gently until the cabbage is tender, about 15 minutes. Turn the cabbage occasionally so that it cooks evenly. Drain in a colander and press well with a potato masher to squeeze out all the moisture.

Add the butter to the hot saucepan and return the cabbage to the pan. Season with salt and plenty of pepper. Toss to glaze the cabbage and serve.

Serves 4

Pancakes

Never cook pancakes in a pan swimming in hot fat. The secret is to cook them in almost no fat at all. The best method is to buy a chunky piece of bacon fat, the sort of bit you find among the bacon scraps or end pieces. Rub it round the hot pan before pouring in the batter. As the pancakes are prepared, keep them hot by stacking neatly between two plates set over a saucepan of simmering water.

100 g/4 oz plain flour	3 dl/½ pint milk
pinch salt	1 tablespoon oil
1 egg	

Sieve the flour and salt into a mixing basin and make a well in the centre. Crack the egg into the well and add half the milk. Using a wooden spoon, mix the egg and milk, gradually drawing in the flour from the edge of the basin. When all the flour has been incorporated, beat well until small bubbles appear on the surface and the mixture is well aerated. Stir in the remaining milk and the oil. Strain into a jug and leave for 30 minutes. Stir before using.

Ideally pancakes should be made in a proper pancake pan which is about 15 cm (6 in) in diameter. Failing this use an omelette pan; as a rule a frying pan is too large. Heat the pan and rub around the inside with the piece of bacon fat to grease it. Pour about 2 tablespoons of the batter into the centre of the pan and tilt the pan so that the batter runs over the base to form a thin pancake. Cook until the underside is brown, then turn and cook the second side.

Repeat the procedure with each pancake, rubbing the pan well with the bacon fat before adding each quantity of batter, until all twelve pancakes are made.

To serve pancakes, sprinkle with sugar and lemon or orange juice and roll up, or fill with jam.
Serves 6

Steamed jam pudding

Remember that a steamed pudding keeps hot perfectly if you don't unmould it but leave it in the steamer off the heat. Red jam such as strawberry is always the popular choice, but as an alternative use marmalade or golden syrup.

175 g/6 oz self-raising flour
pinch salt
75 g/3 oz mixed fats (use margarine and white cooking fat)
75 g/3 oz castor sugar

1 large egg
few drops vanilla essence
3–4 tablespoons milk to mix
1 heaped tablespoon jam

for the jam sauce:
2–3 heaped tablespoons jam
2 level teaspoons cornflour

2 dl/⅓ pint (1 teacup) water
juice of ½ lemon

Sift the flour and salt into a bowl. Blend the fats to mix and then rub into the dry ingredients. Stir in the sugar. Lightly mix the egg and vanilla essence and stir into the ingredients. Add sufficient milk to make a medium-soft consistency.

Place the heaped tablespoon of jam in the base of a well-greased

1-litre (1½-pint) pudding basin. Spoon in the sponge mixture and spread level. Cover with a double thickness of greased greaseproof paper, folding a pleat to allow the pudding to rise. Tie tightly and steam briskly for 1½–2 hours.

Meanwhile prepare the jam sauce. Sieve the jam into a saucepan, add the cornflour blended with the water and lemon juice and stir over the heat until the sauce is boiling and thickened. Unmould the pudding and serve hot with the sauce.
Serves 4-6

Butterscotch flan

Brown sugar and evaporated milk give the rich butterscotch flavour to this flan. The lemon juice thickens the mixture and on baking it sets to a firm custard. It's a strange recipe but one that works.

100 g/4 oz shortcrust pastry

for the filling:

1 small can evaporated milk   1 tablespoon lemon juice
225 g/8 oz soft brown sugar

Roll out the pastry on a lightly floured working surface, and use to line an 18-cm (7-in) flan ring or tart tin, preferably one with a loose base. Trim the edges neatly and fill the centre with a piece of crumpled kitchen foil – this helps to keep the centre of the pastry case flat while baking. Place above the centre of a hot oven (220°C., 425°F., Gas Mark 7) and bake for 10 minutes. Remove the foil a few moments before the end of the baking time. Remove the pastry case from the oven and set aside while preparing the filling.

Pour the evaporated milk into a mixing basin, add the sugar and lemon juice and stir well to mix. Pour into the baked pastry case. Replace in the centre of a moderate oven (180°C., 350°F., Gas Mark 4) and bake for 30 minutes. Remove from the oven and allow to stand for 15 minutes to set firm. Serve warm or cold with cream.
Serves 4-6

Chocolate mousse

This chocolate mousse needs no gelatine. A useful recipe, it can be made up for as few as two servings, or as many as six, so long as you allow 1

*egg and 25 g (1 oz) chocolate per person. Use a plain chocolate,
preferably Chocolat Menier for the best flavour.*

100 g/4 oz plain chocolate   4 eggs
15 g/½ oz butter

Break the chocolate into a basin and set over a saucepan half filled
with hot water. Stir occasionally until the chocolate has melted. Stir
in the butter and blend well. Separate the eggs, adding the yolks to
the chocolate mixture and placing the whites together in a basin.
Stir to blend the egg yolks and chocolate and remove the basin from
the heat.

Whisk the egg whites until stiff and, using a metal spoon, fold gently
but firmly into the chocolate mixture. Pour the mousse into
individual serving dishes and chill for several hours.

It is always advisable to make this kind of mousse several hours in
advance; thorough chilling is required to develop a firm texture. For
a party, the dishes look pretty if decorated with a little whipped
cream or small pineapple cubes. The sharp taste of the pineapple
makes a pleasant contrast to the rich chocolate flavour.
Serves 4

Orange- and lemon-flavoured sugars
Orange- and lemon-flavoured sugars used in place of ordinary sugar
give a real fruit flavour to recipes. Grate the orange or lemon rind on the
finest possible grater and mix it with castor sugar allowing 100 g (4 oz)
sugar for each fruit used. Using a wooden spoon, work the sugar and
zest together. The sugar will take on the colour and absorb the
flavouring oils of the fruit. Spread the sugar out on a square of greaseproof paper or foil and set in a warm place to dry. Crush any lumps or
sieve if necessary, store ready to use in a covered jar.

Follow your own recipe for a sandwich layer cake and use flavoured
sugar instead of ordinary castor sugar. Use lemon sugar to flavour
apples in apple pie and orange sugar to sweeten any dessert recipe using
rhubarb. Either is good sprinkled over pancakes.

Rhubarb with bananas and rum

*Gentle slow cooking is required to keep pieces of rhubarb whole and
neat in shape. Baking them in the oven usually gives very good results.*

450 g/1 lb early rhubarb	pinch salt
100 g/4 oz castor sugar	2 large bananas
juice of 1 orange	1 tablespoon rum

Trim and wash the rhubarb and cut into 2.5-cm (1-in) lengths. Place in an ovenproof dish, sprinkle over the sugar and add the orange juice and salt. Leave to stand for at least 2 hours, so that the sugar draws the juices from the rhubarb. Stir occasionally to help the sugar dissolve.

Cover the dish with a lid and place in the centre of a slow oven (150°C., 300°F., Gas Mark 2) and bake for 45 minutes or until the rhubarb is tender. Cool and then chill. When ready to serve, peel the bananas and slice into a serving dish. Add the rum to the rhubarb and then pour over the bananas. Serve with cream.

Serves 4

Date and walnut bread

The ready-prepared and packaged sugar-coated chopped dates are ideal for this recipe. Find them in most supermarkets.

350 g/12 oz self-raising flour
½ level teaspoon salt
75 g/3 oz soft brown sugar
50 g/2 oz walnuts, finely chopped

100 g/4 oz dates, chopped
2 eggs
2.5 dl/scant ½ pint milk
50 g/2 oz butter, melted

Sift the flour and salt into a large bowl. Stir in the sugar, walnuts and dates. Crack in the eggs and add the milk. Using a wooden spoon, stir to mix the ingredients together and then beat thoroughly to make a fairly soft mixture. Add the melted butter and stir in thoroughly.

Spoon the mixture into a greased and lined large (23- by 13- by 7.5-cm, 9- by 5- by 3-in) loaf pan. Spread the mixture level. Place in the centre of a moderate oven (180°C., 350°F., Gas Mark 4) and bake for 1 hour. When baked remove from the tin and leave until quite cold. Serve sliced and buttered.

Makes 1 large loaf

Malt bread

Children love malt bread and it's good for them. Bake two loaves in this easy way and serve sliced and buttered. Malt extract can be bought from a chemist.

450 g/1 lb self-raising flour
1 level teaspoon salt
25 g/1 oz butter
25 g/1 oz soft brown sugar
100 g/4 oz sultanas

3 dl/½ pint milk
1 tablespoon black treacle
2 heaped tablespoons pure malt
  extract

Sift the flour and salt into a large basin. Rub in the butter. Add the sugar and sultanas. Measure the milk, treacle and malt extract into a saucepan. Place over low heat and warm gently, just until the ingredients have blended together. Pour into the flour mixture all at once. Using a wooden spoon, stir to blend the ingredients together. Then beat thoroughly for a moment to make a smooth, fairly soft mixture.

Divide the mixture equally between two greased and lined small (18- by 10- by 5-cm, 7- by 4- by 2-in) loaf pans. Spread the mixture level. Place in the centre of a very moderate oven (160°C., 325°F., Gas Mark 3) and bake for 1 hour.

Towards the end of the baking time prepare a glaze by measuring 1 tablespoon each castor sugar, milk and water into a saucepan. Stir over the heat to dissolve the sugar, then bring up to the boil. When the malt loaves are baked and while still hot from the oven, brush over the entire surface with hot glaze. This makes them shiny and attractive. Leave the malt bread until quite cold, preferably overnight. Serve sliced and buttered.

Makes 2 small loaves

Raisin bread

Traditional recipes often use cold tea for mixing. It gives a good flavour and makes the fruit in the bread deliciously moist. This loaf keeps well.

225 g/8 oz seedless raisins or other mixed dried fruit
100 g/4 oz soft brown sugar
2 dl/⅓ pint (1 teacup) cold strained tea

225 g/8 oz self-raising flour
½ level teaspoon mixed spice
finely grated rind of 1 orange
1 egg

Measure the dried fruit and brown sugar into a large mixing basin. Pour over the cold tea and stir well with a wooden spoon. Cover the basin and leave for 12–24 hours.

Sift the flour and mixed spice on to a plate. Add the grated orange rind and lightly mixed egg to the fruit mixture and stir in the sifted flour. Mix all ingredients thoroughly and spoon into a greased and lined small (18- by 10- by 5-cm, 7- by 4- by 2-in) loaf pan. Spread

59

the mixture evenly and place in the centre of a very moderate oven (160°C., 325°F., Gas Mark 3) and bake for 1½ hours.

Allow the baked loaf to cool in the pan for 20 minutes, then turn out and leave until cold. Wrap in greaseproof paper and store in a tin with a tight-fitting lid. Serve sliced and buttered.
Makes 1 large loaf

Banana nut bread

Bananas are an all-year-round fruit but for February teas banana bread is a special treat. The loaf is moist and keeps well. Serve it sliced and buttered.

175 g/6 oz self-raising flour
½ level teaspoon salt
1 level teaspoon mixed spice
100 g/4 oz castor sugar

40 g/1½ oz chopped walnuts
2 medium-sized ripe bananas
1 large egg
25 g/1 oz butter, melted

Sift the flour, salt and mixed spice into a mixing basin. Stir in the sugar and walnuts. Peel the bananas and mash to a purée with a fork. Add to the dry ingredients along with the egg and melted butter. Using a wooden spoon stir to blend the ingredients and then beat thoroughly to mix.

Spoon the mixture into a greased and lined small (18- by 10- by 5-cm, 7- by 4- by 2-in) loaf tin. Spread the mixture evenly. Place in the centre of a moderate oven (180°C., 350°F., Gas Mark 4) and bake for 1 hour. Turn out and leave until cold.
Makes 1 small loaf

Soda bread

Soda bread is surprisingly quick to make. Buy the buttermilk required from a supermarket or health food shop.

450 g/1 lb plain flour
1 level teaspoon salt
1 level teaspoon bicarbonate of
 soda

1 level teaspoon cream of tartar
25 g/1 oz butter or lard
3 dl/½ pint buttermilk

Sift the flour, salt, bicarbonate of soda and cream of tartar into a large basin. Add the butter and rub into the dry ingredients. Make a well in the centre and stir in the buttermilk.

Turn out and knead lightly on a floured surface. Shape quickly into a round loaf, about 5 cm (2 in) thick. Place on a floured baking sheet and score the top lightly three times with a sharp knife. Place in the centre of a moderately hot oven (200°C., 400°F., Gas Mark 6) and bake for 35–40 minutes or until well risen and brown. Leave until cold. Serve sliced with butter.
Makes 1 loaf

Teabreads

Even the most reluctant cook will find teabreads rewarding to bake. These mixtures require no tiresome creaming of fat and sugar, nor is yeast among the ingredients as the term 'bread' might imply. Teabreads are made using self-raising flour, or plain flour and a raising agent. They are more interesting than plain bread but not so rich as cake and are marvellous for children's teas, when they can be served sliced and buttered. They are also very good for picnics.

Bake these breads the day before you want them, then they should slice easily and spread without crumbling. Use loaf pans in preference to bread tins. Loaf pans are not so deep, they make teabreads a more attractive shape and one which is better for slicing. Loaf pans come in two sizes – a larger approximately 23- by 13- by 7.5-cm (9- by 5- by 3-in) pan and a smaller 18- by 10- by 5-cm (7- by 4- by 2-in) pan.

Grease the tins well and line with a strip of greaseproof paper cut the width of the tin and long enough to cover the base and overlap the opposite two ends. When baked loosen the unlined sides with a knife and ease the loaf out of the tin using the ends of the greaseproof paper.

Using the freezer in February

Dishes made with cooked fish, particularly the more traditional ones, freeze well. Recipes like *haddock fish cakes* (see page 42) can be prepared, then egg-and-breadcrumbed ready to fry. Freeze uncovered on wax paper-lined trays until firm. Then pack in containers or polythene bags. To use they can be fried from frozen. Prepare the *old-fashioned fish pie* (see page 43) in family or individual-sized foil freezer trays. Cool as quickly as possible and then chill in the refrigerator. Place containers inside polythene bags to overwrap and freeze. To use, thaw overnight in the refrigerator and then place in a moderately hot oven (190°C., 375°F., Gas Mark 5) for 40 minutes to reheat before serving. Cooked fish dishes keep for 1 month.

Brussels sprouts soup (see page 39) freezes well and can be added to your stock of freezer soups for inclusion in supper menus.

One of the most versatile standbys to have in the freezer is prepared pancakes. To prevent pancakes going rubbery, the batter used must be an enriched one, with a tablespoon of oil added to the basic mixture. Use the recipe for *pancakes* (see page 53), and as they are cooked spread them out to cool quickly. Then stack neatly in numbers that you are likely to use at one time. Wrap in foil and freeze. Pancakes store well for up to 2 months.

To use thaw for 2–3 hours at room temperature or overnight in the refrigerator. Loosen the foil packet so the air can circulate and reheat in a moderately hot oven (200°C., 400°F., Gas Mark 6) for about 20 minutes. Serve them with sweet or savoury fillings. A well-seasoned white sauce including pieces of chicken and mushrooms or prawns turns them into a good supper dish.

Freezing fish

Fish to be frozen at home must be absolutely fresh and unless you can be certain of this, it is better to rely on commercially frozen fish. Likely sources of fresh fish are sea or river fish caught by a member of the family, or for those who live near the sea, a local fisherman who sells direct.

Keep any fish iced or in the refrigerator prior to freezing. Large fish can be cut into cutlets or portions while small fish are better frozen whole. Use heavy-duty aluminium foil for wrapping and turn the edges firmly together, folding them in to seal the package airtight. Pieces of fish can be laid in shallow foil dishes into which they fit neatly and then placed inside a polythene bag and sealed airtight. Where fillets or portions of fish are packed together, they are easier to separate for cooking if a small piece of thin plastic film is placed between the pieces of fish.

Mackerel, trout and herrings These are small fish usually served whole. Scale, clean and rinse under water. Leave heads and tails on or not as preferred. Pack individually or in single layers of two to four fish side by side. Store for up to 3 months.

Salmon or salmon trout Clean and rinse under cold water. The smaller salmon trout can be left whole. As a rule it is better to cut larger salmon into serving portions – one or more pieces of 'middle cut' and the 'tail end'. Alternatively salmon can be cut across the bone into 2.5-cm (1-in) 'steaks'. Wrap and freeze. Store salmon for 2–3 months.

To use frozen fish Separate small fish or cutlets while partially frozen and cook from the frozen or partially frozen state. Large whole fish or pieces of fish should be thawed overnight in the refrigerator.

Note With bulk buys of commercially frozen fish fingers or fish cakes it is very important to repack them in smaller quantities. Constantly opening one large container to extract a few can speed up deterioration of the remainder.

March

March is traditionally the first month of spring, and this is a good time to take stock of the kitchen store-cupboard and to use up what remains in the freezer, making the necessary space for inevitable additions during the summer months. Spring sees the start of an excellent supply of poultry including small poussins, plump ducklings and nice fat pigeons. It heralds the start of the salmon season, although too expensive yet for most people. White fish become plump and plentiful and there should be quantities of fresh roe on the market.

Make the most of what remains in the way of main-crop vegetables for the early arrivals of the new season's crops are still expensive. Bring a fresh flavour to recipes with citrus fruits, particularly grapefruit and colourful oranges and lemons for desserts.

Almond soup

Almond soup has a delicate flavour. For best results use freshly blanched and ground almonds. Bought ground almonds can be used instead, but they are inclined to froth up in the pan as the soup comes to the boil.

100 g/4 oz unblanched almonds
2–3 stalks celery
1 small onion
1.75 litres/3 pints chicken stock
25 g/1 oz butter
25 g/1 oz flour
3 dl/½ pint milk
salt and freshly milled pepper
2–3 tablespoons cream
1 egg yolk
few toasted slivered almonds

Blanch the almonds and grind in a Mouli grater or a blender. Place in a saucepan along with the washed and cut up celery and the chopped onion. Add the hot chicken stock and bring up to the boil. Lower the heat, cover and simmer gently for 1 hour. Draw off the heat and strain the liquid, pressing well to extract all the flavour.

Melt the butter and stir in the flour. Gradually add the almond-flavoured stock, stirring well to get a smooth mixture. Add the milk and bring up to the boil. Draw off the heat and add the blended cream and egg yolk. Check seasoning and stir in the toasted slivered almonds.

Serves 6

Chicken broth

The liquor in which a chicken has been boiled, with a stock cube for added flavouring, or home-made stock from a chicken carcass should be used as the basis for this tasty broth. Save any scraps of cooked chicken to add as well.

100 g/4 oz carrots
2 medium-sized onions
2 leeks
1 stalk celery
25 g/1 oz butter
a generous litre/2 pints chicken
  stock

bouquet garni
salt and freshly milled pepper
25 g/1 oz fine short noodles
scraps of cooked chicken
chopped parsley

Peel the carrots and cut into matchstick-thin slices. Peel and shred the onions. Wash and shred the leeks and the celery. Melt the butter in a large saucepan, add the prepared vegetables and sauté gently to soften but not brown. Add the hot chicken stock and the bouquet garni. Cover with a lid and simmer gently until the vegetables are tender.

Remove the bouquet garni and taste the broth for seasoning. Add the rinsed noodles and cook without a lid until the noodles are tender, about 5–8 minutes. Stir in any scraps of cooked chicken and chopped parsley to garnish. Heat for a moment, adding a little more chicken stock if a thinner broth is required. Serve hot.
Serves 4-6

Egg mayonnaise

Other garnishes for egg mayonnaise could include a sprinkling of finely chopped chives or a few soaked anchovy fillets arranged criss-cross over the top.

4 eggs
4 rounded tablespoons mayonnaise
2–3 tablespoons cream

4 crisp lettuce leaves
paprika

Simmer the eggs to hard-boil, then drain and plunge into cold water to prevent further cooking. Peel away the shells and leave the eggs covered with cold water until required.

When ready to serve, drain the eggs and slice in half lengthways. Thin down the mayonnaise to a coating consistency with the cream. Arrange the egg halves in pairs, cut side downwards, on the crisp lettuce leaves. Coat with the mayonnaise. Either sprinkle with the paprika, or for a more effective finish, garnish with a line of paprika running the length of the egg. To do this simply place a little paprika on a square of greaseproof paper, then take up a small amount along the edge of a knife blade. Tip this sharply on to the egg and the paprika should fall off in a neat line. Serve with thinly sliced brown bread and butter.

Serves 4

Grapefruit with cottage cheese

Cottage cheese has just the right bland flavour to combine perfectly with citrus fruits. Both are popular as a salad but in this recipe grapefruit and cottage cheese together make an unusual first course.

3 grapefruit
350 g/12 oz cottage cheese
2–3 tablespoons oil and vinegar
  dressing

1 teaspoon finely chopped parsley

Cut the grapefruit across the centre and loosen the segments of fruit in each half. Tip the grapefruit segments and juice out into a basin. With the fingers pull away the membrane and pith from the centre of the grapefruit so that the shells may be used for serving. With a pair of scissors snip a zig-zag round the rim of each shell and then set aside.

Remove the pips from the segments of grapefruit and strain off the juice. Add the cottage cheese and the dressing to the grapefruit and

using a fork, toss to mix. Taste and add more dressing if liked. Finally mix in the chopped parsley and spoon the mixture back into the prepared shells for serving.
Serves 6

Spiced mustard mayonnaise

Use this mustard mayonnaise as a dip for hot sausages or a dressing for cold ham. Make it in a blender for best results, extra spices contribute to the unusual flavour.

2 egg yolks
¼ level teaspoon salt
1 level teaspoon made mustard
freshly milled pepper
pinch curry powder
1 level teaspoon castor sugar

2 tablespoons wine vinegar
1 level teaspoon concentrated
    tomato purée
3 dl/½ pint salad oil
2 teaspoons cream or top of the
    milk

Place the egg yolks, salt, mustard, a seasoning of pepper, curry powder and sugar in the blender container. Add 1 tablespoon of the wine vinegar. Cover and blend on low speed for a moment. Measure the oil into a jug.

Remove the centre cap in the blender top. Switch on to slow speed and begin adding the oil slowly. The mayonnaise will not thicken until the blades are covered. Continue adding the oil in a thin steady stream and when the mixture gets very thick thin it down with the remaining vinegar. When all the oil is added stir in the tomato purée. Stir in the cream just before using.
Makes 3 dl (½ pint)

Leeks with ham in cheese sauce

A cheese sauce served over any cooked vegetables helps to supply the protein necessary to make them into a nourishing supper dish. On another occasion use chicory in place of the leeks in this recipe, they are just as nice and should be cooked in the same way.

4–6 leeks

for the cheese sauce:
25 g/1 oz butter
25 g/1 oz flour
3 dl/½ pint milk

4–6 slices ham

salt and freshly milled pepper
½ teaspoon made mustard
100 g/4 oz hard cheese, grated

Slice away the root and trim the green top down to within 2.5 cm (1 in) of the white stem on each leek. Wash well in cold water and then add to a pan of boiling salted water. Simmer for about 15–20 minutes or until just tender, then drain thoroughly.

Melt the butter for the sauce over low heat. Stir in the flour and cook gently for 1 minute. Gradually stir in the milk, beating well all the time to get a smooth sauce. Bring up to the boil and simmer for 1–2 minutes. Season well with salt and pepper, stir in the mustard and half the cheese.

Wrap each cooked leek in a slice of ham. Spoon a little of the sauce into a well-buttered shallow baking dish and arrange the leeks on top. Pour over the remaining sauce and sprinkle with the rest of the cheese. Place in a moderately hot oven (190°C., 375°F., Gas Mark 5) and bake for 15–20 minutes or until bubbling hot and brown.
Serves 4

Croquettes using cold meat

Any leftover cold roast chicken, lamb or cold boiled bacon can be used to make delicious croquettes. Egg and breadcrumb them ready for frying well in advance.

225–275 g/8–10 oz cooked chicken, lamb or bacon	salt and freshly milled pepper
1 small onion	50 g/2 oz hard cheese, grated.
25 g/1 oz butter	1 egg
25 g/1 oz flour	toasted breadcrumbs
1.5 dl/¼ pint chicken stock or milk	oil for deep-frying

Remove any skin or fat and mince the cold meat. Peel and finely chop the onion. Melt the butter in a saucepan and add the onion. Cover and fry gently for 5 minutes or until the onion is tender but not brown. Stir in the flour and cook for a few minutes, then stir in the stock. Bring up to the boil, stirring all the time to make a very thick sauce. Season well with salt and pepper, then stir in the grated cheese. Draw the pan off the heat and beat very thoroughly to get a smooth mixture. Add the minced meat and mix well.

Separate the egg and stir the yolk into the mixture, reserving the white for coating the croquettes. Cover the pan and set the mixture aside until quite cold.

Take tablespoons of the mixture and with wetted hands roll each spoonful into a ball. First coat each one in the lightly mixed egg white and then roll in toasted breadcrumbs. Deep-fry in hot oil for about 5 minutes until brown, then serve.
Serves 4

Baked fish in egg and milk

Here's a very Scottish way of baking white fish. You can use any white fish like cod, haddock or, nicest of all, fillets of plaice. The recipe may sound unusual but it is very nourishing and an easy one to make.

225 g/8 oz filleted white fish	2 eggs
salt and freshly milled pepper	3 dl/½ pint milk

Skin the fish fillets and cut into neat pieces or fold in half if plaice is used. Arrange in a well-buttered 1-litre (1½- to 2-pint) pie dish. Season well with salt and pepper.

Whisk together the eggs and milk and strain over the fish. Cover with a buttered paper and place the dish in a larger roasting or baking tin with 2.5 cm (1 in) cold water. Set in the centre of a moderate oven (180°C., 350°F., Gas Mark 4) and bake for 40–45 minutes or until the custard is nicely browned and set. Serve hot.
Serves 2

Omelette Arnold Bennett

One good fat smoked haddock cutlet poached in milk for about 10 minutes then cooled and flaked should give you sufficient smoked haddock for this recipe.

4 tablespoons smoked haddock, cooked and flaked	pepper and salt
	4 tablespoons cream
50 g/2 oz butter	2 tablespoons grated Parmesan
4 eggs	cheese

Toss the haddock in a saucepan with half the butter to heat it through. Meanwhile crack the eggs into a mixing basin and add a good seasoning of pepper and a dash of salt. Add 1 tablespoon of the cream and mix the ingredients thoroughly with a fork. Add the smoked haddock and 1 tablespoon of the cheese.

Melt the remaining butter in a frying pan and when frothing pour in the omelette mixture. Stir for a moment, then allow the omelette to cook gently until the underside is brown and the mixture is set but still moist.

Draw the pan off the heat and pour over the remaining cream. Sprinkle with the remaining cheese and brown under a hot grill. Slide the omelette out on to a plate and serve.
Serves 2

Oatcakes

Oatcakes go well with all cheeses. Serve them on any dinner party cheese tray or spread with butter and sandwich in pairs with a chunk of Cheddar for a sandwich lunch. Use extra oatmeal, not flour, on the working surface when rolling out the dough. You will find them very easy to make following this recipe.

225 g/8 oz medium oatmeal	1 level teaspoon salt
75 g/3 oz plain flour	50 g/2 oz mixed white vegetable fat
¼ level teaspoon bicarbonate of	and margarine
soda	boiling water (see method)

Measure the oatmeal into a mixing basin. Sift in the flour, bicarbonate of soda and salt. Melt the fat and pour into the dry ingredients. Mix with a palette or table knife, adding just enough boiling water from the kettle to make a soft but not sticky dough.

Turn out on to a clean pastry board sprinkled with extra oatmeal. Roll out thinly; if the dough is a little on the soft side for handling, knead in a little extra oatmeal and give the dough a moment to firm up. Cut the mixture with a knife into two wide strips and then into triangles, or use a 5- to 7-cm (2- to 3-in) round cutter and stamp out circles.

Place the oatcakes on ungreased trays. Set above centre in a hot oven (220°C., 425°F., Gas Mark 7) and bake for 15 minutes or until crisp. When quite cold, store in an airtight container.
Makes 2 dozen oatcakes

Lamb guard of honour

This simple method of roasting lamb does not require any stuffing. Ask the butcher to chine the joints, this will make them easier to carve. He will also remove a strip of fat from along the end of the rib bones, so that

the bones protrude about an inch. Buy some cutlet frills and slip them
on to the bones when you serve the roast.

2 joints best end of neck of lamb, with 6–7 cutlets on each
1 clove garlic or a little dried rosemary
seasoned flour
25 g/1 oz dripping

Rub the surface of the meat with a cut clove of garlic or sprinkle
with rosemary. Dredge a little seasoned flour over the fatty part of
the meat and rub well in to get a crisp golden finish. Wrap the bone
tips with foil to prevent them from browning.

Place the two joints flat in a roasting tin and add the dripping. Set
the pan in the centre of a moderate oven (180°C., 350°F., Gas Mark
4) and roast for 1¼ hours. Baste occasionally.

When the roast is done, lift the joints from the tin and stand close
together on a serving dish. The tips of the rib bones should cross
each other like swords. Garnish the rib bones with cutlet frills.
To serve cut each joint downwards into cutlets; serve with
redcurrant or mint jelly and gravy made using the pan drippings.
Serves 6

Roast duckling with honey

*A glaze of honey encourages the skin on duckling to roast a golden brown.
This is an excellent way of roasting a bird which is to be served cold.*

1 oven-ready duckling, about
 2–2.25 kg/4½–5 lb

2 tablespoons clear honey
1 tablespoon boiling water

Remove the giblets from inside the duckling. Rub the skin all over
with salt and prick the surface with the prongs of a fork. Place the
duckling in a roasting tin and add 2 tablespoons cold water – no fat.
Place the tin in the centre of a moderate oven (180°C., 350°F., Gas
Mark 4) and roast allowing 25 minutes per 0.5 kg (1 lb).

After 1 hour of roasting time, pour away the duckling fat from the
roasting tin. Blend the honey and boiling water and brush over the
surface of the duckling. Return to the oven and complete the roasting
time. Brush the duckling once or twice again with the honey
mixture until the skin is glazed and golden brown. Leave until cold.
Before serving carve into joints.
Serves 4

Simmered chicken

An excellent method of cooking a tender young chicken is to simmer it in a small quantity of water with vegetables and herbs. This is a good way to prepare a chicken for salad, or for serving in a cold sauce, when the small quantity of stock used is very well flavoured, and the bird is nice and moist.

1 oven-ready chicken, about 1.25 kg/3 lb
½ lemon
1 onion, cut in quarters
1 carrot, sliced
1 stalk celery
1 level teaspoon salt
4 peppercorns
small bay leaf
few sprigs fresh parsley or tarragon

Rub the surface of the chicken with the cut lemon half to keep the flesh white. Select a pan with a tight-fitting lid, that will hold the chicken neatly.

Pour 2.5 cm (1 in) cold water into the pan and add the onion, carrot pieces, celery, a piece of pared lemon rind, salt and peppercorns, bay leaf and parsley or tarragon. Bring to the boil and add the chicken. Cover with the lid and reduce the heat to a simmer. Cook until tender – about 1 hour for a 1.25-kg (3-lb) bird.

Draw the pan off the heat. Set the pan in a cold larder and allow the bird to cool in the stock overnight.
Serves 6

Noisettes of lamb with wine and herbs

Sweet, tender lamb and vegetables all cooked in one dish make this a recipe which takes care of itself. Choose a spacious, pretty casserole so you can serve it straight from the oven to the table.

6 noisettes of lamb (see method)
seasoned flour
25 g/1 oz butter
12 button onions (about 450 g/1 lb)
pinch dried rosemary
1 tablespoon finely chopped parsley
1.5 dl/¼ pint red wine
100 g/4 oz button mushrooms, trimmed and sliced
12 small new potatoes
1 packet frozen peas, thawed

Either buy a piece of lamb with six loin chops on it and ask the butcher to bone, roll and cut the joint into six, or, alternatively, buy six loin chops and with a small sharp knife remove the T-bone at the base. Then roll and tie them up individually yourself. Dip both sides of the meat in seasoned flour. Heat the butter in a frying pan, add the meat and brown gently on both sides for about 15–20 minutes. Lift the chops from the pan and place in a large casserole.

Peel the button onions, leaving them whole. Add to the hot butter in the pan and fry quickly, turning often to brown them slightly. Add these to the lamb along with a good pinch of rosemary which has been crushed. Pour away all but about 1 tablespoon of the fat in the frying pan, taking care to leave as much of the sediment behind as possible. Add the wine and bring back to the boil, stirring and scraping to mix the sediment into the sauce. Pour this over the meat, add the chopped parsley, sliced mushrooms and scraped new potatoes – cut in half if large.

Cover with a buttered paper and a lid, place in the centre of a moderate oven (180°C., 350°F., Gas Mark 4) and bake for 1 hour. About 10 minutes before the cooking time is completed add the peas, re-cover and complete cooking time. Remove the string from around the lamb noisettes before serving.
Serves 6

Oven-fried chicken with bacon

Oven-fried chicken suggests rather a contradiction in terms, but the result is very similar to pan-fried chicken. In fact, the chicken is less greasy and crisper as a result of being cooked in the oven. Fixing the bacon rashers on skewers means that they stay neatly rolled up for serving.

4 chicken joints	50g/2 oz butter
1 egg	1 tablespoon olive oil
toasted breadcrumbs for coating	100 g/4 oz lean bacon rashers

Trim the chicken joints and remove the skin. Lightly mix the egg and place in a shallow dish. Dip the pieces of chicken in the egg and then roll in the breadcrumbs to coat each piece thoroughly.
Put the butter and oil in a roasting tin, place in the centre of a moderately hot oven (190°C., 375°F., Gas Mark 5) and allow to heat through until the butter has melted and is quite hot. Place the pieces of chicken in the tin and baste with the hot fat, then cook for 1 hour. Baste all the chicken pieces occasionally; there is no need to turn them as they will become evenly cooked and brown.

Trim the rinds from the bacon rashers and stretch each rasher slightly by pressing it out along the working surface using the blade of a knife. Cut the rashers in half, roll up and fix on skewers. About 15 minutes before the end of the cooking time, baste the chicken joints again and add the bacon rolls. When cooking time is complete, lift the chicken pieces from the pan and remove the bacon rolls from the skewers. Serve both together.

Serves 4

Lyonnaise potatoes with anchovy

Fried potatoes made using blanched, sliced raw potato are a great improvement on leftover boiled potatoes which are all too often used. Blanched potato slices rarely break up on frying and they cook to a golden brown. Onion and anchovy add extra flavour and make them specially nice to serve with cold chicken or ham.

675 g/1½ lb potatoes
1 large onion
50 g/2 oz bacon dripping or butter
salt and freshly milled pepper

1 teaspoon tarragon or wine vinegar
6–8 anchovy fillets, soaked in milk
chopped parsley

Peel the potatoes and cut into 0.5 cm (¼-in) thick slices. Add to a saucepan of boiling water, bring back to the boil and simmer for 5 minutes, then drain. Peel and slice the onion.

Melt half the fat in a good-sized frying pan and add the onion. Cook gently for about 5 minutes until the onion is soft but not brown. Remove the onion from the pan with a slotted spoon. Add the remaining fat and raise the heat. Tip in the potato slices and fry fairly quickly to brown them. Turn the potato slices over and shake the pan occasionally. Fry the potatoes in batches if the pan is small and keep the cooked ones hot along with the onions.

Finally return the onions and all potatoes to the pan. Cook them together to heat them through and brown the onion. Sprinkle with salt and freshly milled pepper and the vinegar. Fry for a further moment, then draw off the heat. Add the finely chopped anchovies and sprinkle with parsley. Toss lightly to mix and serve hot.

Serves 4

Cauliflower, egg and watercress salad

Cauliflower can be used to make an attractive winter salad.
Ready-cut cauliflower sprigs packed in boxes are often on sale alongside
whole cauliflower heads; usually they are cheaper and are ideal for
this kind of recipe.

1 head cauliflower	3 eggs
4–6 tablespoons prepared French dressing	2 bunches watercress

Remove the outer green leaves and break the cauliflower neatly into
sprigs. Trim away any long pieces of stalk and add the sprigs to a
pan of boiling salted water. Simmer for 8–10 minutes until the sprigs
are tender but not broken. Test by piercing the stalks with the point
of a sharp knife. Drain and place in a mixing basin. Pour over half
the dressing while the cauliflower is still warm – this prevents the
cooked cauliflower going dark in colour.

Meanwhile, hard-boil the eggs, drain and plunge into cold water.
When cold shell and cut into quarters. Add the egg to the cauliflower
and toss with a little extra dressing if necessary. Wash the watercress
well and remove the long stalks. Arrange round the outer edge of a
salad bowl. Spoon the cauliflower and egg into the centre. Pour the
remaining dressing over the watercress and serve.
Serves 4-6

Buttered noodles

Ribbon noodles are also called tagliatelle. They can be plain, or green
with spinach added to the dough. Noodles make a good accompaniment
for recipes with a rich sauce.

225g/8 oz ribbon noodles	25–50 g/1–2 oz grated Parmesan
25 g/1 oz butter	cheese
freshly milled black pepper	

Add the noodles to a pan filled with plenty of boiling salted water.
Bring back to the boil and cook for 12 minutes. Fork out a small
piece of pasta and test by biting it – pasta when cooked should be
tender but still a little chewy. Drain the noodles at once in a colander.
Add the butter to the hot pan, return the noodles and add a good
seasoning of freshly milled black pepper. Using two forks lift and

turn the noodles in the melted butter. Tip into a hot serving dish and serve with the Parmesan cheese for sprinkling on top.
Serves 4

Orange and onion salad

Salads, especially those including oranges, are an important part of winter menus. Serve this one with cold sliced pork, roast duck or chicken.

3 oranges   2 medium-sized onions

for the dressing:
salt and freshly milled pepper   4 tablespoons salad oil
pinch paprika pepper   little chopped garlic (optional)
pinch sugar
2 tablespoons tarragon or wine
  vinegar

Cut a slice from the top and base of each orange then set the orange upright and using a knife cut the peel and white pith away by slicing through to the orange flesh. Slice the oranges thinly across and arrange in a shallow dish. Peel the onions, leaving them whole, then slice thinly across and separate the rings. Add these to the orange slices.

Into a small basin measure a good seasoning of salt and freshly milled pepper, a pinch of paprika pepper and a pinch of sugar. Add the vinegar and mix well then add the oil and a little chopped garlic if liked. Mix thoroughly, pour over the orange and onion slices and leave to marinate for at least 1 hour before serving.
Serves 4

Sweet and sour baked onions

Unusual as they sound, these onions make an excellent accompaniment to grilled or fried foods. They have a clean, sweet-sharp flavour and make a pleasant change from fried onions.

6 medium-sized onions   1 level tablespoon cornflour
salt and freshly milled pepper   1 tablespoon wine vinegar
50 g/2 oz soft brown sugar
3 dl/½ pint stock (use water and
  stock cube)

Peel the onions leaving them whole. Place in a saucepan, cover with cold water and bring to the boil. Simmer for 10 minutes then drain. Place in a casserole, season with salt and pepper and sprinkle over the sugar. Add the stock. Cover with a lid, place in a moderate oven (180°C., 350°F., Gas Mark 4) and bake for 25–30 minutes or until tender.

Remove the onions from the casserole and place in a hot serving dish. Pour the juices into a saucepan. Blend the cornflour with the vinegar, dilute with a little of the hot juice, then stir into the saucepan. Bring to the boil, stirring all the time until thickened and clear. Check the flavour and pour over the onions. Serve with grilled pork or lamb chops or with steak.

Serves 6

Lemon sorbet

Snowy white and fresh to taste, a lemon sorbet should be made several days before serving so that the mixture has a chance to become quite firm. For a dinner party treat, pour a measure of Cointreau over each portion of sorbet when serving.

a scant litre/1½ pints water	rind and juice of 4 large lemons
350 g/12 oz castor sugar	2 egg whites

Measure the water and sugar into a saucepan. Stir over low heat until the sugar has dissolved. Add the finely pared lemon rind – use a vegetable parer and pare off only the fine outer yellow zest. Bring to the boil and cook rapidly for about 5 minutes. Draw off the heat and allow to cool.

Add the lemon juice and strain the mixture into a basin. Add the unbeaten egg whites and whisk with a fork to break them up. Pour into a plastic freezer container and freeze until the mixture is mushy – about 2 hours.

Spoon the partially frozen mixture into a chilled bowl and whisk until smooth and white. The whiteness comes from the air whisked into the mixture. Spoon the mixture back into the container, cover and refreeze.

Serves 6

Fresh orange jelly

A home-made jelly does not set sparkling and clear like a bought jelly. It tends to be a little cloudy, but this in no way affects the delicious, fresh fruit flavour.

3 dl/½ pint water
175 g/6 oz castor sugar
15 g/½ oz powdered gelatine
finely pared rind and juice of
 3 oranges

finely pared rind and juice of
 1 lemon

Measure 4 tablespoons of the water into a teacup and pour the remaining water into a saucepan. Add the sugar and set the pan over moderate heat. Stir to dissolve the sugar and then allow the mixture to come up to the boil to form a sugar syrup.

Meanwhile sprinkle the gelatine over the water in the cup and set aside to soak for a few minutes. Draw the pan of sugar syrup off the heat and add the soaked gelatine. Stir until dissolved; the heat of the pan should be sufficient to do this.

Using a vegetable parer, thinly pare the rinds off the washed oranges and lemon into a basin. Pour over the hot sugar syrup. Squeeze the juices from the fruits and add to the basin. Set the mixture aside to stand for 1 hour so that the orange and lemon flavour is extracted from the peels. Then strain into a jug, pour into a wetted mould and leave until set firm. Unmould and serve with cream.
Serves 4-6

Easter eggs

Gaily decorated eggs are a traditional part of Easter and they can provide hours of amusement for children. If they plan to paint a design or faces on the eggs, make sure you prepare the surface first, otherwise the paint will smear. Hard-boil the eggs – cover with cold water and bring slowly to the boil to avoid cracking. Simmer for 6–8 minutes then drain and run under cold water until the eggs are cool enough to handle.

Beat an egg white with a fork just enough to break it up, but not enough to make it frothy. Using a pastry brush paint the egg shell all over to seal the surface. The egg white will dry very quickly since the eggs are still warm. It is advisable to give each egg two coats. When dried the eggs will look just the same, except that they have a slightly shiny surface. Coloured felt-tipped pens, water colours or poster colours will go on quite smoothly and can be used to make quite elaborate designs. Little hats made from scraps of material, or wool for hair can be added to those with faces.

Lemon cream

This delicately flavoured mixture makes a lovely party dessert. Use any 1-litre (1½-pint) jelly mould – a fluted ring shape is the most attractive – and serve with the orange sauce.

1.5 dl/¼ pint water	juice and finely grated rind of
15 g/½ oz powdered gelatine	3 lemons
225 g/8 oz castor sugar	3 dl/½ pint double cream

for the orange sauce:

50 g/2 oz castor sugar	juice and finely grated rind of
1 level teaspoon cornflour	1 orange
pinch salt	knob of butter
1.5 dl/¼ pint water	

Measure the water into a small saucepan. Sprinkle in the gelatine and set aside for 5 minutes to soften. Place over low heat and stir occasionally until the gelatine has dissolved but do not allow to boil. Draw off the heat.

Put the sugar with the lemon juice and rind into a medium-sized mixing basin. Stir to blend, then add the cream and whisk until thick and light. Gradually whisk in the dissolved gelatine mixture. Pour in a thin steady stream directly into the centre of the lemon mixture and whisk continuously to incorporate the gelatine immediately. As soon as the mixture begins to thicken pour at once into a wetted 1-litre (1½-pint) mould. Chill until set firm.

To make the orange sauce, put the sugar, cornflour, salt and water into a saucepan. Blend with a wooden spoon until the cornflour has dissolved. Add the finely grated orange rind and bring up to the boil, stirring all the time. When thickened and clear draw off the heat. Add the strained orange juice and a small nut of butter. Blend well and leave until cold before serving.

To serve, unmould the pudding and pour some of the sauce over. Serve the remainder separately in a sauceboat.
Serves 6

Apricot Bavarian cream

A smooth custard and cream mould flavoured with apricots makes a delicious dessert at a time of year when the variety of fresh fruit available is limited. Served with a compote of sliced oranges this would make a lovely dinner party dessert.

225 g/8 oz dried apricots
3 tablespoons cold water
15 g/½ oz powdered gelatine
juice of 1 lemon

100 g/4 oz castor sugar
3 dl/½ pint milk
2 egg yolks
1.5 dl/¼ pint double cream

Place the apricots in a saucepan and just cover with boiling water. Cover and leave for 2 hours to soak. Simmer over gentle heat for 40 minutes until tender. Keep the pan covered and simmer very gently; if the water is allowed to evaporate too quickly the apricots may burn. Check the pan occasionally and add more water if necessary. Meanwhile, measure the cold water into a small basin and sprinkle in the gelatine. Set aside to soak.

When the apricots are soft, draw the pan off the heat and stir in the lemon juice and half the sugar. Then pass the apricots and the juices in the pan through a sieve to make a purée. Discard any pieces of skin left in the sieve. Return the apricot purée to the saucepan and add the soaked gelatine. Stir over very low heat just long enough to dissolve the gelatine. Pour into a mixing basin.

Measure the milk into a saucepan and bring almost to the boil. Blend the egg yolks and remaining sugar in a basin, stir in the hot milk and blend well. Pour this custard into the milk pan and stir over low heat for 1–2 minutes, but do not allow to boil.

Combine the hot custard with the fruit purée and set aside until cold. When beginning to thicken, fold in the lightly whipped cream. Pour into a 1.25-litre (2-pint) mould and chill until set firm. Unmould before serving.
Serves 8

Oranges with candied peel

Whole oranges piled high in a serving bowl with a scattering of finely shredded peel are a feature of the dessert trolley in most smart restaurants. Now they are a popular dinner party dessert and one that can be made all year round. Cutting the skin off the oranges is the most exacting part of the preparation and should be done carefully. Otherwise they are easy to make and should be prepared well in advance so they are thoroughly chilled before serving.

8 oranges	1.5 dl/¼ pint water
175 g/6 oz castor sugar	juice of ½ lemon

Using a potato peeler or very sharp knife, pare the top peel or zest only from two oranges. Be very careful not to take any of the bitter white pith. Shred the peel finely, place in a saucepan and cover with cold water. Bring up to the boil, drain immediately and re-cover with fresh cold water. This initial blanching removes any bitter taste. Reboil the peel, and this time cook for about 25–30 minutes or until tender. Drain and reserve.

Slice both ends off each orange, then stand the fruit upright and slice down and round the sides of the orange to remove both the peel and white pith, leaving only the flesh. Place the oranges in a serving dish.

Measure the sugar and water into a saucepan. Stir over low heat to make a sugar syrup, then bring up to the boil. Add the cooked peel and simmer in the syrup for 2–3 minutes or until the peel begins to look glazed and candied. Add the lemon juice and then pour the hot syrup and candied peel over the oranges. Cool, then chill for several hours before serving. Serve plain or with vanilla ice cream.

Serves 8

Wholemeal baps

Serve these warm with a cold supper of chicken or ham salad or with hot soup. They are ideal for a packed lunch – fill them with cheese, tomato, egg or salami and lettuce or cucumber.

225 g/8 oz strong plain flour	a scant 3 dl/½ pint warm mixed
2 level teaspoons salt	milk and water
225 g/8 oz wholemeal flour	15 g/½ oz lard or white cooking fat
25 g/1 oz fresh yeast or 1 level	
tablespoon dried yeast and 1 level	
teaspoon castor sugar	

Sift the white flour and salt into a warm mixing basin. Add the wholemeal flour. Blend the fresh yeast with the warm mixed milk and water. If using dried yeast, dissolve the sugar in the hand-hot milk and water and sprinkle in the dried yeast. Set aside in a warm place for 10 minutes or until frothy.

Rub the cooking fat into the mixed flour and stir in the yeast liquid. Mix by hand to a rough dough, then turn out on to an unfloured working surface and knead thoroughly until the dough is smooth and no longer sticky. Rough the dough up and replace in the basin. Set inside a large polythene bag and leave in a warm place until the dough is double in size.

Turn the risen dough out on to a floured surface and press all over with the knuckles to knock out the air. Roll out the dough to about 1 cm (½ in) in thickness. Using a floured 7-cm (3-in) round cutter, stamp out about twelve circles of dough. Place on a greased baking tray. Cover and leave in a warm place until risen and puffy. Dust with a little wholemeal flour and bake in a hot oven (220°C., 425°F., Gas Mark 7) for about 15 minutes.
Makes 12

Lemon sandwich cake

To a standard Victoria sandwich cake recipe you can add lemon or orange rind and the juice of the fruit as the flavouring. The finely grated rind gives flavour to the cake layers, while the juice is used in the icing.

100 g/4 oz self-raising flour	100 g/4 oz castor sugar
pinch salt	2 large/standard eggs
100 g/4 oz butter or margarine	finely grated rind of 1 lemon

for the filling:

| 40 g/1½ oz butter or margarine | 75 g/3 oz icing sugar |

for the lemon icing:

| lemon juice (see method) | 75 g/3 oz icing sugar |

84

Sift the flour and salt and set aside. Cut up the butter or margarine and place in a warm mixing bowl. Add the sugar and beat until light and fluffy. Lightly mix the eggs and lemon rind and gradually beat into the creamed mixture. This should be done in several additions: if added too quickly the egg will not be absorbed by the fat and a curdled mixture will result. If necessary add a little of the flour with the last few additions of egg. Using a metal spoon, fold in the remaining flour half at a time.

Divide the mixture evenly between two greased and lined 18-cm (7-in) round sandwich cake tins. Spread the mixture level and place in the centre of a moderate oven (180°C., 350°F., Gas Mark 4) and bake for 20–25 minutes, or until the cakes are firm to the touch and have shrunk away from the sides of the tin. Allow the cakes to cool for a few minutes in the tin before turning out, then leave until cold.

Cream the butter for the filling and gradually beat in the sieved icing sugar. Use to sandwich the two cake layers. Warm the strained lemon juice for the icing and sieve the icing sugar into a mixing basin. Gradually beat in sufficient lemon juice to make a smooth coating consistency. Pour the icing over the top of the cake and spread evenly. Warming the liquid for mixing encourages the icing to set more quickly.
Makes one 18-cm (7-in) sandwich cake

Bread-making
For bread-making you need wholemeal flour or strong plain flour and yeast. Where fresh yeast is not obtainable dried yeast can be used. Usually available from most grocers or chemists, dried yeast will keep in the tin for up to 6 months. Dried yeast is twice as concentrated as fresh yeast and in a recipe listing fresh yeast, only half as much dried yeast is required, i.e. 15 g ($\frac{1}{2}$ oz or 1 level tablespoon) dried yeast equals 25 g (1 oz) fresh yeast.

Fresh yeast needs only to be blended with the warm liquid in the recipe before adding to the flour. Dried yeast needs to be reconstituted first. The water used should be slightly hotter than for mixing fresh yeast, about 43°C. (110°F.) or hand-hot. A drop on the wrist should feel hot, but not burning. To start yeast working a little sweetness is required, and this can take the form of sugar. You may like to use a little honey in white bread or treacle in brown bread. Once blended with liquid, dried yeast needs to stand in a warm place for about 10 minutes or until frothy. Then the yeast can be added to the flour.

A dough which is 'proving' or rising likes a damp, warm atmosphere. Nowadays a roomy polythene bag has taken over from the old-fashioned damp cloth for covering the dough. Pop the basin of dough inside the polythene bag and tie closed, leaving it rather baggy so the dough has room to rise. The atmosphere inside will be perfect, retaining all the moisture and warmth necessary.

Normally a kitchen temperature is about right for proving dough but in cold weather it may be necessary to set the bowl of dough over a saucepan half filled with *warm* water – check that the base of the bowl does not touch the water. An excellent 'proving chamber' can be made by running about an inch of hot water into the sink. Put in a cake rack and stand the bread on the rack. Cover the sink completely with a large tray and teacloth. This provides the warm, steamy atmosphere for bread to prove in.

White bread

Persevere with home bread-making once you start. It may not turn out right the first time, but with experience you will get to know the right feel and texture of the dough at different stages. Then bread-making is easy and loaves turn out right every time.

675 g/1½ lb strong plain flour
15 g/½ oz (1 level tablespoon) salt
15 g/½ oz lard or white cooking fat

25 g/1 oz fresh yeast or 1 level tablespoon dried yeast and 1 level teaspoon castor sugar or honey
4.25 dl/¾ pint warm water

Sift the flour and salt into a large mixing basin and rub in the fat. Blend the fresh yeast in 3 dl (½ pint) of the warm water. If using dried yeast dissolve the sugar or honey in 3 dl (½ pint) of the water; it should be 43°C. (110°F.) or hand-hot. Sprinkle in the yeast and leave in a warm place until frothy – about 10 minutes.

Stir the yeast liquid and the remaining warm water into the dry ingredients and mix to a rough dough in the basin. Turn the dough out on to a clean working surface. Knead and stretch the dough by folding towards you, then pushing down and away with the palm of the hand. Give the dough a quarter turn and repeat the kneading. Continue for about 10 minutes. At first the dough will be sticky but as you work it will become very smooth.

Replace the dough in the mixing basin and set the whole thing inside a large polythene bag. Leave the dough on the kitchen table until risen and doubled in size – about 1½ hours.

Turn out the risen dough on to a floured surface and press all over with the knuckles to knock out air bubbles and flatten.

For one large loaf, grease a 1-kg (2-lb) loaf tin. Stretch the dough into an oblong the same width as the tin. Fold into three and turn over so the seam is underneath. Smooth over the top, tuck in the ends and place in the greased tin.

For two small loaves grease two 0.5-kg (1-lb) loaf tins. Divide the dough into two portions, shape each one as above and place in the tins.

Place the shaped bread to rise again. Put the tins inside a lightly greased polythene bag and leave to rise until the dough comes to the tops of the tins and springs back when pressed with a floured finger. This takes about 30–45 minutes at room temperature.

Set the loaves to bake in the centre of a hot oven (230°C., 450°F., Gas Mark 8) for 30–40 minutes according to size. The baked loaves shrink slightly from the sides of the tin and sound hollow when tapped underneath with the knuckles. For a crusty loaf turn out of the tin and replace in the oven for a further 5 minutes. For a soft crust rub the loaf all over with a buttered paper when hot from the oven.
Makes 1 large or 2 small loaves

Hot cross buns

Bake your own hot cross buns, and a warm spicy fragrance will fill the kitchen. Those not eaten fresh are lovely toasted.

450 g/1 lb strong plain flour
1 level teaspoon salt
1 level teaspoon mixed spice
1 level teaspoon ground cinnamon
½ level teaspoon ground nutmeg
50 g/2 oz castor sugar
25 g/1 oz fresh yeast or 1 level tablespoon dried yeast and 1 level teaspoon castor sugar

a scant 3 dl/½ pint warm mixed milk and water
1 egg
50 g/2 oz melted butter
100 g/4 oz currants
50 g/2 oz chopped mixed peel

for the glaze:
1 tablespoon each water, castor sugar and milk

Sift the flour, salt, spices and sugar into a warm mixing basin. Stir the fresh yeast into the warmed mixed milk and water. If using dried yeast, stir the teaspoon of sugar into the hand-hot mixed milk and water. Sprinkle in the dried yeast and leave for about 10 minutes until frothy.

Stir the yeast liquid, egg, melted butter, currants and peel into the centre of the dry ingredients. Mix to a soft dough, turn out on to an unfloured surface and knead well until the dough is smooth. Shape into a round and replace in the basin. Set inside a polythene bag and leave in a warm place until double the size.

Turn out the risen dough, flatten with the knuckles and knead again lightly. Divide into twelve equal portions and shape into buns. Place on greased baking trays, cover and leave in a warm place until the buns look puffy.

To make the crosses, either slash the buns with a knife or use a smooth paste made by mixing flour with water. Spoon the flour paste into a piping bag and pipe a cross on each bun. Bake in the centre of a hot oven (220°C., 425°F., Gas Mark 7) for 15–20 minutes. When baking time is almost complete combine the ingredients for the glaze in a saucepan. Stir over the heat until just boiling. Brush over the hot buns to make them shiny. Serve warm with butter.

Makes 12

Brown bread

To make brown bread tin loaves, follow the directions for shaping and baking in the recipe for white bread. Otherwise bake crusty round cobs or rolls with your brown bread dough. A mixture of brown and white flour makes a loaf that slices better. All brown flour makes a crumbly texture, but it is the best from a flavour and health point of view. Use either in this recipe.

350 g/12 oz strong plain flour
350 g/12 oz wholewheat flour ·
15 g/½ oz (1 level tablespoon) salt
15 g/½ oz lard or white vegetable
   fat

25 g/1 oz fresh yeast or 1 level
   tablespoon dried yeast and 1 level
   teaspoon castor sugar or black
   treacle
4.25 dl/¾ pint warm water
cracked wheat for the tops

Sift the white flour into a basin and add the wholewheat flour and salt. Add the fat and rub into the mixture. Blend the fresh yeast with the warm water. If using dried yeast dissolve the sugar or treacle in 3 dl ($\frac{1}{2}$ pint) of the water which should be 43°C. (110°F.) or hand-hot. Sprinkle in the yeast and leave in a warm place until frothy – about 10 minutes.

Stir the yeast liquid and the remaining warm water into the dry ingredients and mix to a rough dough in the basin. Turn the dough out on to a clean working surface. Knead the dough well for about 10 minutes to make a smooth dough.

Shape the dough into a round and replace in the mixing basin. Set the whole thing inside a large greased polythene bag. Leave the dough on the kitchen table until risen and doubled in size – about $1\frac{1}{2}$ hours. Turn the risen dough out on to a floured surface and press all over with the knuckles to knock out air bubbles and flatten.

For two cob loaves grease two baking trays. Divide the dough into two equal portions and knead each one into a neat round ball. Flatten slightly and place on the greased baking trays. Sprinkle with cracked wheat and put to rise until puffy – 30–45 minutes. Set in a very hot oven (230°C., 450°F., Gas Mark 8) and bake for 40 minutes.

To make brown rolls divide the dough into 18 equal portions – each should weigh about 50 g (2 oz). On an unfloured surface roll each piece of dough into a ball inside your cupped hand. Press down hard at first, then ease up to shape them nicely. Arrange on greased baking trays about 2.5 cm (1 in) apart and sprinkle with cracked wheat. Place the baking tin inside a greased polythene bag and leave to rise until the rolls are puffy – 25–30 minutes. Set in a hot oven (230°C., 450°F., Gas Mark 8) and bake for 15–20 minutes.
Makes 2 round cobs or 18 rolls

Using the freezer in March

With schools breaking up at the end of the month, early March is a good time to batch-bake bread and cakes for holiday teas. Victoria sandwich cake layers freeze well wrapped in polythene freezer bags. Thaw at room temperature and fill as required. Cake layers can be sandwiched with buttercream like this month's recipe for *lemon sandwich cake* (see page 84). For freezing it is advisable to omit the glacé icing, which tends to become thin and runny on thawing, and simply give the cake a dusting of icing sugar before serving.

Decorated or iced cakes can be cut in wedges before freezing, then you can take out a few slices as required.

Freezing bread

Bought sliced and wrapped bread freezes well in the wrapper providing the seal is not broken. If you intend to take out slices of bread a few at a time, it is better to overwrap the loaf with a polythene bag. You can then rewrap each time to a smaller size.

Ordinary *white and brown loaves* (see pages 86 and 88) keep well for up to 1 month and enriched breads like the teabreads in February (see pages 58 to 61) for 6 weeks. Place loaves in polythene bags and seal before freezing to avoid drying out of the crust. White or brown loaves wrapped in foil can be taken straight from the freezer and placed in a moderately hot oven (200°C., 400°F., Gas Mark 6) for 45 minutes, when they will taste like freshly baked bread. It's useful to know that sliced bread can be toasted from frozen and takes very little longer than fresh bread slices.

Crusty breads like French or Vienna loaves and rolls do not freeze well since the crusts begin to shell off after a week. After short-term storage you should allow them to thaw, then place in a hot oven (200°C., 400°F., Gas Mark 6) for 20 minutes or until the crusts are crisp.

Your own home-made *wholemeal baps* (see page 83) are marvellous for packed lunches and picnics. Place in polythene bags to freeze and allow to thaw at room temperature before using – about 1 hour. Other items, such as Danish pastries, croissants and brioches from a good baker, are excellent so long as they are fresh and quite cold before being placed in the freezer. Bake a batch of *hot cross buns* (see page 87) so they can be warm and fresh for Easter teas.

Never throw away leftover bread – remember that fresh breadcrumbs keep well in the freezer and are very useful. If you have a blender then the crumbs can be made in a moment. Trim crusts from bread slices and break the bread into pieces. Remove the centre cap from the lid of the blender and switch the blender on. Drop pieces of bread on to the rotating blades through the hole. When the blades are covered stop the machine and empty out. Repeat the procedure until all the breadcrumbs are made. Packed in a polythene bag the crumbs remain quite loose on freezing and you can extract any small quantity required. Use them for puddings, stuffings and bread sauce.

April

April is the most climatically unpredictable month of the year, so menus need to be as flexible as possible. For holiday meals there is plenty of poultry and a fat capon is a good buy for a long weekend. Egg dishes also make a welcome change from meat recipes on spring days. Root crops dwindle this month but there is an increasing supply of spring vegetables. With luck we should find sprouting broccoli, young spinach, excellent cauliflowers, spring onions and the first radishes to indicate that summer is on its way. Watch out for supplies of outdoor-grown rhubarb which build up this month. These early samples are particularly good for preserving.

Marinated mushrooms and prawns

To get the true delicate flavour of mushrooms, they must be really fresh. Button or the slightly open cup mushrooms should be used. Slice them almost paper-thin with a razor-sharp knife and dress them in a shallow china dish for serving as a first course.

225 g/8 oz button mushrooms	finely chopped parsley
100 g/4 oz frozen prawns, thawed	

for the dressing:

salt and freshly milled pepper	4 tablespoons olive oil
2 tablespoons lemon juice or wine vinegar	

Wash the mushrooms and trim the stalks level. Slice thinly, then place in a bowl along with the prawns. Combine a good seasoning of salt and pepper, the strained lemon juice and the olive oil for the dressing. Pour over the mushrooms and shrimps, toss well and leave to marinate for 1 hour before serving. Sprinkle with chopped parsley before serving.

Serves 4

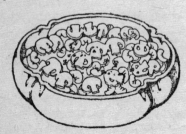

Grilled sugared grapefruit

Grilled grapefruit should be crunchy and brown on top; they should also be warm. So prepare them in advance, but grill them only when required for serving.

3 grapefruit   demerara sugar (see method)
25 g/1 oz butter

Halve the grapefruit and using a grapefruit knife or a small sharp knife cut around each segment to loosen the flesh. Turn upside-down on a large plate to drain until ready to grill.

Melt the butter over low heat and liberally brush the surface and outer rim of each grapefruit half. Sprinkle with plenty of demerara sugar – about 2 rounded teaspoons on each half – and place 5–7 cm (2–3 in) away from the heat under a hot grill. Grill until the sugar has melted and becomes brown. Spoon any juices which have drained from the grapefruit halves over the hot sugar on each one and serve at once.

Serves 6

Leeks and tomatoes à la Grecque

Serve this recipe with plenty of crusty French bread for mopping up the delicious wine- and garlic-flavoured dressing.

6 medium-sized leeks   4 tablespoons olive oil
½ small onion, finely chopped   bouquet garni
6 tomatoes   ½ small clove garlic, crushed
1.5 dl/¼ pint dry white wine   salt and pepper

Remove the outer damaged leaves from the leeks. Trim away the bases and tops. Slice through to the centre lengthways, open carefully and wash well under running cold water. Cut across into pieces about 3 cm (1½ in) long.

Place in a saucepan with the onion, the peeled and deseeded tomatoes, the wine, olive oil and enough water to cover. Add the bouquet garni and garlic and season well with salt and pepper.

Cover the pan with a lid and simmer very gently for 30 minutes until the leeks are tender. Remove from the heat and allow to become quite cold. Remove the bouquet garni and garlic before serving.

Serves 6

Cucumber vichyssoise

This charming spring soup should be served very cold. Purée the mixture in a blender to get a really smooth creamy soup.

450 g/1 lb new potatoes
1 cucumber
50 g/2 oz butter
1 small onion

a generous litre/2 pints chicken
  stock
1 teaspoon castor sugar
1.5 dl/¼ pint single cream

Scrape the potatoes and cut them and the unpeeled cucumber into chunky pieces. Peel and chop the onion. Melt the butter in a large saucepan and add the prepared vegetables. Cover with a lid and cook gently for about 10 minutes to draw out the juices and soften the vegetables. Add the stock and bring up to the boil. Cover and allow to simmer for about 15–20 minutes or until the vegetables are quite tender.

Remove from the heat and pass the liquid and vegetables through a vegetable mill (or use a blender) to make a purée. Pour into a bowl, stir in the sugar – this counteracts the slightly bitter flavour of the cucumber skin – and season with salt and pepper. Cool, then stir in the cream and chill thoroughly before serving.

Serves 6

Smoked salmon with devilled eggs

Smoked salmon is an expensive item but in this recipe you need allow no more than 25 g (1 oz) per person. Or you can use smoked salmon trimmings which are cheaper to buy, but be a little more generous with the quantity you allow.

6 eggs
2 tablespoons mayonnaise
½–1 teaspoon made mustard
pinch curry powder

salt and freshly milled pepper
175 g/6 oz smoked salmon
6 slices buttered brown bread

Hard-boil the eggs, drain and plunge immediately into cold water to prevent further cooking. Peel away the shells and leave the eggs covered with cold water until required.

Halve each egg lengthways. Dip the knife blade in cold water before cutting; this helps to prevent the egg from breaking. Tip out the yolks and set the whites aside. Press the egg yolks through a sieve, or mash with a fork, and beat in the mayonnaise. Add mustard to taste, a pinch of curry powder and a good seasoning of salt and pepper. Refill each egg white with a heaped teaspoon of the mixture.

Arrange the smoked salmon to cover each slice of buttered brown bread. Trim the edges so that the salmon fits neatly on the bread. Reserve the salmon trimmings. Arrange the devilled eggs in pairs on the smoked salmon. Chop the reserved trimmings and sprinkle over the tops of the eggs as a garnish.
Serves 6

Spaghetti with tomato and onion

If your children like canned spaghetti in tomato sauce, they'll love this. The flavour is important, so use the concentrated tomato purée from a tube, not tomato ketchup. Serve the spaghetti with sliced ham, grilled sausages or fried eggs.

225 g/8 oz spaghetti
25 g/1 oz butter
1 medium-sized onion, finely
  chopped

2 tablespoons concentrated
  tomato purée
1 tablespoon water

Add the spaghetti to a pan of boiling salted water. Push the spaghetti slowly into the water and as it softens wind it round the inside of the pan to keep the strands whole. Bring back to the boil and cook for 12 minutes, then drain.

Melt the butter in the hot saucepan. Add the chopped onion. Cover with a lid and fry gently for a few minutes until the onion is tender but not brown. Add the tomato purée and the water and stir to make a tomato, onion and butter glaze. Draw the pan off the heat. Add the hot cooked spaghetti and using two forks toss and turn the spaghetti so that it is well glazed and coloured. Turn into a hot dish and serve. **Serves 4**

Shepherd's pie

Minced cooked meat provides the basis for many made-up dishes, one of the most popular being shepherd's pie. The addition of curry powder and mixed herbs gives this recipe a slightly spicy flavour which makes it particularly tasty.

275–350 g/10–12 oz cold roast beef
1 onion
40 g/1½ oz butter
salt and freshly milled pepper
¼ level teaspoon curry powder

¼ level teaspoon mixed herbs
1.5 dl/¼ pint thickened gravy (see method)
450–675 g/1–1½ lb mashed cooked potato

Trim the fat from the meat and pass the meat through the mincer.

96

Finely chop the onion and add to 25 g (1 oz) of the butter melted in a saucepan. Fry gently until the onion is soft and lightly brown. Stir in the meat and add a good seasoning of salt and pepper, the curry powder and mixed herbs. Stir in the gravy, preferably gravy left over from the roast. If the gravy is unthickened blend 1 level tablespoon flour with a generous 1.5 dl (¼ pint) gravy (or use stock) and stir over the heat until thickened and boiling.

Blend the ingredients together (the meat mixture should be nice and moist) and spoon into a greased pie dish. Cover with mashed potato and rough up the surface with a fork. Dot with the remaining butter and reheat near the top of a moderately hot oven (180°C., 350°F., Gas Mark 4) for 30 minutes.
Serves 4

Swiss eggs

Make a dish of eggs as the Swiss do, with cream and cheese. In individual gratin dishes the eggs can be prepared for one or two. They should be served in and eaten from the cooking dish.

4 eggs	40–50 g/1½–2 oz Gruyère cheese,
4 tablespoons double cream	grated
salt and freshly milled pepper	

Choose two individual gratin or egg dishes and thoroughly butter them inside. Crack two eggs into each dish and spoon a tablespoon of cream over each egg. Season with salt and pepper. Sprinkle a wreath of grated cheese around each egg, over the white. Place in a moderate oven (180°C., 350°F., Gas Mark 4) and bake for 15–20 minutes. The whites should be set and the yolks still soft.

If you like the cheese slightly browned, pop them under the grill for a moment but not too long otherwise the egg yolks become overcooked. Serve in the dish with French bread and butter.
Serves 2

Vol-au-vent cases for the freezer

Vol-au-vent cases are one of the most useful items to have in the freezer. They can be taken out at a moment's notice and require only a short time to thaw before baking. Use them for serving scraps of cooked chicken left over from a roast when even a small amount in these crisp hot cases can make a lovely meal.

To make the cases Roll out 450 g (1 lb) bought puff pastry to a thickness of 0.5 cm (¼ in). Lightly flour a board or baking tray and slide the pastry on to it. Leave in a cool place – preferably the refrigerator – for the pastry to firm up. Stamp out twelve circles using a floured 7-cm (3-in) round cutter. Using a palette knife to lift the circles (so that they are not pulled out of shape) transfer six of them to a flat tray. Prick them well with a fork and brush with lightly mixed egg. Cut out the centre from the remaining circles using a 5-cm (2-in) round cutter. Lift these rings carefully and *turn them over* on to the pastry circles. Press gently to seal. Freeze the prepared cases and the small centre circles, which will become the lids, uncovered until hard. Then pack in a polythene freezer bag for storage.

To use simply transfer as many as required – not forgetting a lid for each one – on to a baking tray. Allow to thaw at room temperature for 1 hour. Then put in the centre of a very hot oven (230°C., 450°F., Gas Mark 8) for 15–20 minutes until well risen and set. Then lower the heat to moderately hot (200°C., 400°F., Gas Mark 6) and bake for a further 10 minutes until the cases are crisp. With a fork remove any soft pastry from the centre of each one and spoon in your filling – about 3 dl (½ pint) well-seasoned white sauce with pieces of cooked chicken and a squeeze of lemon juice to sharpen the flavour. Top with the lids and they are ready to serve.
Makes 6 cases

Potato omelette

A potato or Spanish omelette includes cooked sliced potato and fried Spanish onion as the main ingredients. This omelette is particularly good served cold, cut in wedges, and it is surprisingly tasty for a packed lunch or picnic.

2 medium-sized potatoes	salt and pepper
1 large onion	25 g/1 oz butter
1 tablespoon olive oil	chopped parsley
4–5 eggs	

Peel the potatoes and cook in boiling salted water until just tender, then drain and cool. Cut into quarters lengthways and slice very thinly. Peel and finely chop the onion.

Heat the oil in a frying pan and add the onion. Fry gently until the onion has softened, then add the potato and fry a little more quickly until both are just beginning to brown. Draw the pan off the heat. Crack the eggs into a mixing basin and add a good seasoning of salt and pepper. Add the potato and onion mixture.

Melt the butter in a clean frying pan. When frothing pour in the omelette mixture. Stir for a moment, then allow the omelette to cook slowly until the underneath has browned and the mixture is set but still moist. Loosen the omelette and turn over on to a hot plate. Slide it back into the pan and cook the second side. Turn out on to a plate and sprinkle with chopped parsley. Serve hot or cold.
Serves 2-3

Pork chops with orange and ginger

The combination of flavours in this recipe is quite unusual and the resulting sauce has a delicious sweet-sour flavour. The same recipe can be prepared using lamb chops.

4 lean pork chops	¼ level teaspoon ground ginger
15 g/½ oz butter	salt and freshly milled pepper
50 g/2 oz soft brown sugar	1 small orange
3 tablespoons wine vinegar	2 level teaspoons cornflour

Trim the pork chops and add to the hot butter melted in a frying pan. Fry over medium heat until the chops are well browned on both sides. Then pour away the excess fat from the pan.

Blend the brown sugar, vinegar, ginger and a seasoning of salt and pepper together in a basin. Cut four slices from the orange. Pour the vinegar and sugar mixture over the chops in the pan. Top each chop with one of the orange slices. Squeeze any juice from the remaining bit of orange into the pan too. Cover with a lid and leave to simmer gently for 30 minutes.

Lift the chops on to a hot serving dish. Drain off the pan liquid, measure and make up to 1.5 dl (¼ pint) with water. Blend the cornflour with a little cold water until smooth, then add to the pan juices and stir over the heat until the sauce is boiling and thickened. Strain over the pork chops and serve.

Serves 4

Blanquette of chicken

A blanquette of chicken should be light in colour with a contrast in the sauce provided by the darker mushrooms. To preserve the colour of the sauce, only the mushroom stalks are used during the first stages of the recipe. The mushroom caps are cooked separately and added later.

4 chicken joints	1 egg yolk
1 onion, peeled and cut in quarters	2–3 tablespoons single cream
225 g/8 oz button mushrooms	squeeze of lemon juice
6 dl/1 pint chicken stock	salt and freshly milled pepper
25 g/1 oz butter	chopped parsley
25 g/1 oz flour	

Trim the chicken joints and place in a saucepan with the onion. Wipe the mushrooms and trim the stalks level with the caps. Add the stalks to the pan and reserve the mushroom caps. Add the stock and bring to the boil. Cover and simmer for 45 minutes or until the chicken is tender. Lift the cooked chicken from the pan. Strain the stock and reserve 4 dl (¾ pint) for the sauce. Remove the chicken flesh from the bones and discard the skin and the onion and mushroom stalks.

Melt the butter in a saucepan and stir in the flour. Cook gently over low heat for 1 minute, then gradually stir in the reserved chicken stock. Beat well all the time to get a smooth sauce. Bring up to the boil and simmer gently for 5 minutes. Meanwhile place the mushroom caps in a small saucepan, cover with cold water and bring just up to the boil. Drain the mushrooms and add to the sauce along with the pieces of chicken flesh. Allow to heat through.

Blend the egg yolk with the cream and stir into the chicken blanquette. Add a squeeze of lemon juice to sharpen the flavour. Heat through but do not boil. Check the seasoning of salt and pepper and serve sprinkled with chopped parsley. Plain boiled rice goes well with this.

Serves 4

Chicken in Parmesan cream sauce

Acknowledged as one of the best cheeses for cooking, Parmesan has a pronounced flavour that comes through marvellously in recipes. Although expensive to buy, it is economical to use for less is required to get a good flavour than would be needed of a milder cheese. The very best flavour comes from Parmesan that is freshly grated, so buy only when required and use it all up at once.

4–6 chicken joints	50 g/2 oz butter
salt and freshly milled pepper	

for the sauce:

40 g/1½ oz butter	2 egg yolks
25 g/1 oz flour	1.5 dl/¼ pint double cream
3 dl/½ pint milk	extra Parmesan cheese
25 g/1 oz grated Parmesan cheese	

Trim the chicken joints or pieces and season with salt and pepper. Heat the 50 g (2 oz) butter in a frying pan. Add the chicken joints, skin side down, and fry gently, turning to brown on both sides. Cover the pan and allow the chicken to fry gently for 25–30 minutes or until tender.

Melt the butter for the sauce in a pan. Stir in the flour and cook gently for a few moments. Gradually stir in the milk, beating well all the time to get a smooth, shiny sauce. Bring up to the boil and simmer for a few minutes. Season to taste with salt and pepper and stir in the grated cheese.

When ready to serve, lift the chicken pieces out on to a hot serving dish. Blend the egg yolks with the cream. Draw the sauce off the heat and stir in the liaison of eggs and cream. Blend well and reheat for a moment. Recheck the seasoning and spoon the sauce over the chicken pieces. Sprinkle with extra Parmesan cheese and set under a hot grill until bubbling and golden brown.

Serves 4-6

Meat loaf

For a recipe like this use best-quality minced beef. A baked meat loaf can be served hot with vegetables one day and sliced cold with salad the next.

1 slice white bread
2 tablespoons milk
450 g/1 lb minced beef
1 small onion (optional)
1 egg

1 level teaspoon salt
freshly milled pepper
seasoned flour
40 g/1½ oz butter for frying

Trim the crusts from the slice of bread and crumble the white part into a basin. Add just enough milk to soak the bread and mix with a fork to break it up. Add the minced beef, the finely chopped onion if you like the flavour, the egg, salt and plenty of pepper. Mix the ingredients with a fork to bind them thoroughly together. Texture at this stage is important; if the meat loaf is going to be juicy and succulent the mixture must be moist, but not wet or difficult to handle.

Using wetted hands pat the meat mixture into a neat loaf shape. Roll in seasoned flour to coat lightly on all sides. Melt the butter in a frying pan, add the meat loaf and fry gently to brown all over. Then lift from the pan and place in a covered roasting tin.

Add about ½ teacup water to the hot butter in the frying pan then stir and swirl the mixture over the heat to form a little gravy. Pour this over the meat loaf and cover with the lid. Place in the centre of a moderate oven (180°C., 350°F., Gas Mark 4) and cook for 45 minutes. If correctly made the meat loaf will keep its shape beautifully and any juices from the roasting tin should be poured over before serving.

Serves 4

Fried turkey escalopes

For this recipe buy the tender pieces of turkey breasts that are available in most supermarkets. Egg-and-breadcrumb them ready for cooking in advance.

4 turkey escalopes
1 egg
salt and freshly milled pepper
toasted breadcrumbs

50 g/2 oz butter
1 tablespoon oil
juice of ½ lemon

Trim the turkey pieces, removing any skin. Lightly mix the egg with a seasoning of salt and pepper. Dip the escalopes first in the egg, then in toasted breadcrumbs to coat all over.

Melt the butter and oil in a large frying pan. The addition of oil helps to prevent the butter from becoming too brown during frying. Add the turkey escalopes to the hot fat, brown both sides and then lower the heat. Fry gently for about 15–20 minutes, turning once.

When tender and golden brown, lift from the pan on to a hot serving dish. Add a good squeeze of lemon juice to the hot butter. Pour over the turkey escalopes and serve.
Serves 4

Green pepper coleslaw

The combination of oil and vinegar dressing and mayonnaise gives coleslaw salad a pleasant bite. Soured cream or yogurt can be used instead of mayonnaise and the cabbage can be tossed with grated carrot or apple, chopped celery, chunks of orange flesh, fresh dates or nuts. In this case sweet green peppers and raisins provide a variation. Serve with cold ham, chicken or pork.

½ white cabbage
2 small green peppers
2 tablespoons raisins
3 rounded tablespoons mayonnaise

4 tablespoons single cream
1 tablespoon finely chopped chives
  and parsley

oil and vinegar dressing:
salt and freshly milled pepper
1 teaspoon castor sugar
pinch paprika

2 tablespoons vinegar
3 tablespoons salad oil

Remove any outer damaged leaves and cut the cabbage in half. Remove the centre core and shred the cabbage finely across the leaves. Halve, deseed and finely shred the peppers. Mix the cabbage, peppers and raisins together in a bowl, and prepare the dressing.

Place the salt, pepper, sugar and paprika in a small basin. Add the vinegar, stir to dissolve the seasonings and then stir in the oil. Pour over the shredded cabbage and peppers, mix well and put to chill for 30 minutes.

Thin down the mayonnaise with the cream and pour over the salad,

toss ingredients to mix and spoon into a salad bowl. Sprinkle lavishly with chives and parsley and serve.
Serves 6

Sour cream potato salad

A salad that tastes good and looks pretty. Serve with cold ham, chicken or tongue.

675 g/1½ lb new potatoes
1 small onion
½ cucumber

3–4 stalks celery
salt and freshly milled pepper
3 hard-boiled eggs

for the dressing:

1 carton soured cream
3 rounded tablespoons mayonnaise

1 teaspoon made mustard

Scrape the potatoes and place in a saucepan. Cover with boiling water and cook for 12 minutes. Drain and allow to cool, then slice thickly. Peel and finely chop the onion. Peel the cucumber, slice lengthways and remove the centre seeds, then dice the cucumber flesh. Wash and shred the celery. Place all the vegetables together in a bowl and season well with salt and pepper.

Cut the hard-boiled eggs in half and separate the whites from the yolks. Chop the egg whites and add to the salad. Mix the soured cream, mayonnaise and mustard in a basin. Add to the salad ingredients and toss lightly to mix. Spoon the mixture into a salad bowl and using a wooden spoon press the egg yolks through a sieve all over the top to decorate.
Serves 6

Carrot and apple salad

Serve this refreshing salad for a lunch menu with cold meat or chicken and crusty bread and butter.

225 g/8 oz new carrots
3 dessert apples
4 tablespoons seedless raisins

1 carton soured cream
2 level teaspoons castor sugar
juice of ½ lemon

Scrape the carrots and grate coarsely into a bowl. Peel, core and grate the apple and add along with the raisins.

Mix together the soured cream, sugar and lemon juice and pour

over the mixture. Toss with a fork to blend the ingredients and
serve.
Serves 4

Broccoli with cream and parsley

*If any sauce is to be served with spring vegetables, it must be light and
delicate in flavour. You can make this recipe using soured cream and
omit the lemon juice. Serve hot over broccoli, new potatoes or broad
beans.*

about 1 kg/2–2½ lb purple sprouting
  broccoli
1.5 dl/¼ pint double cream

salt and freshly milled pepper
1 tablespoon finely chopped parsley
squeeze of lemon juice

Cut away the outer green leaves from the broccoli and separate the
small heads. Soak in cold water for about 30 minutes. Drain and add
to a pan of boiling salted water. Bring back to the boil and cook
rapidly for 10 minutes for young small heads, 15 minutes for others.
When cooked the stalks will feel tender when pierced with the point
of a knife. Drain thoroughly and return the broccoli to the hot pan.

Heat the cream with a seasoning of salt and pepper, the chopped
parsley and a squeeze of lemon juice. Pour over the broccoli and
serve.
Serves 4

Broccoli soufflé

Vegetable soufflé can be served with the lighter kinds of meat, like roast chicken or veal. Carrot or spinach soufflé is just as easy to make if you cook and purée the vegetable first and then follow the method given in this recipe.

450 g/1 lb fresh broccoli	salt and freshly milled pepper
25 g/1 oz butter	juice of ½ lemon
1 rounded tablespoon flour	4 egg yolks
1.5 dl/¼ pint milk	5 egg whites

Trim away the outer leaves and coarse stalks from the broccoli. Leave only the tender inner leaves and cut the heads in half if necessary. Add to a pan of boiling salted water and simmer for 15 minutes until tender. Draw off the heat, drain and mash or blend to a purée.

Meanwhile, melt the butter in a large saucepan. Stir in the flour and cook over a low heat for 1 minute. Do not allow to brown. Gradually add the milk, stirring all the time to make a smooth sauce. Bring to the boil – at this stage the mixture will be very thick. Allow to cook for 2–3 minutes, then season with salt and pepper and stir in the lemon juice and broccoli purée. Beat the egg yolks into the sauce one at a time. Whisk the egg whites until stiff, then with a metal spoon gently fold into the mixture. Pour into a well-buttered 1-litre (2-pint) soufflé dish. Place in the centre of a moderate oven (180°C., 350°F., Gas Mark 4) and bake for 1 hour. Serve hot.
Serves 4

Rum and coffee cream

In most recipes double cream and evaporated milk are interchangeable – the cream makes a more luxurious version and the evaporated milk a less expensive recipe. Use 3 dl (½ pint) double cream here if you prefer.

3 tablespoons water	2 teaspoons coffee essence
2 level teaspoons powdered gelatine	1 tablespoon dark rum
50 g/2 oz castor sugar	chopped walnuts for decoration
1 small can evaporated milk, chilled (see note)	

Measure the water into a small saucepan, sprinkle on the gelatine and set aside to soak for 5 minutes. Add the sugar and stir over low heat until both the sugar and gelatine have dissolved, but do not allow to boil. Draw off the heat and cool for a few minutes.

Whisk the evaporated milk until thick and light. Whisk in the coffee essence and rum, then gradually whisk in the gelatine mixture, pouring from well above the bowl so that it is added in a thin steady stream. Continue to whisk the mixture until thick and beginning to set. Pour into six individual goblets to set. Top with chopped walnuts.
Serves 6

Note Small cans of evaporated milk should be brought to the boil from cold, simmered for 15 minutes, then cooled and chilled. Evaporated milk so treated will whisk up thick and fluffy.

Banana mousse

This is an ideal recipe to make using a blender, so that the bananas are reduced to a lovely smooth purée.

4 tablespoons water
2 level teaspoons powdered
  gelatine
3 large bananas

75 g/3 oz castor sugar
juice of 1 large lemon
1 small can evaporated milk,
  chilled (see previous recipe)

Measure the water into a small saucepan, sprinkle on the gelatine and set aside to soak for 5 minutes. Then place over low heat and stir until the gelatine has dissolved – do not allow the mixture to boil. Draw the pan off the heat.

Peel the bananas and cut into chunks. Place in a blender, along with the sugar and lemon juice. Cover and blend to a purée. Alternatively, the mixture may be well mashed together with a fork.

Whisk the chilled evaporated milk until thick. Whisk in the gelatine mixture and then fold in the banana purée. Pour into a glass bowl and chill until set firm. Serve with cream.
Serves 4-6

Pots de crème au chocolat

The chocolate does not need to be melted when the cream is heated in a recipe as the heat of the cream is sufficient to soften it. This is a rich dessert and portions should be small.

175 g/6 oz chocolate chips or plain chocolate broken in pieces
3 dl/½ pint single cream

1 egg
pinch salt
½ teaspoon vanilla essence

Put the chocolate in the goblet of a blender. Heat the cream until just under boiling point, then pour on to the chocolate. Cover, switch on and blend until smooth. The heat of the cream will melt the chocolate.

Add the egg, salt and vanilla essence and blend again quickly. The mixture at this stage will be quite thin. Pour into six small individual pots, or failing this, small glasses. Chill for several hours or overnight until the mixture is quite firm.
Serves 6

Lemon freeze

This recipe makes a delicious, sharp-flavoured lemon ice cream. It has an excellent creamy smooth texture.

50 g/2 oz crushed cornflakes
50 g/2 oz castor sugar

50 g/2 oz melted butter

for the lemon ice cream:

2 eggs
1 small can sweetened condensed milk
1.5 dl/¼ pint double cream

juice and finely grated rind of 2 lemons
25 g/1 oz castor sugar

Measure the cornflake crumbs into a basin and add the sugar. Using a fork stir in the melted butter and mix well until all the crumbs are buttery. Line a large refrigerator ice tray or an oblong polythene freezer box with a strip of kitchen foil. This makes the dessert easier to lift out afterwards. Reserve 2 tablespoons of the crumb mixture and pat the remainder over the base of the container.

Separate the eggs, placing the yolks in one basin and the whites in a second basin. Add the condensed milk and cream to the egg yolks and blend well. Add the strained lemon juice and the finely grated lemon rind. Stir until the mixture thickens. Beat the egg whites until stiff. Add the sugar and beat until glossy. Fold the egg whites into the lemon mixture and then pour into the prepared container. Spread level and sprinkle with the reserved crumb mixture. Freeze for several hours or until quite firm.

Loosen the sides of the dessert with a knife blade. Then, using the foil, lift the dessert out of the container. Allow to stand at room temperature to soften slightly. Then serve cut in bars.
Serves 6

Meringues

Never use eggs that are cold from the refrigerator. Bring out the number required and allow them to come up to room temperature before using in a recipe. Egg whites in particular whisk up to a better volume when at room temperature.

Meringue toppings A meringue mixture used to decorate a pudding or pie should be made using 40–50 g (1½–2 oz) castor sugar per egg white.

A pudding served hot from the oven will require the smaller quantity of sugar. This produces a soft, less sweet meringue which combines deliciously with the pudding. About 10 minutes in a moderate oven (180°C., 350°F., Gas Mark 4) will brown the meringue attractively; serve at once.

For a meringue topping on a pie which is to be served cold, the full 50 g (2 oz) castor sugar should be used. This meringue is baked more slowly to dry the mixture out; it will hold a better and more attractive shape this way. Place in a cooler oven (150°C., 300°F., Gas Mark 2) and bake for 30 minutes or more. Allow the meringue to brown – it looks and tastes better.

Remember to sprinkle any meringue toppings with a little castor sugar before baking; this helps to ensure a crisp crust.

Meringue shells Ideally egg whites for meringue shells should be cracked and allowed to stand at room temperature for 24 hours before using. Egg whites that have been left over from a previous recipe and which have been standing for 2–3 days are excellent.

Beat egg whites until very stiff before adding the sugar. Use castor sugar; make sure it is dry and sieve out any lumps. Allow 50 g (2 oz) per egg white. The sugar should be added slowly – ideally in three equal parts. The first two additions should be whisked in very thoroughly, but the final addition simply lightly folded in using a metal spoon to blend. Over-mixing at this final stage is what causes meringue mixtures to go soft.

Sprinkle unbaked meringue shells with sugar for a crisp crust. Try chopped walnuts or hundreds and thousands – they bake on prettily. Dry shells out in a cool oven (110°C., 225°F., Gas Mark ¼) with the oven door open. Meringues take 2–3 hours to dry out. Rotate the trays so that they dry evenly and when the shells are crisp turn them over to dry the underneath. Store in an airtight tin when cold – they keep well for several weeks so may be made in advance.

Chilled lemon cheesecake

This cheesecake, set with gelatine, has a smooth, mousse-like texture and a crunchy biscuit base. It makes a very nice spring dessert and is particularly good served with strawberry or raspberry sauce (see page 164).

4 tablespoons water
15 g/½ oz powdered gelatine
3 large eggs
100 g/4 oz castor sugar
juice and finely grated rind of
  2 lemons

450 g/1 lb cream cheese
1 170-g/6-fl oz carton double
  cream

for the crumb base:
8 digestive biscuits
1 level tablespoon castor sugar

50 g/2 oz butter

Measure the water into a saucepan, sprinkle in the gelatine and set aside to soak for 5 minutes. Stir over low heat until the gelatine has dissolved; draw off the heat ready to use.

Separate the eggs, placing the yolks in one basin and the whites in a second larger basin. Add the sugar, lemon juice and finely grated lemon rind to the egg yolks. Place the basin over a saucepan half filled with simmering water and whisk until the mixture is frothy and light in colour. Remove from the heat and whisk in the dissolved gelatine.

Blend the cream cheese until smooth and then gradually whisk in the gelatine and egg mixture. This is easiest done on a machine or with a hand mixer if you have one. Beat the mixture well until thick and light; by now it will be almost at setting point. Lightly whip the cream and stiffly beat the egg whites. Fold both into the cheese mixture gently but thoroughly. Pour into a 20-cm (8-in) round deep cake tin, lined on the base with a circle of greaseproof paper.

Crush the digestive biscuits and mix with the sugar. Melt the butter and stir in the crumbs with a fork. Spoon over the top of the cheese-cake mixture and chill until firm.

When ready to serve, loosen around the top and turn the cheesecake out on to a plate. The biscuit crumb topping will now be on the base. Serve with cream or fresh fruit.
Serves 8

Lemon spice cakes

A mixture that can be baked in a large tin and then cut into several smaller pieces is always quicker to make and less trouble to cope with. Once cut, store these cakes in a covered tin to keep them fresh and moist.

100 g/4 oz plain flour	175 g/6 oz butter
1 level teaspoon baking powder	225 g/8 oz soft brown sugar
½ level teaspoon ground cinnamon	2 large eggs
¼ level teaspoon ground nutmeg	½ teaspoon vanilla essence
100 g/4 oz quick-cooking rolled oats	finely grated rind of 1 lemon
	2 tablespoons lemon juice
50 g/2 oz walnuts, finely chopped	3 tablespoons milk

for the lemon glaze:

175 g/6 oz icing sugar	2 tablespoons lemon juice

Sift the flour, baking powder, cinnamon and nutmeg on to a plate, add the rolled oats and chopped walnuts and set aside.

Cream the butter in a basin, then beat with the sugar until light. Lightly mix the eggs with the vanilla essence, lemon rind and juice and beat into the creamed mixture a little at a time. Fold in the flour mixture, along with the extra milk if needed, to make a soft consistency. Spoon into a medium-sized greased and lined shallow baking or roasting tin and spread the top smoothly. Bake in the centre of a moderate oven (180°C., 350°F., Gas Mark 4) for 30–35 minutes until golden brown. Remove from the oven and set aside while preparing the glaze.

Sift the icing sugar and mix to a smooth glaze with the lemon juice. Pour over the top of the warm cake and spread smoothly. When the cake is cold, loosen the sides and lift from the tin. Cut into squares.
Makes about 2 dozen squares

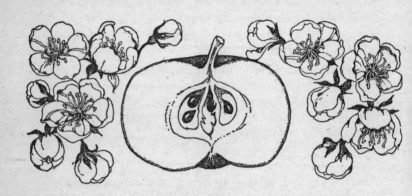

Apple slice

Apple slice made in a big rectangular tin can be served at home as a dessert with ice cream or custard, or taken on a picnic. Use the tart cooking apples, like Bramley's Seedlings, if there are still some available.

225 g/8 oz self-raising flour
175 g/6 oz butter

50 g/2 oz castor sugar
1 large egg

for the filling:

450 g/1 lb cooking apples
75–100 g/3–4 oz castor sugar
½ level teaspoon ground cinnamon

1 tablespoon seedless raisins (optional)

Rub or cut the butter into the flour until the mixture resembles coarse crumbs. Stir in the sugar and then mix to a dough with the egg. Leave in a cool place for 30 minutes.

Roll out half the dough to line a rectangular roasting or baking tin.

On top, grate the peeled and cored apples, sprinkling layers of apple with the mixed sugar and cinnamon. A tablespoon of washed seedless raisins may also be added. Top with the remaining dough rolled out to fit. Mark into squares lightly, using a knife. Bake in a moderate oven (180°C., 350°F., Gas Mark 4) for 1 hour. Sprinkle thickly with icing sugar and cut into pieces when cold.
Makes 12 pieces

Rock cakes

The 'rock' in rock cakes should apply to the rough appearance only. This mixture is a rich one and the cakes should be light and crumbly. Another time try them with chopped dates, currants or mixed peel in place of the sultanas.

225 g/8 oz self-raising flour
¼ level teaspoon salt
pinch mixed spice
75 g/3 oz butter
75 g/3 oz castor sugar

75 g/3 oz sultanas
1 large egg
2 tablespoons milk
demerara sugar

Sift the flour, salt and mixed spice into a basin. Add the butter cut in pieces and rub into the flour. Add the sugar and sultanas and mix. Lightly mix the egg and milk and pour into the centre of the ingredients. Using a fork mix to a rough dough. The mixture should be fairly firm.

Pile the mixture into twelve rough heaps on greased baking trays, not too close together, since they flatten out slightly on baking. Sprinkle a little demerara sugar on the top of each one. Place in the centre of a moderately hot oven (200°C., 400°F., Gas Mark 6) and bake for 10–15 minutes, or until lightly browned. Loosen the base of each with a palette knife and cool on a wire tray.
Makes 12

Raspberry buns

Quick and easy to make, these jam-flavoured 'cakes' are fine for the children's tea, or for mid-morning with a glass of milk. Make them with different jams – raspberry, apricot or marmalade – so the children can choose their favourites.

225 g/8 oz self-raising flour
pinch salt
75 g/3 oz butter

75 g/3 oz castor sugar
1 large egg
2 tablespoons milk

for the decoration:
raspberry jam
little milk

castor sugar

Sift the flour and salt into a mixing basin. Add the butter in pieces and rub into the flour. Add the sugar. Lightly mix the egg and milk and pour into the centre of the ingredients. Using a fork mix to a rough dough in the basin.

Turn out on to a floured board and knead lightly. Divide in half and roll each piece into a sausage about 30 cm (12 in) long. Cut each roll into eight equal pieces and form each piece into a ball. Space a little apart on two greased baking trays and using a floured thumb make a small indent in each bun.

Fill the space in each bun with a little raspberry jam, then with floured fingers pinch up the sides to keep the jam in. Brush with a little milk and sprinkle with a little castor sugar. Place in the centre of a moderately hot oven (200°C., 400°F., Gas Mark 6) and bake for 15 minutes. Cool on a wire tray.
Makes 16

Queen cakes

Queen cakes are traditionally baked in small round fluted tins. A tray of lined bun or tartlet tins will do as well.

75 g/3 oz self-raising flour
pinch salt
50 g/2 oz butter
50 g/2 oz castor sugar
1 egg

little finely grated lemon rind
40 g/1½ oz currants
15 g/½ oz chopped mixed peel
milk to mix

Sift together the flour and salt and set aside. Cream the butter and sugar until light and creamy. Lightly mix the egg and grated lemon rind. Gradually beat into the creamed mixture, adding a little of the flour along with the last addition of egg. Fold in half the flour mixture, then the remaining flour and fruit, adding a little milk to make a medium-soft consistency.

Spoon dessertspoonfuls of the mixture into either well-greased

queen cake moulds or deep bun tins lined with paper baking cases. Place in the centre of a moderate oven (180°C., 350°F., Gas Mark 4) and bake for 15–20 minutes or until risen and brown. Cool before serving.
Makes 9

Using the freezer in April

Plan Easter holiday menus carefully. A capon or small turkey can be useful to have in the freezer for long weekends. Small turkeys of 3½–4 kg (8–9 lb) in weight are readily available and make a marvellous roast, providing enough for eight hearty appetites with a little left over for cold. Use the carcass for soups and the pickings of the cold bird in a white sauce as a filling for pancakes or hot *vol-au-vent cases* (see page 97). Stock up the freezer with some turkey pieces to use for *fried turkey escalopes* (see page 102).

Rhubarb is a food not to be ignored this month. Wash, trim stalks and cut into 2·5-cm (1-in) lengths; freeze in polythene bags in quantities of 450 g (1 lb). Rhubarb that has been frozen makes up best into compotes. Do not thaw first, just use frozen. You will find that the *chilled lemon cheesecake* (see page 110) will also freeze. Freeze uncovered until firm. Dip the tin in very hot water for a few seconds, loosen around the top with a knife, and turn out. Wrap in cling wrap and foil for storage. Remove from the freezer about 6–8 hours before serving, unwrap, and allow to thaw slowly on a plate in the refrigerator.

Freezing poultry

Both fresh and frozen poultry are for sale all year round and it is doubtful whether it is worth taking up valuable freezer space with whole birds. Small poussins are seasonable however, and can be frozen whole or cut in half. The small spring chickens of 1 kg (2–2½ lb) can be very useful for a dinner party when they can be roasted unstuffed with fresh herbs and butter.

Whole birds can be cut into portions for storage. A bird of up to 1.25 kg (3 lb) should give four portions and a larger bird up to six or eight pieces. Chicken portions cut at home from the carcass will be much neater and less bulky. Pack leg pieces for casseroles and breast portions for grilling and frying. Use the carcass, bones and trimmings to make a concentrated stock. Strain and freeze for soups, sauces and casseroles.

Use a coating of egg and breadcrumbs to form an extra protective coating layer for foods in the freezer. Fresh sliced turkey breasts available in supermarkets can be egg-and-breadcrumbed and frozen in freezer bags. They are ready for thawing and quick frying. A boiling fowl, an economical cooking bird, is not a good item for the freezer. It's better to make it up into a cooked dish and freeze like that.

Chill chicken in the refrigerator before freezing. Whole birds should be trussed as for roasting to give the bird a neat shape, and frozen unstuffed. Polythene bags are the most satisfactory wrapping material for chicken. Press out as much air as possible before freezing. Joints or breast portions can be laid side by side in one layer on a foil tray. To aid separation pack with cellophane paper between each one.

Freeze all stuffings separately. Bread stuffings are more perishable than the chicken so it is always advisable to pack them separately. A stuffed bird makes an excellent place for harmful bacteria to grow, particularly during thawing and the early stages of cooking.

Poultry must be properly thawed before cooking and preferably in the refrigerator. Room temperature is fine for small birds but for larger ones it must be a cold larder. Leave a shop-frozen bird in the wrapper and as soon as it is pliable, remove the giblets to speed thawing.

Thawing time for poultry

	Refrigerator	Room temperature
Joints	6 hours	3 hours
Whole chicken or duck up to 1.75 kg (4 lb)	12 hours	overnight in cold larder
Capon, large duckling or small turkey up to 3.5 kg (8 lb)		up to 16 hours in cold larder
Small turkey or goose up to 5.5 kg (12 lb)		up to 24 hours in cold larder
Large turkey over 5.5 kg (12 lb)		up to 48 hours in cold larder

May

May is a forward-looking month and cooks need to be particularly alert to take full advantage of the first summer vegetables as they come on the market. These can make a dramatic difference to our menus. The young fresh flavours make them suitable for serving as a first course and for adding to salads. We can expect broad beans, young beetroot and bunched carrots, soon followed by courgettes, French beans and sugar peas. May brings good avocados, the start of the summer supply of globe artichokes from Brittany and our own asparagus season.

As spring gets under way mint should be sprouting in the garden for the new season's lamb. Herrings are at their best and along with them come mackerel, a real sea fish with a strong flavour. Towards the end of the month the season of summer fruit starts, with imported apricots and the early gooseberries which are green and hard, but the ones for cooking generally and preserving. Small pineapples are also plentiful and inexpensive to serve.

Cream of watercress soup

Watercress soup is also delicious served cold. Allow the soup to cool, then stir in the cream, chopped watercress and a little extra stock to thin it down. Chill well before serving.

2 bunches watercress	6 dl/1 pint chicken stock
450 g/1 lb potatoes	3 dl/½ pint milk
1 onion	salt and freshly milled pepper
25 g/1 oz butter	1.5 dl/¼ pint single cream

Thoroughly wash the watercress, dipping it head downwards in plenty of cold water. Set one bunch aside for the garnish. Cut away the stalks from the remaining bunch and then coarsely chop the leaves and top parts of the stalks. Peel and dice the potatoes. Peel and finely chop the onion.

Melt the butter in a large saucepan, add the onion and fry gently for a moment. Add the potatoes, chopped watercress, stock and milk. Season with salt and pepper and bring up to the boil. Simmer gently for 1 hour.

Meanwhile nip the leaves off the stalks from the reserved bunch of watercress and chop finely. Draw the soup off the heat and pass the vegetables and liquid through a vegetable mill or purée in a blender. Return to the pan and reheat. Stir in the cream and chopped watercress, check the seasoning and serve.

Serves 6

Summer pâté

Both soft and hard herring roes are sold by the fishmonger – take care to choose the right ones for this recipe.

75 g/3 oz butter	juice of ½ lemon
100 g/4 oz fresh soft herring roes	2 teaspoons finely chopped parsley
salt and freshly milled pepper	

Melt 25 g (1 oz) of the butter in a frying pan, add the roes and season with salt and pepper. Fry gently for about 5 minutes, turning the roes over to cook them evenly. Draw the pan off the heat and spoon the roes and butter from the pan into a mixing basin. Using a wooden spoon beat the mixture to a smooth paste. Gradually beat in the remaining butter, softened, lemon juice to taste and chopped parsley.

Alternatively the pâté may be mixed in a blender. In this case spoon the hot roes and butter from the pan into the container. Cover and blend until smooth, then blend in the remaining butter, 15 g (½ oz) at a time, and the lemon juice. When the mixture is smooth stir in the chopped parsley.

Spoon the prepared pâté into a small dish and chill for several hours. Serve with hot toast and butter.

Serves 4

Egg and anchovy mousse

Egg mousse can be rather bland unless the recipe is well seasoned. This mixture includes Worcestershire sauce and salty anchovy fillets to add to the flavour. Serve as a first course with thinly sliced brown bread and butter, or include it as part of the cold foods for a buffet supper.

8 eggs	1.5 dl/¼ pint double cream
1 can anchovy fillets	1 teaspoon Worcestershire sauce
3 dl/½ pint chicken stock	salt and freshly milled pepper
15 g/½ oz powdered gelatine	

Bring the eggs to the boil from cold and simmer for 6–8 minutes to cook hard. Drain the eggs and submerge in cold water to prevent over-cooking. Shell the eggs and leave covered in cold water until required. Sieve the yolks into a basin. Chop the whites and add to the yolks. Remove about six anchovy fillets from the can, chop coarsely and add to the eggs. Measure about 3 tablespoons of the stock into a saucepan. Sprinkle in the gelatine and allow to soak for a few minutes. Add the remaining stock and stir over low heat until the gelatine has dissolved. Draw off the heat and allow to cool.

When the stock is beginning to thicken and shows signs of setting, pour at once into the egg mixture. Add the lightly whipped cream, Worcestershire sauce and a seasoning of salt and pepper. Blend the ingredients quickly and evenly. Pour into a 1-litre (1½-pint) wetted mould – a 15-cm (6-in) cake tin is quite a good size – and chill until set firm.

Turn the mousse out on to a serving plate. Criss-cross the remaining anchovy fillets on the top and surround with watercress.
Serves 6

Cucumber soup with mint

A white sauce can be used as part of the liquid in a soup recipe. It provides the thickening agent and gives a rich smooth flavour. Cream soups made from salad vegetables like lettuce and cucumber are often prepared in this way. This recipe has mint added for flavour. Serve it hot or cold.

2 large cucumbers	½ onion
60 g/2½ oz butter	bay leaf
3–4 sprigs fresh mint	25 g/1 oz flour
pinch sugar	4 dl/¾ pint chicken stock
salt and freshly milled pepper	2–3 tablespoons single cream
3 dl/½ pint milk	freshly chopped mint

Peel the cucumbers, slice in half lengthways and remove the centre seeds. Chop the cucumbers up and blanch in boiling water for 2 minutes. Drain well. Melt 25 g (1 oz) of the butter in a saucepan, add the cucumber, the sprigs of mint, sugar and a seasoning of salt and pepper. Cover and cook gently for about 15 minutes, or until tender.

Meanwhile infuse the milk with the onion and bay leaf for about 15 minutes. Melt the remaining butter in a saucepan and stir in the flour. Cook over the heat for a minute and then gradually stir in the strained milk. Beat well and bring up to the boil to make a smooth sauce. When the cucumbers are tender, add the chicken stock and the sauce to the pan. Stir and bring up to the boil. Cover with a lid and simmer gently for a further 15 minutes.

Using a fork, remove the stalks of mint. Pass the soup through a food mill or purée in a blender. Return to the saucepan, check the seasoning and reheat. Stir in the cream and sprinkle with chopped mint before serving.
Serves 6

Gulls' eggs

The season for gulls' eggs is short, only about 6 weeks in all, and finishes by the end of May. Allow 2–3 eggs per person. If uncooked add to boiling water and simmer for 5 minutes. Drain and cool. In most cases the eggs are sold already hard-boiled. Serve as a first course unshelled – guests peel the eggs themselves. Pass slices of brown bread and butter and coarse salt or celery salt.

Globe artichokes with vinaigrette

Here is something easy and new to serve. Globe artichokes are not only delicious eating but they look so pretty too. In Brittany they serve the artichokes warm or cold with vinaigrette dressing. If your pan is not large enough to hold all the heads at once, serve them cold and cook them in batches.

4 globe artichokes

for the dressing:

salt and freshly milled pepper	3 tablespoons wine vinegar
dash of French mustard	6 tablespoons oil

Globe artichokes have a stem of about 15 cm (6 in) attached when bought and the first task is to cut or snap the stalk off close to the head. Rub the fleshy base over with the cut side of a lemon to prevent any discolouration and remove any small leaves around the base.

Bring plenty of well-salted water to the boil and add the globe artichokes. They may bob to the surface, but just make sure that the base is downwards in the water. Simmer them gently, uncovered, for 40 minutes. When ready a leaf should easily detach itself when gently pulled. Drain the artichokes from the pan with a slotted spoon, holding each over the pan for a moment so that all the boiling water trapped in the leaves drains out.

When the artichokes are cool enough to handle, open the upper leaves at the top and you will see a cone of tightly closed leaves underneath. Gently pull these out and discard them. Look back inside the artichoke and you will now see what is called the 'choke', a hairy bit which lies on the surface of the artichoke heart. With a teaspoon scrape out and discard this. Your artichoke is now ready to serve; arrange them on individual serving plates.

Blend together the ingredients for the dressing and pass separately. It can be spooned into the space in the centre of the artichokes or on to the plate so that the tender base of each leaf can be dipped as you eat it. When you get down to the *fond* or heart which is the most succulent bit of all, a knife and fork will be required for cutting it up and eating it.

Serves 4

Smoked salmon tart

An 85-g (3-oz) packet of sliced smoked salmon from the freezer is just the right amount for making this savoury tart. Use a shortcrust pastry mixed with egg to get a pastry crust that is short and crisp.

100 g/4 oz shortcrust pastry

for the filling:

3 eggs
3 dl/½ pint milk
salt and freshly milled pepper
pinch nutmeg

15 g/½ oz butter
75–100 g/3–4 oz sliced smoked
  salmon

Roll the pastry out to a circle on a lightly floured board. Use to line a 20-cm (8-in) quiche tin with a loose base or a flan ring set on a baking tray. Set aside while preparing the filling.

Lightly mix the eggs, milk, a seasoning of salt and pepper and the nutmeg. Strain into a jug and pour into the flan case. Dot with the butter cut in small pieces and then cover the surface with the thin slices of smoked salmon.

Place in the centre of a moderately hot oven (190°C., 375°F., Gas Mark 5) and bake for 40 minutes. Serve warm. Excellent as a first course or as a lunch or supper dish with a tossed salad.

Serves 4

Grilled herrings

Grilling is a method of cooking that conserves the flavour of fish and is particularly suitable for herrings. Prepared in this way they taste especially good with a mustard sauce.

4 fresh herrings   oil

for the mustard cream sauce:

4 tablespoons double cream   salt and freshly milled pepper
1 tablespoon prepared English
  mustard

Rinse the herrings and remove the scales by scraping gently with a knife from the tail end towards the head. Trim off the fins with scissors. If the fish is not already cleaned, cut off the head, slit the fish down the belly and draw out the entrails and roes. Make three shallow, slanting slashes through the skin on each side of the fish – this prevents the fish from curling up when the skin contracts on cooking. Rinse the fish and pat dry.

Grease the grill bars or tray and brush the fish with a little oil. Place under a medium hot grill and cook gently for 3–4 minutes on each side.

Meanwhile measure the cream, mustard and a pinch of salt and pepper into a bowl. Whisk until thick and light. Serve the fish with the mustard cream sauce spooned over – it melts deliciously over the hot fish.

Serves 4

Mackerel with brown butter

Mackerel are particularly good filleted and fried in butter. Ask the fishmonger to clean the mackerel for you and cut each one into two fillets. He will do this by making a cut down the length of the fish along its back, then inserting the knife and gently pulling the flesh away from the bone.

2 large or 4 small mackerel, cut into fillets	juice of $\frac{1}{2}$ lemon
seasoned flour	1 tablespoon finely chopped parsley
50 g/2 oz butter	lemon slices

Dip the mackerel fillets in seasoned flour and shake off the surplus. Melt the butter in a heavy frying pan until slightly frothing. Put in the fish fillets flesh side down, and cook gently for about 5 minutes. Turn and cook the second side. Lift on to a serving dish and keep warm.

Increase the heat under the pan until the butter turns a golden brown. Add the lemon juice and shake the pan over the heat for a minute to mix. Add the chopped parsley and pour over the fish. Garnish with a few slices of lemon and serve.
Serves 4

Trout meunière

Trout is the most delicately textured and deliciously flavoured fish, but it is rarely served at home which is a pity because it is one of the quickest and easiest to cook. For family eating it is simple to serve the fish at its best – straight from the pan to the table.

4 fresh trout	1 tablespoon oil
seasoned flour	juice of $\frac{1}{2}$ lemon
50–75 g/2–3 oz butter	

Ask the fishmonger to clean out the trout. Holding each one by the tail, roll in seasoned flour to coat all over. Heat the butter and oil in a large frying pan and when hot, but not brown, add the fish one at a time.

Cook over moderate heat for about 5 minutes until nicely browned, then turn and cook the second side for a further 5 minutes. Lift from the pan on to a hot serving platter. Add the juice of the lemon to the hot butter. Heat for a moment, then pour over the fish and serve.
Serves 4

Anchoide

Anchoide is a well-seasoned paste made using anchovy fillets. Spread it on French bread and serve it hot for a snack, preferably with a glass of chilled white wine.

2 cans anchovy fillets	1 teaspoon red wine vinegar
2 cloves garlic	freshly milled pepper
1 tablespoon olive oil	slices of French bread
50 g/2 oz soft butter	

Pound the anchovies to a smooth paste with the peeled cloves of garlic. Add the olive oil, butter and wine vinegar. Season with plenty of pepper.

Toast slices of French bread on one side only. Spread the anchoide thickly on the untoasted side, pressing down so that the flavour soaks in. Place in a hot oven for a few minutes before serving.
Serves 4

Cream in sauces

Cream has the ability to complement other flavours and it adds a rich smoothness to a recipe. Cream mellows flavours too and seasonings in a recipe should be rechecked before serving. The most simple use of cream is to add a tablespoon or two to a recipe just before serving. This is particularly good for soups, especially chilled summer soups. Cold cream poured over a hot dessert is a marvellous combination. Try it over hot baked peaches, apricots, pears or flambéed bananas.

One of the best-known uses of cream is as a liaison of 2–3 tablespoons cream and an egg yolk. This is added to give a richness and texture to sauces in recipes like blanquette of veal or chicken. Blend the liaison with a little of the hot sauce first, then stir in at the last minute and reheat but do not boil.

Use cream as a sauce over ingredients that cook quickly like steak, chicken joints or veal escalopes. Sauté them first in butter with onion, garlic, tarragon, thyme or parsley added for flavour. When the cooked ingredients are lifted out of the pan, pour the cream into the hot flavoured butter. Swirl round and then tip out over the food. When combining wine and cream in a sauce for meat and poultry, reduce the wine well to concentrate the flavour. Then when you stir in double cream there should be no risk of separation and the ingredients will blend perfectly.

Frikadeller

All Scandinavian countries make marvellous meatballs. These are the Danish kind and are particularly good served with seasonal vegetables like carrots, French beans or peas. Remember that any left over are very good cold with a salad; the Danes also serve them sliced on open sandwiches.

225 g/8 oz lean beef	1 level teaspoon salt
225 g/8 oz pork fillet	freshly milled pepper
1 medium-sized onion	2–3 tablespoons milk
flour (see method)	50–75 g/2–3 oz butter
1 egg	

Trim the meat and mince two or three times with the onion – you may, if you prefer, use veal in place of the beef. Mix well and then pat evenly over the base of a mixing bowl. Spoon a quarter of the mixture to the side and fill the space with flour. Blend the flour with all the meat and stir in the egg, seasoning and enough milk to make a fairly soft mixture.

At this stage a little should be tasted to see if the seasoning is correct. Do this by dropping a teaspoon of the mixture into boiling water. Cook for 5 minutes, then taste and correct the seasoning if necessary.

Drop the mixture by tablespoons into the hot butter in a frying pan – you should get about eight. Fry over moderate heat on both sides until well browned, about 20 minutes. Then remove from the pan. Add a little extra butter to the frying pan, heat for a moment and pour over the frikadeller.
Serves 4

Lamb cutlets en croûte

Meat cooked in a puff pastry crust retains essential juices and flavours and has the added advantage of a pretty covering that is nice to eat. Lamb cutlets en croûte are delicious served hot or cold for a picnic.

450 g/1 lb ready-made puff pastry	50 g/2 oz liver pâté
6 lamb cutlets	egg for glazing
salt and freshly milled pepper	

On a lightly floured surface roll the pastry out thinly and cut into six pieces approximately 15 cm (6 in) square. Allow to rest while preparing the cutlets.

Trim the cutlets and scrape the fat back from the bone so that 2.5 cm (1 in) of the bone shows. Season with salt and pepper and spread each cutlet on both sides with a little liver pâté. Lay a cutlet diagonally across each of the pastry squares so that the bone extends over the edge. Fold the pastry over, completely wrapping the cutlets inside, and seal the joins. Trim the pastry-covered cutlets and put sealed side down on a baking tray.

Glaze with beaten egg. Set in a hot oven (220°C., 425°F., Gas Mark 7) and bake for 10 minutes, then reduce the heat to moderate (180°C., 350°F., Gas Mark 4) and cook for a further 20 minutes. **Serves 6**

Loin of lamb with glazed carrots

Roast meats seem to have more flavour when they are served cold. Cook with care so that the joint remains moist and serve with an attractive garnish of seasonal vegetables. Lamb with glazed carrots makes an easy-to-serve meal for a summer party.

1 1.25- to 1.75-kg/3½- to 4-lb loin of lamb, boned but not rolled
salt and freshly milled pepper

small bunch fresh mint
little sugar
50–75 g/2–3 oz dripping

for the glazed carrots:
675–900 g/1½–2 lb new carrots
salt and freshly milled pepper
1 level tablespoon castor sugar

25 g/1 oz butter
1–2 tablespoons fine-shred orange marmalade

Open out the piece of meat and season the inside with salt and pepper. Wash and finely chop the mint, pound with a little sugar to bruise the leaves and draw the juices, and then spread over the inside of the meat. Roll up the joint starting with the thicker side and tie securely with string, then set in a roasting tin with the dripping. Roast in the centre of a moderate oven (180°C., 350°F., Gas Mark 4) for 1½–1¾ hours for a joint which is a little pink in the centre. Extend the cooking time to 2 hours for a joint cooked right through. Remove the meat from the oven and allow to stand on a rack to cool in its own time – do not refrigerate. Cut away the strings when the meat is cold.

Meanwhile, scrape and thinly slice the carrots. Put in a saucepan with cold water to half cover the carrots. Add a seasoning of salt and pepper, the sugar and butter. Cover with a lid and simmer gently for 30 minutes or until the carrots are quite tender. Then remove the lid and boil rapidly until the water has evaporated and only the butter remains in the pan – watch the pan carefully towards the end for scorching.

Draw off the heat, add the marmalade and toss well to glaze the carrots. Allow to cool. Serve the glazed carrots as a colourful, sweet garnish to the sliced cold meat.

Serves 6

Lamb chops with mint butter

Loin or chump chops are even nicer when marinated before grilling. When ready to serve, place a pat of mint butter on top of each one so it melts over the surface.

4–6 loin or chump lamb chops

for the marinade:

3 tablespoons oil
2 tablespoons dry cider or white wine

½ clove garlic, finely crushed and chopped
little freshly milled black pepper

for the mint butter:

50–75 g/2–3 oz butter
½ teaspoon vinegar

1 heaped tablespoon freshly chopped mint
salt and freshly milled pepper

Trim the chops neatly and cut away any loose tissue. Mix together the ingredients for the marinade and pour into a shallow dish. Place the chops in the dish and leave them to marinate for about 10 minutes, turning the meat once.

Lift the chops from the marinade and arrange on the grill pan. Place under a hot grill about 7 cm (3 in) below the heat and grill for about 15 minutes. Turn halfway through the cooking time.

Prepare the mint butter in advance if possible. Cream the butter until soft then gradually work in the vinegar. Beat in the freshly chopped mint and a seasoning of salt and pepper. Spoon the butter into a square of greaseproof paper and roll up like a log shape, twisting the ends like a cracker. Chill until ready to serve.

When the chops are ready remove from the heat. Strip the paper from the mint butter and serve each chop topped with a slice.
Serves 4-6

Veal escalopes with cream sauce

Vermouth, which has a slightly herby flavour, gives a very good taste to the sauce when used in veal or fish recipes.

4 veal escalopes
salt and freshly milled pepper
juice of ½ lemon
50 g/2 oz butter

4 tablespoons dry vermouth
1.5 dl/¼ pint double cream
few fresh tarragon leaves

Melt the butter in a frying pan, add the escalopes and fry gently for about 5 minutes turning once. Remove them and keep hot. Pour in the vermouth, stir and allow to bubble briskly until syrupy – it is important to reduce the mixture well. Add the cream and a few fresh chopped tarragon leaves. Cook for a few moments. Replace the veal escalopes in the pan and simmer very gently, shaking the ingredients so that they heat thoroughly. Serve hot.
Serves 4

Florida salad

Most fruits combine very well with an oil and vinegar dressing. They make colourful salads that go well with cold meats of any kind.

225 g/8 oz black and green grapes
2 oranges
2 bananas
2–3 tablespoons oil and vinegar
  dressing

1 tablespoon finely chopped mint
crisp lettuce leaves for serving

Halve and deseed the grapes. Mark the orange skins into quarters and peel as for eating. Scrape away all white pith and then cut the oranges downwards through the centre, first in half and then in quarters. Cut the orange quarters across into chunky pieces so that each bit has a minimum amount of skin attached. Peel and slice the bananas.

Mix all the fruits together with the dressing. Add the chopped mint and pile into crisp lettuce leaves for serving.
Serves 4

Mint

Mint is a herb that is common in most gardens. Once it becomes established – usually in some damp shaded corner – it will provide a constant supply of one of summer's most refreshing herbs. There are different kinds of mint but your garden is most likely to boast a clump of the common garden or spearmint.

Gather up a bunch when you next need mint sauce for roast lamb and remember that if you pound the mint leaves you get a much better flavour. Take a good handful of mint and strip the leaves from the stems. Chop them up or pass them through a 'parsmint' and place in a mortar. Sprinkle with a tablespoon of castor sugar and using the pestle pound the leaves until well crushed and mushy. You can do this in a mixing basin with the end of a plain wooden rolling pin. Let the mixture stand and the sugar will draw the juices and flavouring oil from the mint. Give it a final mix and stir in wine vinegar to taste.

Fresh, very bright green mint sauce can be made in the blender. Take a good handful of fresh mint, strip the leaves from the stems and place them in the blender. Add 1 tablespoon of sugar and 1 tablespoon boiling water to dissolve the sugar. Then add 4 tablespoons wine vinegar, cover and blend until the mint leaves are finely chopped.

Sweet glazed carrots

Certain vegetables are naturally sweet in flavour. Carrots and onions are a good example, and in cooking the sweetness should be emphasized. Carrots taste lovely in a shiny butter glaze and when fresh peas are available combine both, as they look pretty together.

450 g/1 lb new carrots	2 teaspoons castor sugar
½ onion, finely chopped	15 g/½ oz butter
bay leaf	1.5 dl/¼ pint water

Scrape the carrots and slice or dice. Place in a saucepan and add the onion, bay leaf, sugar, butter and water. Cover with a lid and bring up to the boil, then cook over moderate heat. After about 20 minutes the carrots should be tender. Remove the pan lid and continue to boil quickly so that the water remaining in the pan evaporates.

When the carrots begin to fry in the butter glaze that remains, draw them off the heat. Toss them, check the seasoning and serve in the

shiny butter glaze. If you add peas, do so towards the end of cooking time as they take less time to cook than carrots.
Serves 4

Cottage cheese and fruit salads

The combination of fruit and cheese is an unusual and delicious one and has the extra advantage of being good for you. Fruits such as sliced banana tossed in lemon juice, peaches or strawberries could be included. For a crunchy texture, sprinkle chopped walnuts over the top before serving.

1 small head lettuce
1 bunch watercress
2 oranges
4 rings pineapple

2 227-g/8-oz cartons cottage cheese
French dressing or mayonnaise for serving

Separate the leaves of lettuce, remove the coarse stems and wash thoroughly. Remove the stems and wash the watercress. Cut a slice from the top and base of each orange. Then cut round each orange removing the peel and white pith. Slice the oranges across thinly.

Arrange the lettuce on a serving platter. Arrange the slices of orange and pineapple around the edge and pile the cottage cheese in the centre. Garnish with sprigs of watercress.

Serve with mayonnaise or French dressing. Crusty brown bread and butter or crispbread would make a good accompaniment for this salad.

VARIATIONS
Slice a peeled orange thinly and arrange attractively round cottage cheese with unpeeled cucumber slices. Spoon over oil and vinegar dressing.

Drain canned peach halves and pile high with chive-flavoured cottage cheese. Serve on crisp lettuce tossed in French dressing.

Slice tomatoes, marinate in oil and vinegar dressing and serve with cottage cheese seasoned with salt and pepper and mixed with seedless raisins and chopped chives.

Buttercrisp new potatoes

Small, even-sized new potatoes can be cooked over direct heat so that they are crisp and brown when ready to serve. Where possible choose a lidded frying pan, so that the potatoes cook evenly and in one layer.

675 g/1½ lb new potatoes   salt
50 g/2 oz butter

Scrub or scrape the potatoes and dry them well. Melt the butter in a pan wide enough to take all the potatoes in one layer. Add the potatoes and stir, turning them so that they are well coated with butter.

Cover the pan with a lid and allow the potatoes to cook gently over low heat for 20–30 minutes. Shake the pan occasionally until the potatoes are crisp and golden outside and soft inside. Draw off the heat, sprinkle with salt (see note) and serve.
Serves 4

Note Use coarse sea salt from a mill if you can.

Spinach en branche

As a straightforward vegetable spinach is not very adaptable. It can be served en branche *when the leaves are whole, and as a purée. Both methods follow the same basic procedure, but for a purée pass the leaves*

*through a vegetable mill before returning to the pan with the butter.
Stir in 4–6 tablespoons cream to make it more delicious.*

675–900 g/1½–2 lb fresh spinach   salt and freshly milled pepper
15 g/½ oz butter

Pull away the centre ribs and wash the spinach in several lots of
cold water. Lift the spinach dripping from the bowl and place
straight in the saucepan. There will be sufficient water clinging to
the leaves and no more will be required. Cover and cook over
moderate heat for 5–10 minutes, shaking the pan occasionally.

Turn into a colander and press well to remove surplus water. Melt
a nut of butter in the hot pan and return the spinach. Season to
taste, toss gently in the butter and serve.
Serves 4

Vanilla cheesecake

*A cheesecake is fragile and not a cake that can be turned out of the
baking tin. Bake it in a tin that opens from the side with a spring clip;
most specialist cook-shops sell them. For the best flavour and texture,
allow the baked cheesecake to stand for 24 hours before serving.*

25 g/1 oz butter   100 g/4 oz castor sugar
6 digestive biscuits   25 g/1 oz cornflour
450 g/1 lb cottage cheese   ½ teaspoon vanilla essence
3 large eggs   1 carton soured cream

Melt the butter in a small saucepan and draw off the heat. Crush the
biscuits to crumbs and, using a fork, stir into the butter. Blend the
mixture well, then spoon into the base of a buttered 20-cm (8-in)
spring clip pan. Spread the crumbs evenly and press down firmly.

Rub the cottage cheese through a sieve into a mixing basin. Separate
the eggs, putting the egg yolks into one basin and the whites into a
second basin. Add the sugar to the yolks and beat with a wooden
spoon until creamy and light. Add the cornflour and vanilla essence
and beat until mixed thoroughly. Beat in the cheese and stir in the
soured cream. Whisk the egg whites until stiff, then fold in gently
but evenly.

Pour the mixture into the prepared tin. Bake in the centre of a
moderate oven (180°C., 350°F., Gas Mark 4) for 1–1¼ hours. Turn
off the oven heat and leave the cheesecake in the oven for a further

15 minutes. Then allow to cool. Loosen the sides of the cheesecake and remove from the tin for serving.
Serves 6-8

Gooseberry mousse

During summer months it is a good idea to have several small cans of evaporated milk ready for whisking. Bring small cans to the boil from cold and simmer for 15 minutes. Cool and then refrigerate. They can easily be whipped up and used in a dessert recipe like this one.

450 g/1 lb green gooseberries	3 tablespoons water
100 g/4 oz castor sugar	juice of ½ lemon
few drops green colouring	1 small can chilled evaporated milk
15 g/½ oz powdered gelatine	2 egg whites

Place the washed gooseberries – no need to top and tail them – in a saucepan along with the sugar and 2 tablespoons water. Bring up to the boil, cover and simmer gently for 10 minutes, stirring occasionally, until the gooseberries are quite soft. Meanwhile, sprinkle the gelatine over the water in a teacup and set aside to soak for 5 minutes.

Draw the pan of cooked gooseberries off the heat and add the soaked gelatine. Stir until dissolved – the heat of the pan should be sufficient to do this. Pass the fruit and juice through a sieve into a large mixing basin to make a purée. Discard the skins and pips left in the sieve. Add a few drops of green colouring to the purée, this improves the appearance of the finished dessert. Add the strained lemon juice and allow to cool.

Whisk the chilled evaporated milk until very thick. Beat the egg white until stiff and fold them both into the fruit purée. Pour into a serving dish and chill until set firm before serving.
Serves 6

Chilled lemon pudding

Most lemon mousse recipes have cream folded into the mixture. This one has the cream on top as a decoration, and the contrast of fresh lemon with smooth cream is a good one.

4 large eggs
175 g/6 oz castor sugar
rind of 1 lemon
juice of 2 lemons

1.5 dl/¼ pint water
15 g/½ oz powdered gelatine
1.5 dl/¼ pint double cream

Separate the eggs, putting the yolks into one basin and the whites into a second. Add the sugar to the yolks along with the finely grated lemon rind and the lemon juice. To get the right lemon flavour, you need about 3–4 tablespoons lemon juice. Using a wooden spoon, stir the egg-yolk mixture well to blend all the ingredients thoroughly.

Measure the water into a saucepan and sprinkle in the gelatine. Allow to stand for a few minutes, then place over low heat and stir until the gelatine has dissolved. Draw off the heat. Holding the pan well above the mixing basin, add the gelatine to the lemon mixture, pouring in a thin, steady stream. Whisk all the time and when the gelatine is blended in set the mixture aside to cool until beginning to thicken and set.

Stiffly beat the egg whites and fold into the lemon mixture. Pour into a serving dish and chill until set firm. Spoon the lightly whipped cream over the mousse about 1 hour before serving. Chill until ready to serve.
Serves 6

Baked fresh apricots

The fresh apricots that come on to the market at the beginning of the season are often slightly under-ripe and rather firm. This is a very good method of cooking them.

675 g/1½ lb fresh apricots
100 g/4 oz castor sugar

juice of 1 lemon

Place the washed, whole apricots in an ovenproof dish. Add the sugar and the strained lemon juice – no water is required since the sugar and lemon juice alone form a delicious syrup for the fruit. Cover with a lid, place in the centre of a slow oven (150°C., 300°F.,

Gas Mark 2) and bake for 45 minutes–1 hour or until the fruit is tender. Serve warm or cold with cream or ice cream.
Serves 4-6

How to serve a fresh pineapple
Pineapples are small and inexpensive during summer months. To serve one with the minimum of fuss and trouble cut up the pineapple as follows:
1 Cut across the top and base to remove a slice. Reserve the leafy top for decoration.
2 Stand the pineapple on end and cut downwards into four or six wedges according to the size of the fruit.
3 Hold each pineapple wedge on end and cut downwards along the inner edge to remove the hard centre core.
4 Place the wedges flat and with a sharp knife cut between the pineapple flesh and skin exactly as one cuts melon flesh from the skin.
5 Cut across the pineapple flesh and zig-zag the segments so that they look attractive.
6 Serve the cut pineapple with a garnish of orange, a black grape or just a sprinkling of sugar.

Banana Chartreuse

Choose pale-coloured jelly for this recipe, so that the decoration shows through clearly – lemon or lime give the best results.

1 568-ml/1-pint packet lime jelly	juice of ½ lemon
3 dl/½ pint cold water	1.5 dl/¼ pint single cream
3 large ripe bananas	1.5 dl/¼ pint double cream

Measure 1.5 dl (¼ pint) of the water into a saucepan, bring up to the boil and draw off the heat. Add the jelly in pieces, stir until dissolved and then add the remaining water. Spoon a little jelly over the base of a deep 15-cm (6-in) round cake tin or 1-litre (2-pint) mould and allow to set firm. Slice one banana thinly and arrange neatly round the edge of the mould on the surface of the jelly. Spoon over a little more jelly to wet the decoration and leave to set firm. Meanwhile allow the remaining jelly to cool until beginning to set.

Mash the remaining bananas with the strained lemon juice to a purée. Whisk the single cream and double cream together until

thick, then fold in the almost set jelly and the mashed bananas. Pour into the mould over the decorative base. Leave in a cool place until set firm. Loosen round the top edges of the mould and dip for a moment into water – as hot as the hand can bear. Place a serving plate over the top and invert the mould on to it, giving a good sharp shake so that the dessert slides out. Serve with pouring cream.
Serves 6

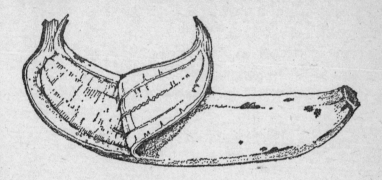

Bourbon biscuits

Many of the manufactured biscuits that we buy are not difficult to make at home. Bourbon fingers, for instance, are quite easy to prepare; no special cutters are required, just a good sharp knife.

100 g/4 oz plain flour
½ level teaspoon baking powder
2 level tablespoons cocoa powder

50 g/2 oz butter
50 g/2 oz castor sugar
1 level tablespoon syrup

for the chocolate filling:

25 g/1 oz butter
50 g/2 oz icing sugar

2 teaspoons cocoa powder
few drops vanilla essence

Sift together the flour, baking powder and cocoa powder and set aside. Cream the butter and sugar until soft and light, then beat in the syrup. Stir in half the flour mixture and mix with a wooden spoon until smooth. Turn the dough out on to a working surface and knead in the remaining flour.

Roll the dough out thinly to about 0.5 cm (¼ in) in thickness on a sheet of greaseproof paper. Scatter a little granulated sugar over the surface of the dough and lightly roll the pin over to fix the sugar grains. Cut the dough into neat fingers about 2.5 cm (1 in) wide and

7 cm (2½ in) long. Using a palette knife lift carefully on to a greased baking tray. Prick each biscuit with the prongs of a fork two or three times. Place in the centre of a slow oven (160°C., 325°F., Gas Mark 3) and bake for 15–20 minutes. Cool before adding the filling.

Cream the butter until soft, then gradually beat in the sieved icing sugar and cocoa powder. Flavour with a few drops of vanilla essence and sandwich the biscuits in pairs.

Makes 1½ dozen

Vienna shortcakes

Avoid using butter straight from the refrigerator; if the butter is not creamed and softened sufficiently, the mixture will be very difficult to pipe.

175 g/6 oz plain flour
50 g/2 oz cornflour
225 g/8 oz butter

75 g/3 oz sifted icing sugar
few drops almond essence

for the topping:
extra sifted icing sugar

raspberry jam

Sift together the flour and cornflour and set aside. Cream the butter very thoroughly until soft. Add the icing sugar and flavouring and cream in thoroughly. Gradually work in the flour and cornflour until smooth and blended.

Spoon the mixture into a large nylon or cotton piping bag, which has been fitted with a large rosette piping tube. Pipe the mixture into paper baking cases arranged in bun tins or on a baking tray. Pipe twice round the outer edge so there is a hollow in the centre.

Place the cakes in the centre of a moderate oven (180°C., 350°F., Gas Mark 4) and bake for about 20 minutes, or until cooked but still very pale in colour. Cool the cakes thoroughly before dusting each liberally with sifted icing sugar. Finish with a little raspberry jam in the centre of each cake.

Makes 12

Honey cookies

These are a cross between a little cake and a biscuit. Serve them plain with morning coffee or sandwiched with jam or buttercream for tea.

200 g/8 oz self-raising flour	1 egg
pinch salt	½ teaspoon vanilla essence
100 g/4 oz butter	50 g/2 oz (1 rounded tablespoon)
100 g/4 oz soft brown sugar	honey

Sift the flour and salt on to a plate and set aside. Cream the butter and sugar together until pale and soft. Lightly mix the egg and vanilla essence, then gradually beat into the creamed mixture a little at a time. Beat in the honey. Add half the sifted flour to the mixture and, using a wooden spoon, work to a soft paste. Add the remaining flour and mix to a soft dough. Cover and chill in the refrigerator for one hour or longer. This makes the dough firmer and easier to handle.

Spoon out rounded teaspoons of the mixture and roll into balls. Set well apart on greased baking sheets and flatten slightly – don't put more than 6–8 cookies on a sheet at one time.

Place in the centre of a moderate oven (180°C., 350°F., Gas Mark 4) and bake for 12 minutes, or until well risen and firm. Lift them from the baking tray and cool on a rack. Serve plain or sandwich with jam or buttercream.
Makes 30 cookies

Chocolate chip cookies

These cookies make a good addition to a picnic basket. The semi-sweet chocolate chips in the mixture soften during cooking but harden up again on cooling to provide crunchy pieces of chocolate throughout each one.

140 g/5 oz plain flour	80 g/3 oz castor sugar
½ level teaspoon bicarbonate of soda	1 egg
¼ level teaspoon salt	few drops vanilla essence
110 g/4 oz butter	1 113-g/4-oz packet chocolate chips
25 g/1 oz brown sugar	50 g/2 oz finely chopped walnuts

Sift together the flour, bicarbonate of soda and salt. Cream the butter and both sugars until soft. Lightly mix the egg and vanilla essence and gradually beat into the creamed mixture. Stir in the sifted flour and beat well. Finally stir in the chocolate chips and the walnuts.

Spoon heaped teaspoonfuls of the mixture on to greased baking trays. Space the cookies a little apart to allow room for spreading.

Place in the centre of a moderately hot oven (190°C., 375°F., Gas Mark 5) and bake for 12 minutes or until golden.

Loosen each cookie with a palette knife and lift on to a cooling tray. They will become crisp as they cook. Store in an airtight tin.
Makes 30 cookies

Rich flan crust

A rich shortcrust pastry keeps its shape well when baked. If made with butter and stored in a lidded tin when quite cold it will keep well for several days. In summer you can bake several flan cases and keep them ready to fill and serve with summer fruits.

100 g/4 oz plain flour	25 g/1 oz sifted icing sugar
pinch salt	1 egg yolk
50 g/2 oz butter	1 tablespoon water

Sift the flour and salt into a mixing basin. Add the butter cut in pieces and rub into the mixture. Add the sifted icing sugar and mix through the ingredients. Blend the egg yolk and water and using a fork stir into the contents of the mixing basin. Mix to a rough dough, then turn out on to a lightly floured surface and knead for a moment until smooth.

Place the dough in a polythene bag and leave to rest in a cool place for 30 minutes before using. If chilled in the refrigerator, allow to come back to room temperature before rolling out.

To make a pastry flan, roll the pastry out on a lightly floured surface to a circle slightly larger all round than a 20-cm (8-in) flan case – preferably one with a loose base, or a flan ring set on a baking tray. Line the case with the pastry, pressing in from the centre out to the edges to exclude any air bubbles. Prick the base with a fork and fill the centre with a piece of crumpled kitchen foil to weight down the middle.

Place above the centre in a moderately hot oven (190°C., 375°F., Gas Mark 5) and bake for 12 minutes. Remove the foil and return the pastry case to the oven for a further 5–8 minutes to dry out the centre. Fill with fruit and glaze in the same way as for sponge flan cases.
Makes 100 g (4 oz) pastry

Using the freezer in May

Think ahead for dinner parties or eating out-of-doors. The *cream of watercress soup* and *cucumber soup with mint* (see pages 118 and 120) are lovely fresh soups that freeze well. Thaw in the refrigerator and serve cold. Keep a small (85-g, 3-oz) pack of frozen smoked salmon for the *smoked salmon tart* (see page 122). It's a good item for a picnic – especially if it's a special occasion like an evening at Glyndebourne. You'll find the *vanilla cheesecake* (see page 133) freezes well too, marvellous and moist for packed lunches.

Pineapples are a good buy and cheap at the moment. For freezing it's best to cut the pineapple in rounds. Stand on end and cut down the sides to remove the outer skin. Then cut across into slices and using a small knife or pastry cutter remove the centre circle of hard core. Layer with sugar into rigid containers; this is good with a drop of kirsch added afterwards or for using in fresh fruit salads.

Freezing summer vegetables
Spread the work by freezing small quantities of vegetables often rather than trying to tackle bulk supplies. Pick vegetables when they are young and tender and freeze them as soon as possible for best flavour.

Vegetables are blanched before freezing to retard the action of enzymes which can spoil colour and flavour during storage. Use about 2.5 litres (2 quarts) water for every 0.5 kg (1 lb) vegetables. The same water may be used each time as long as it's for the same type of vegetable. Blanch vegetables in small quantities at a time so that the water reboils within a minute – this avoids over-cooking. Bring the water to the boil. Add the vegetables in a wire blanching basket so that they can be quickly removed when blanching time is complete. Drain and plunge into iced water to cool for the same length of time as the vegetables were blanched.

Pack vegetables in polythene bags or waxed cartons and exclude air. Seal and freeze. Some vegetables like peas and beans can be frozen using the 'free-flowing' method. Spread out on a tray – a Swiss roll tin is ideal – and freeze uncovered until firm. Then pack, seal and freeze.

Broad beans Select small, very tender beans. Pod and blanch for 2 minutes. Pack in polythene bags.

French beans Top and tail the beans leaving small ones whole and cut larger ones in half. Blanch for 2–3 minutes. Pack in polythene bags.

Broccoli and calabrese Trim any leaves and stalks and cut into heads of even size. Soak in salt water. Blanch for 3–4 minutes. Pack in rigid cartons or polythene bags.

Carrots Freeze only very small new carrots. Trim tops and bases. Blanch whole for 4 minutes, then rub off the skins. Pack in polythene bags.

Peas Select tender young peas and pod. Blanch for 1 minute. Freeze 'free-flowing' and then tip into polythene bags for storage.

Courgettes Wash and cut into 2.5-cm (1-in) slices. Blanch for 1 minute. Freeze in polythene bags. Courgettes are often better frozen as a recipe – see *courgette soup* (July, page 172).

Spinach Pick tender young leaves and remove the stalks. Wash thoroughly and blanch for 2 minutes. Press out moisture and pack in polythene bags.

June

June is a month when home-grown vegetables are prolific, varied and of excellent quality. This is a month for salads with plenty of tomatoes, cucumbers, spring onions, watercress and many varieties of lettuce. Serve them with cold meats and barbecue suppers, for June is the first month when meals can take place out-of-doors.

Besides plenty of herring and mackerel, there should be fine trout and salmon trout readily available, all excellent to use for light summer recipes. Garden herbs are flourishing and they should be used liberally over fish, meat and salad dishes for their flavour and colour.

This month heralds the start of the strawberry season and brings a good supply of English cherries on the market. With the gooseberries and apricots already there we have no shortage of lovely fruits for summer desserts.

Avocado fromage

This attractive pale green mixture will surprise your guests if you serve it rather as you would a pâté – that is, with hot toast. Avocado fromage has a soft, spreadable consistency and a delicious flavour.

2 ripe avocados	1 teaspoon onion juice
225 g/8 oz fresh cream cheese	1 level teaspoon salt
juice of ½ lemon	dash of Worcestershire sauce

Halve the avocados, remove the stones and scoop out the flesh with a spoon. Mash the flesh well and then beat in the cream cheese, lemon juice, onion juice, salt and Worcestershire sauce. Blend the ingredients very thoroughly to form a smooth mixture – it's best to purée the ingredients in a blender.

Spoon into individual china soufflé dishes and cover close to the surface with a piece of clear cling wrap to prevent discolouration. Chill for several hours before serving.
Serves 6

Curry mayonnaise

A curry-flavoured mayonnaise is a lovely sauce to serve over cold sliced chicken for a main course, or over hard-boiled eggs to start a menu. Make it up the day before if necessary.

1 tablespoon oil
1 small onion, finely chopped
1 level tablespoon curry powder
1.5 dl/¼ pint stock
1 teaspoon concentrated tomato
  purée

juice of ½ lemon
2 tablespoons apricot jam or sweet
  mango chutney
3 dl/½ pint mayonnaise
3 tablespoons single cream

Heat the oil in a saucepan. Add the onion, cover and fry very gently for about 5 minutes or until the onion is soft but not brown. Stir in the curry powder and cook for a further few moments to bring out the flavour. Stir in the stock, tomato purée, strained lemon juice and the jam or chutney. Stir until boiling and then simmer for 5 minutes. Strain the sauce into a basin and leave until quite cold.

Blend together the curry mixture and the mayonnaise. Stir in the cream just before using.

Makes 4.5 dl (¾ pint)

Tomato and cucumber soup

Chilled tomato soup with a garnish of chopped cucumber is cool and fresh on a hot summer day. Make this recipe when there are plenty of inexpensive tomatoes to be had.

50 g/2 oz butter
1 medium-sized carrot
1 small onion
675 g/1½ lb fresh tomatoes
a scant litre/1½ pints chicken stock

salt and freshly milled pepper
1 level tablespoon castor sugar
1 level tablespoon flour
½ cucumber
single cream

Melt half the butter in a large saucepan. Add the peeled and diced carrot and finely chopped onion. Cover and cook gently for 5 minutes until the onion is soft. Halve the tomatoes and add to the pan, re-cover and fry gently for 15 minutes to soften the tomatoes and extract the juice.

Stir in the stock, a good seasoning of salt and freshly milled pepper and the sugar. Bring to the boil, then simmer gently for 1 hour. Draw the pan off the heat and rub the soup through a sieve, pressing through as much of the soft vegetables as possible. Return the strained soup to the pan. Cream the flour with the remaining butter to make a *beurre manié* then add this a little at a time to the hot soup. Stir over low heat until the soup has thickened and is boiling. Draw off the heat.

Meanwhile peel the cucumber and slice in half lengthways. Discard the seeds and chop the cucumber flesh in small dice. Add to a pan of boiling salted water, reboil and simmer for 2 minutes to soften the cucumber and give it a pleasant green colour. Drain and add to the tomato soup. Check seasonings, cool and then chill for several hours.

Just before serving pour in a little single cream but do not stir in. **Serves 6**

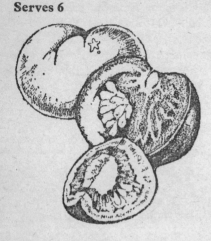

Summer soup

Lettuce, spinach and mint all flourish in the garden now. Together, they make a delicious blend of flavours. Serve this soup well chilled.

25 g/1 oz butter
1 medium-sized onion
225 g/8 oz (1 large) potato
a scant litre/1½ pints chicken stock

225 g/8 oz mixed lettuce and spinach
handful fresh mint
salt and freshly milled pepper

Melt the butter in a saucepan. Peel and chop the onion and add to the butter. Fry gently for about 5 minutes or until the onion is soft and tender but not brown. Peel and dice the potato and add to the pan. Toss in the onion-flavoured butter and then stir in the stock. Bring up to the boil, then lower the heat and allow to simmer for about 15 minutes or until the potato is tender.

Meanwhile wash the lettuce, spinach and mint well in two or three lots of cold water. Strip away the lettuce stalks and pull away the stem and mid-rib from the spinach leaves. Strip the mint leaves from the stems. Add all the greens at once, bring back to the boil

and simmer for 10 minutes. Draw the pan off the heat and pass the soup through a vegetable mill. If preferred blend the soup to a purée in a blender, in which case sieve the soup afterwards to remove the small stalky pieces that will inevitably come from the mint. Check seasoning with salt and pepper and allow to cool. Chill for several hours before serving.
Serves 6

Asparagus with white butter sauce

Hot asparagus is usually served with melted butter; a white butter sauce is similar but a little more complicated to prepare. It's a soft butter sauce which has the texture of cream, subtly flavoured with shallot and sharpened with vinegar. Not a sauce to make for a crowd, but definitely as a treat for two.

1 bundle fresh asparagus

for the sauce:
1 shallot
2 tablespoons white wine vinegar

salt and freshly milled pepper
100 g/4 oz butter (see method)

Scrape the asparagus stalks, rinse and trim level. Retie in a bundle for boiling with a 2.5-cm (1-in) gauze bandage. The asparagus can't slip out and the gauze won't cut into the stems. Place in a saucepan of boiling salted water and simmer for 10 minutes with the bundle standing upright, then for a further 10 minutes downwards in the pan on its side.

Meanwhile peel and finely chop the shallot. Place in a saucepan with the vinegar. Heat gently until the shallot is tender and the vinegar has almost evaporated – take care not to allow any scorching. Draw off the heat. Add the butter (which has been well chilled and cut into 15-g ($\frac{1}{2}$-oz) pieces) one or two pieces at a time, whisking well. As the butter softens in the hot pan it takes on the texture of thin cream. Serve at once with the hot, well-drained asparagus.
Serves 2

Mackerel with gooseberry sauce

Mackerel should be cooked with sharp or spicy ingredients that give them plenty of flavour. At this time of year they can be served with their traditional gooseberry sauce.

| 2 large or 4 small mackerel | 50 g/2 oz butter |
| seasoned flour | juice of ½ lemon |

for the gooseberry sauce:

| 450 g/1 lb green gooseberries | 15 g/½ oz butter |
| 2 tablespoons water | 25 g/1 oz castor sugar |

Have the mackerel cleaned and cut into fillets. You can do it yourself by cutting the length of the fish along one side of the backbone. Insert the knife blade between the flesh and bone and gently lift the flesh away. Repeat on the second side of the fish to get two fillets from each.

Dip each fillet in seasoned flour and shake off the surplus. Melt the butter in a frying pan, put in the mackerel fillets, flesh side down, and cook gently for 5 minutes. Turn and cook the second side. Lift the fish fillets from the pan and keep warm. Continue to heat the butter in the pan until it becomes a rich golden brown, then draw off the heat and add the lemon juice. Shake over the heat for a moment and pour over the fish. Serve with the hot gooseberry sauce, made as follows.

Top and tail the gooseberries and place in a small saucepan with the water and butter. Cover and cook very gently until the gooseberries are quite soft. Rub the fruit through a sieve and return the purée to the saucepan. Add the sugar and cook gently until the sauce is smooth and about the consistency of apple sauce.

Serves 4

Quiche aux fines herbes

If you are lucky enough to have a root of French tarragon and some chervil in the garden, you can make up a fines herbes *mixture of both with parsley – a marvellous flavouring for egg dishes.*

100 g/4 oz shortcrust pastry

for the filling:

15 g/½ oz butter	salt and freshly milled pepper
1 shallot or small onion	2–3 tablespoons chopped *fines*
3 eggs	*herbes* (see method)
1.5 dl/¼ pint single cream	

Roll out the pastry and use to line a 20-cm (8-in) quiche tin or tart tin with a loose base. Prick the base with a fork and fill the centre with crumpled kitchen foil. Bake blind in a hot oven (220°C., 425°F., Gas Mark 7) for 12–15 minutes. Remove the foil towards the end of the cooking time. Set the partly baked case on a baking tray.

Melt the butter and add the finely chopped shallot or onion. Fry gently for a few minutes to soften but not brown. Sprinkle over the base of the pastry case. Crack the eggs into a basin, add the cream and a seasoning of salt and pepper. Whisk well to mix and add the herbs. The filling should be fairly green with herbs, and of the quantity used about half should be chopped parsley and the rest chopped tarragon and chervil.

Pour the filling into the pastry case and replace in the oven at a lower temperature (180°C., 350°F., Gas Mark 4) and bake for 20–25 minutes or until the filling has set. Serve warm.
Serves 4

Salmon trout in foil

Salmon trout, being a smaller fish than salmon, is ideal for cooking whole. Wrapping the fish in foil keeps the fish moist and preserves all the juices.

1 salmon trout,	½ lemon, cut in slices
about 1–1.25 kg/2–3 lb	few parsley stalks
butter or oil (see method)	

Have the fish cleaned but left whole. Place in the centre of a large square of foil – buttered for serving hot and oiled for serving cold. Arrange the lemon slices and parsley stalks over the fish. Fold the foil over the top and turn up the ends to wrap the fish completely in a loose foil parcel. Place in a large roasting tin or on a baking tray. Set in the centre of a moderate oven (180°C., 350°F., Gas Mark 4) and bake allowing 15 minutes per 0.5 kg (1 lb).

To serve hot, let the baked trout stand in the wrapped package for 5 minutes to allow the flesh to settle. To serve cold, leave the fish wrapped in the packet until quite cold.

Open the foil, discard the lemon and parsley and lift the skin away from the fish. Separate the flesh down the centre following the line

of the bone. Serve the flesh in pieces, lifting the centre bone away to
get at the flesh underneath.
Serves 4-6

Note A 1-kg (about 2- to 2½-lb) fish will serve 4; a 1.25-kg (2½- to
3-lb) fish will serve 6 and a 1.5 to 1.75-kg (3½- to 4-lb) fish will
serve 8.

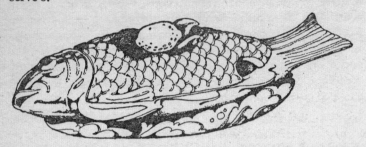

Stroganoff sauce

*Few of us can afford the steak for beef stroganoff any more but you can
serve the stroganoff sauce and it's delicious over hamburgers or chicken.
Use button or closed mushrooms in the sauce so it retains a light colour.*

1 small onion
25 g/1 oz butter
50 g/2 oz button mushrooms
½ teaspoon concentrated tomato
 purée

1 carton soured cream
salt and freshly milled pepper

Peel and finely chop the onion. Melt the butter in a frying pan, add
the onion and fry gently for a few minutes to soften. Trim and slice
the mushrooms, add to the pan and cook gently for about 5 minutes.

Stir in the tomato purée and soured cream and bring just up to the
boil. Season to taste with salt and pepper and serve at once.
Serves 2-3

Sweet pepper and salami salad

*Sweet green peppers can be served raw in a salad. Blistering them under
a hot grill or over a flame so that you can peel off the skins has the same
effect as blanching – it removes the bitter flavour. This is a good method
for salads, since it preserves the bright green colour of the pepper flesh.*

2 green sweet peppers
100 g/4 oz salami
50 g/2 oz hard cheese
4 tomatoes

crisp lettuce leaves
4–6 tablespoons oil and vinegar
 dressing

Place the peppers under a hot grill and cook them until the skins crinkle and split. Turn occasionally so they grill on all sides – about 5 minutes. Alternatively spear the peppers with a fork and hold over a gas flame until the skins char and split. While hot, peel or scrape away the skins under cold water. Halve the peppers and remove the seeds from inside, then shred the pepper flesh.

Remove any rind from around the slices of salami and coarsely grate the cheese.

Arrange a bed of crisp lettuce in a serving bowl, top with the shredded peppers, the slices of salami and then the grated cheese. Decorate with the tomatoes cut in slices and spoon over the dressing. Serve with crusty rolls and butter.

Serves 4

Beef kebabs with barbecue sauce

On beautiful skewers, kebabs look sufficiently dramatic to serve at a dinner party. They may need last-minute cooking, but at least there's a minimum of kitchen preparation time.

675 g/1½ lb rump steak
4 medium-sized onions

12 small mushrooms
oil for brushing

for the barbecue sauce:

2 tablespoons oil
1 onion, finely chopped
1.5 dl/¼ pint tomato ketchup
1.5 dl/¼ pint water
3 tablespoons wine vinegar
2 rounded tablespoons soft brown sugar

2 teaspoons made mustard
2 tablespoons Worcestershire sauce
½ level teaspoon salt
1 level tablespoon cornflour blended with 2 tablespoons water

Trim the steak and cut into neat pieces for skewering – try to allow about four pieces of meat per person. Peel the onions and cut in half, then separate out into pieces. Skewer pieces of meat, pushing them close together with onion at either end if they are to be cooked 'rare' or separate the pieces of meat and skewer alternating with pieces of onion and mushrooms for meat that's to be well done. Brush with oil and set aside while preparing the sauce.

Heat the oil in a saucepan and add the onion. Fry gently for a few minutes to soften the onion, then stir in the tomato ketchup, water, vinegar, sugar, mustard, Worcestershire sauce and salt. Bring up to the boil and simmer for 5 minutes. Blend a little of the hot sauce with the cornflour blend, mix well and return to the saucepan. Stir until boiling and slightly thickened.

Meanwhile, preheat the grill until hot. Set the kebabs under the grill at least 7 cm (3 in) below the heat. Grill under high heat for the first few moments, then lower the heat and cook gently for 15–20 minutes. Turn the skewers to cook evenly.

Serve the kebabs on a mound of rice with the sauce separately.
Serves 6

Chicken in a basket

Use chicken legs only for chicken in a basket. They can be taken from a carcass where the breast portions have been used for another recipe, or they can be specially purchased chicken-leg portions. Deep-fried so they are deliciously crisp, the pieces are best served hot, but are also good cold for a picnic. Serve them in the traditional manner arranged in a basket lined with a gay napkin so that they can be picked up and eaten with the fingers. Provide extra paper napkins.

4 chicken joints, leg portions
seasoned flour
beaten egg

fresh white breadcrumbs
fat for deep-frying

Remove the skin from the chicken portions. Cut each portion through at the joint to make two pieces, so that in all you have eight small pieces of chicken – smaller pieces of chicken deep-fry more evenly and quickly.

Dust the pieces with seasoned flour, then dip in lightly beaten egg and finally roll in fresh white breadcrumbs. Chill the pieces for 1 hour so that the coating sets.

Place in a frying basket and fry in hot deep fat for 8–10 minutes, by which time they should be crisp, brown and cooked through. Serve hot.
Serves 4

Roast duckling with glazed turnips

In France small tender new turnips are a traditional choice to serve with duckling.

1 oven-ready duckling, about
   2–2.5 kg/4½–5 lb
450 g/1 lb small turnips

25 g/1 oz butter
1 tablespoon castor sugar

for the brown sauce:

25 g/1 oz butter
1 onion, finely chopped
1 carrot, finely chopped
2 rashers streaky bacon
25 g/1 oz flour

4 dl/¾ pint giblet stock (see
   method)
1 teaspoon concentrated tomato
   purée
salt and freshly milled pepper

Remove the giblets from the duckling. Cover the giblets generously with cold water, add salt and a peeled onion for flavour if liked and bring up to the boil. Simmer gently for 30–40 minutes to make the stock, then strain and reserve 4 dl (¾ pint) for the sauce. Rub the skin of the duckling over with salt, prick the surface and place in a roasting tin. Add 2 tablespoons water – no fat – and place in the centre of a moderate oven (180°C., 350°F., Gas Mark 4). Roast, allowing 20 minutes per 0.5 kg (1 lb).

Melt the butter for the sauce in a pan and add the prepared onion and carrot and the bacon cut in small pieces. Fry gently until the onion is soft and beginning to brown. Stir in the flour and continue to cook, stirring occasionally, until the mixture is a nutty brown colour, about 15 minutes. Gradually stir in the strained stock and bring to the boil. Add the tomato purée and allow to simmer very gently for 20 minutes.

Meanwhile peel the turnips and cut into quarters; cut larger ones again into eighths, and then using a sharp knife trim each piece into a neat 'barrel' shape. Place in a saucepan, cover with cold water, add a little salt and bring up to the boil. Simmer gently for 10–15 minutes until just tender and drain. Add the butter to the hot pan, return the turnips and sprinkle with the sugar. Replace over the heat and sauté gently until the turnips are brown and glazed.

Lift the cooked duckling from the roasting tin and using a sharp knife cut into four portions. Place in a hot serving dish and add the glazed turnips. Check the seasoning in the sauce, then strain over the duckling and serve.
Serves 4

Veal in white wine with herbs

Veal is always more popular in summer. It's a meat that lends itself to quick, simple methods of cooking and fresh summer flavours. Serve this recipe with some of the lovely summer vegetables in season now.

4 veal escalopes	1.5 dl/¼ pint dry white wine
seasoned flour	1 teaspoon each finely chopped
75 g/3 oz butter	fresh chives, tarragon and mint

Ask the butcher to beat the escalopes out flat. Dip both sides in seasoned flour then add to 50 g (2 oz) of the butter melted in a frying pan. Fry till brown then turn to cook the second side – takes about 8 minutes altogether. Lift from the pan.

Add the wine to the pan and boil quickly to reduce by half. Add the chopped herbs and stir in the remaining butter. Pour over the veal and serve.
Serves 4

Chicken with tarragon

One of the nicest things about this recipe is the delicious aroma of
tarragon that fills the kitchen while the chicken pieces are cooking.

4 chicken joints
salt and freshly milled pepper
small bunch fresh tarragon

50 g/2 oz butter
1.5 dl/¼ pint double cream

Wipe and trim the chicken joints. Season well with salt and pepper.
Wash the tarragon, strip the leaves from the stems and chop finely.
Then, using a knife, cream the butter with the tarragon on the
chopping board.

Place the chicken joints in a baking or roasting tin, skin side upwards.
Spread the tarragon butter on each one. Place in the centre of a
moderate oven (180°C., 350°F., Gas Mark 4) and cook for 1 hour.
Baste the joints several times with the butter as it melts in the
roasting tin. About 5 minutes before cooking time is completed,
pour the cream over the chicken joints and return to the oven.

To serve, lift the chicken pieces out on to a hot serving plate. Stir
the cream and butter in the roasting tin to blend the juices together.
Check the seasoning, adding a little salt if necessary. Spoon over the
chicken joints and serve.
Serves 4

Green beans with onions

By 'green' beans in this recipe I mean either French or runner beans.
The simple addition of an onion and butter glaze makes either quite out
of the ordinary, and this is a lovely way to serve the French beans in
season now and the runner beans that follow. Use it to give extra interest
to frozen beans in winter. It takes only a minute to fry the onion and the
difference in flavour is well worth it.

450–680 g/1–1½ lb fresh green
  beans

25 g/1 oz butter
1 small onion

Top and tail French beans and string and slice runner beans. Cook
in boiling salted water for 10–15 minutes or until tender, then drain
well.

Put the butter in the hot rinsed-out pan and add the finely chopped
onion. Fry for a few minutes until the onion is softened and

beginning to brown. Return the beans to the pan and toss to blend with the butter and onion. When hot and glazed serve at once.

Serves 4

Lettuce and avocado salad

At the last minute, toss sliced avocado into a favourite green salad and you've got something very special to serve. A sprinkling of tiny cubes of crisp fried bacon may sound unusual too, but serve a salad this way and wait for the compliments.

1 cabbage lettuce
½ cucumber
1 bunch watercress
1 ripe avocado

3–4 tablespoons prepared oil and vinegar dressing
1–2 lean bacon rashers, trimmed and finely chopped

Remove any coarse outer lettuce leaves, separate and wash the remainder. Remove any coarse stems and pat the leaves dry. Place in a salad bowl and add the peeled and sliced cucumber and the washed sprigs of watercress.

Peel the avocado, halve it and remove the centre stone. Slice the flesh and toss immediately in a few tablespoons of the oil and vinegar dressing. When ready to serve, add to the salad and toss with the remaining dressing. Fry the chopped bacon in a dry pan until the fat runs and the pieces are crisp. Sprinkle over the salad and serve at once.

Serves 4-6

156

Herbs

Fresh herbs are with us for only a short season each year so make the most of them. Cultivate a few in your garden or on the kitchen window-sill.

Thyme This is a low-growing, sun-loving little herb. Use it to flavour almost any food; a little finely chopped will enliven vegetable soups or chicken casserole.

Fennel This tall and willowy herb, slightly reminiscent of aniseed, gives fish a marvellous flavour. Snip over cucumber salad or use sprigs to garnish cold fish dishes.

Basil This is a native of Mediterranean countries and dislikes our cold winters and frosts. It needs to be sown from seed every year. Sprinkle chopped leaves over tomato salads, or use in tomato recipes.

Sage This herb on the other hand is a sturdy perennial, and is a strongly flavoured herb to be used with discretion. It goes well with rich fatty foods and can be included in the stuffings for pork, goose or duck. Try a little in cheese dishes.

Chives Use scissors to cut bunches of spiky green chives and snip them over egg and salad dishes. Chives impart a delicate onion flavour to dishes; sprinkle over buttered new potatoes or tomato salad or mix with soured cream as a delicious topping for baked potatoes.

Marjoram This is a member of the mint family and has a warm spicy flavour. It is a good herb to use in made-up meat dishes like croquettes and shepherd's pie.

Mint Perhaps the easiest of all herbs to grow is mint. Use it to add a fresh flavour to summer foods. Strip the leaves from the stems and add a pinch of granulated sugar when chopping, to get a really fine mixture. Mint sprigs look pretty in drinks.

Parsley Useful as a garnish. Sow from seed each year and you have your own; parsley must be fresh. Remember parsley stalks have flavour too and add them to poaching liquor, soups and casseroles for extra taste.

Rosemary Of all the herbs rosemary is the most pungent, so use it with caution. A beautiful evergreen herb that will grow into a fine bush, it is unrivalled for use with lamb, pork and ham. A sprig in the water for simmering gammon or cauliflower makes a great improvement in the flavour of the dish.

Tarragon Choose the French variety of tarragon with its delicately flavoured soft green leaves. Tarragon is popular for its delicate aniseed flavour. It is wonderful with chicken dishes and is an essential ingredient of Béarnaise sauce. Put 1–2 sprigs of French tarragon in a bottle of wine vinegar and flavour it perfectly for salad dressings.

Bay leaves These can be used fresh or dried. Most stocks, soups and casseroles are improved by the addition of a bouquet garni, made using bay, thyme and parsley stalks.

New potato salad

This potato salad has lots of flavour. The cream and mayonnaise dressing, which has a taste of curry, makes it quite unusual and very suitable for a party menu.

900 g/2 lb new potatoes
1 tablespoon wine vinegar
1 small clove garlic, crushed
salt and freshly ground black pepper
1 green pepper, halved and deseeded

50 g/2 oz bacon rashers, trimmed and chopped
1.5 dl/¼ pint double cream
2 good tablespoons mayonnaise
1 teaspoon lemon juice
1 level teaspoon curry powder

Scrub the potatoes and plain-boil until just barely tender, about 15 minutes, then drain and when cool enough to handle, peel away the skins and slice.

Rub around the inside of a medium-sized basin with the crushed garlic then add the warm potatoes, sprinkle over the vinegar and add plenty of salt and freshly ground black pepper and set aside until cold.

Finely chop the green pepper and add to the potatoes, along with the bacon rashers, crisply fried and crumbled. Blend together the cream, mayonnaise, lemon juice and curry powder and pour over the potato mixture, mixing carefully with a spoon to avoid breaking up the potatoes.
Serves 6

Salad of French beans

French beans are so lovely served cold in a salad that it is surprising they are not served this way more often. Make the dressing with tarragon vinegar for the best flavour.

450 g/1 lb French beans
6 tablespoons prepared French dressing

Trim the beans, add to a pan of boiling salted water and simmer rapidly until tender, about 10–15 minutes. Drain and place in a basin. Spoon over the French dressing while the beans are still hot and leave to cool before serving.

Serves 4

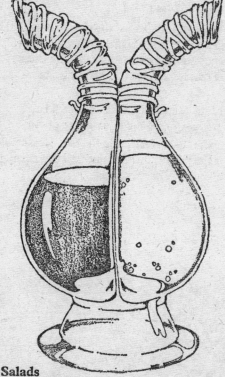

Salads

Keep salad greens fresh during hot weather. If not to be used immediately don't wash them, but simply trim away unusable outer leaves and wrap up closely in polythene or kitchen paper. Store in a covered box and place low down in the refrigerator. Otherwise pack the wrapped salad into a covered container – a saucepan with a lid is ideal. Stand in the coolest part of the larder: a stone floor is ideal. The important thing is to exclude the air. Lettuce, spring onions, parsley and even watercress will keep crisp and fresh for several days if stored in this way.

Quick fried asparagus

This unusual method of cooking asparagus is one of the quickest ways of serving fresh asparagus as a vegetable. Buy less expensive, thinner green sticks.

450–675 g/1–1½ lb fresh asparagus 2 tablespoons water
3 tablespoons olive oil salt

Wash the asparagus then snap off and discard the woody base of the stalks. Line up several stalks on a cutting board and using a sharp knife cut across the asparagus on the extreme bias making slices about 0.5 cm (¼ in) thick. This should give thin slanting slices about 2.5 cm (1 in) long.

Measure the oil and water into a saucepan, cover with a lid and bring up to the boil. Add the asparagus and a seasoning of salt.

Re-cover and cook over moderate heat, shaking the pan occasionally, for about 5 minutes. Draw the pan off the heat and test the asparagus – the pieces should be tender-crisp. Serve at once.

Serves 4

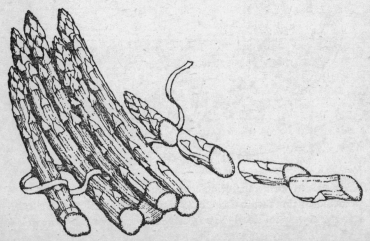

Raspberry and strawberry mousse

A frothy, pink summer mousse, this has a lovely flavour and is very easy to make. Serve it along with some fresh berries.

225 g/8 oz mixed raspberries and
    strawberries
1 packet strawberry jelly

3 eggs
25 g/1 oz castor sugar

Hull the berries then press the fruit through a sieve to make a purée. Measure the purée and make up to 4 dl (¾ pint) with water. Pour the mixture into a saucepan and bring up to the boil. Draw off the heat, add the strawberry jelly and stir until melted.

Separate the eggs, placing the yolks together with the sugar in one basin and the whites in a second basin. Whisk the yolks and sugar until thick and light and gradually whisk in the warm jelly mixture. Set aside until the mixture is cold and beginning to thicken.

Whisk the egg whites until stiff and fold into the fruit mixture. Pour into a serving dish and chill until ready to serve.
Serves 4

Gooseberry cream snow

All fruit fools, of which this is one, can also be used to make very good fruit-flavoured ice creams. For an alternative dessert, freeze the mixture, giving it a stir once or twice.

450 g/1 lb green gooseberries
2 tablespoons water
100 g/4 oz castor sugar

1 egg white
3 dl/½ pint double cream

Wash the gooseberries; there is no need to top and tail them. Place in a saucepan with the water. Bring up to the boil, cover and simmer very gently for 10 minutes until tender and quite soft. Draw off the heat, add the sugar and stir to dissolve it in the heat of the pan. Then rub the fruit and juices through a sieve to make a purée. Discard the skin and pips that remain in the sieve and allow the purée to cool.

Add the unbeaten egg white to the cream and whisk both together until thick and light. Fold in the gooseberry purée. Spoon into a serving dish or individual glasses and chill for several hours until firm before serving. This looks pretty sprinkled with a few chopped pistachio nuts for decoration.

Serves 6

Strawberries with Devonshire sauce

The addition of soft cream cheese to fresh cream gives a flavour not unlike Devonshire clotted cream. The blend goes particularly well with strawberries, but take care to use fresh cream cheese or a foil-wrapped packet of full fat soft cheese, both of which are very mild in flavour.

450 g/1 lb fresh strawberries

for the Devonshire sauce:

1 85-g/3-oz packet cream cheese
1.5 dl/¼ pint single cream
1 level tablespoon castor sugar

¼ teaspoon finely grated lemon rind
1 teaspoon lemon juice

Wash and hull the strawberries, place in a serving dish and put to chill. Beat the cream cheese until soft and smooth and gradually beat in the cream. Stir in the sugar, lemon rind and lemon juice and blend well. Chill well. Pour over the strawberries and serve.

Serves 4

Tutti frutti liqueur

Tutti frutti liqueur, an exotic-sounding home-made liqueur, is one that can be added to throughout the summer as the fruits come into season. Select a large screw-topped preserving jar and start the recipe with 450 g (1 lb) ripe strawberries and 450 g (1 lb) granulated sugar. No preparation of the fruit is required other than removing any hulls or stalks. To the strawberries and sugar in the jar add 1 bottle brandy. Cover tightly.

When raspberries come into season add 450 g (1 lb) fresh raspberries and 450 g (1 lb) granulated sugar. Cover tightly. In turn add 450 g (1 lb) loganberries and 450 g (1 lb) sugar and finally 450 g (1 lb) acid cherries. Leave the stalks on about half the cherries and leave them unstoned for flavour. Tie down tightly.

Leave the jar in a cool place for several months. Decant the liqueur into clean dry bottles. Use the fruit in trifles or desserts.

Orange and strawberry dessert

The specially prepared syrup draws out the natural juices from both fruits, resulting in a delicious combination of flavours. This is a recipe to make a few strawberries go a long way at the start of the season.

3 oranges	1.5 dl/¼ pint water
450 g/1 lb strawberries	juice of 1 lemon
225 g/8 oz castor sugar	1–2 tablespoons Grand Marnier

Mark the peel of the oranges into quarters with a sharp knife. Put the oranges together in a large basin and cover with boiling water. Allow to stand for 5 minutes, then drain and peel away the skins. Using this method both the outer skin and white pith should come away together. Scrape away any white pith remaining on the oranges with a knife.

Cut the oranges across into thin slices and place in the base of a glass serving dish. Hull and wash the strawberries and cut any large ones in half. Arrange the strawberries on top of the oranges and set aside while preparing the syrup.

Measure the sugar and water into a small saucepan. Place over a low heat and stir until the sugar has dissolved. Bring to the boil, simmer for 1 minute and then draw off the heat. Add the strained lemon juice and the liqueur. Allow the syrup to stand for 10 minutes, then pour the warm syrup over the fruit. Cool, then chill for several hours.
Serves 6

Fresh mint ice cream

You need a blender for this recipe. Mint has a most refreshing flavour and makes a delicious ice cream. The mixture tends to be rather pale, but one drop of green food colouring added to the mixture brings up the colour nicely.

100 g/4 oz castor sugar
1.5 dl/¼ pint water
1 teacup mint leaves, stripped
  from the stem

juice of ½ lemon
3 dl/½ pint double cream

Place the sugar and water in a saucepan. Stir over low heat until the sugar has dissolved, then bring up to the boil. Wash the mint leaves and squeeze dry. Place in a blender. Pour in the hot syrup, cover and blend for a few minutes until the mint is very finely chopped. Leave the mixture until quite cold, then strain into a mixing basin.

Add the strained juice of the lemon half and stir in the double cream. Whisk lightly to blend the ingredients and add a little green food colouring if liked. Pour into a large refrigerator ice tray or a polythene freezer box. Cover and place in the freezer. As the mixture becomes icy round the sides, turn the edges into the centre with a fork. When the mixture is half frozen turn out into a chilled basin and give it a really good mix. Return to the container and refreeze. Leave for several hours until quite firm.

Before serving, remove the container to the refrigerator compartment for about 30 minutes before serving, to allow the ice cream to soften slightly.
Serves 6

Ice cream toppings

You can make some lovely sauces to serve with vanilla ice cream and they take only a few moments to prepare.

Raspberry sauce
Pick over 225 g (8 oz) fresh raspberries and then mash them down in a saucepan. Add 2 tablespoons redcurrant jelly and stir over low heat until the jelly has melted and the raspberries are quite soft. Blend 2 level teaspoons cornflour with 1 tablespoon cold water and stir into the contents of the pan. Stir until boiling, when the mixture will thicken and become clear. Strain into a basin, add a squeeze of lemon juice to sharpen the flavour and serve warm or cold.
Serves 4-6

Chocolate sauce
Measure 100 g (4 oz) castor sugar and 1.5 dl (¼ pint) water into a saucepan and stir over low heat to dissolve the sugar. Bring up to the

boil and simmer for 1 minute. Then tip in 50 g (2 oz) cocoa powder. Whisk until the sauce is smooth and bring back to the boil. Draw off the heat and pour into a basin. Stir occasionally; the sauce will thicken up as it cools. Serve warm or cold.
Serves 6

Butterscotch sauce
Measure 100 g (4 oz) granulated sugar into a dry pan and stir over moderate heat until the sugar has melted and turned to a golden brown. Draw off the heat and add a scant 2.5 dl ($\frac{1}{2}$ pint) water – take care for the mixture will boil up on the addition of a cold liquid. Replace the pan over the heat and add a pinch of salt, 2 teaspoons golden syrup and $\frac{1}{2}$ teaspoon vanilla essence. Stir until the caramel and syrup have dissolved. Add 1 level tablespoon cornflour blended with 2 tablespoons cold water and stir until the sauce is boiling and slightly thickened. Add 15 g ($\frac{1}{2}$ oz) butter and 2 tablespoons seedless raisins. Leave to cool, stirring occasionally. Serve warm or cold.
Serves 6

Mint sauce to keep

If you have lots of mint growing in the garden it's a shame not to put some of it away for use in winter. Chop fresh mint with a stainless steel knife to keep the green colour – you can even whizz the whole lot in a blender if you take the trouble to strip the stalks from the leaves and put the leaves in the blender goblet along with the dissolved sugar and vinegar mixture.

1 large bunch (about 100 g/4 oz) fresh mint	3 dl/$\frac{1}{2}$ pint distilled malt vinegar 175 g/6 oz granulated sugar

Strip the mint leaves from the stems. Wash the leaves and shake or squeeze dry in a towel. Chop the mint very finely and put in a bowl.

Measure the vinegar and sugar into a saucepan. Stir over low heat to dissolve the sugar. Bring to the boil, then draw off the heat and pour over the mint. Leave until cold. Pour into one or more clean screw-topped bottles. Cover tightly and store away from the light.

To serve, spoon out the amount required and stir in more vinegar to taste.
Makes about 4 dl ($\frac{3}{4}$ pint) mint sauce

Home-made salad cream

Make up salad cream as you require it. This quantity will fill two 3-dl (½-pint) bottles. Store in a cool place or in the refrigerator.

25 g/1 oz plain flour
4 level teaspoons dry mustard
50 g/2 oz castor sugar
1 level teaspoon salt

3 dl/½ pint milk
3 dl/½ pint distilled malt vinegar
100 g/4 oz butter
1 egg

Measure the flour, mustard, sugar and salt into a saucepan and mix together. Gradually stir in the milk and whisk well to make sure there are no lumps.

Place the pan over the heat and bring slowly to the boil, stirring all the time. As the mixture begins to thicken in the pan, remove from the heat and beat *very* thoroughly – this helps to make a smooth mixture.

Replace over the heat and allow to come up to the boil. Stir in the vinegar and add the butter cut in pieces. Continue to stir over the heat until the butter has melted and the mixture is blended. Remove from the heat and cool for a few minutes.

Lightly mix the egg in a basin. Whisk in a little of the sauce. Blend well and pour the mixture back into the saucepan. Stir over the heat just for a few moments to cook the egg. Pour the salad cream into wide-necked bottles and seal. Leave until cold. Shake the bottle before using.

Makes 6 dl (1 pint)

Wine cups

Wine cups are coming right back into fashion for serving at summer parties. Besides being cool, fresh and pretty to look at, they are light to drink and you can be generous with the quantities. Though particular wines are used in these recipes, similar wines are equally suitable. For example, Chablis cup doesn't have to be made with Chablis; any good dry white wine will do.

Serve a choice of red or white wine cup in tall glass jugs – it's easier for you to fill any empty glasses while you mingle with guests. Jugs are better too for retaining the fruit. The fruit in a wine cup should be there to garnish the contents of the jug and should *not* be poured into the glasses. Don't hesitate to serve these wine cups throughout a meal; they are pleasantly informal and relaxing.

Chablis cup

2 bottles Chablis
50 g/2 oz lump sugar
1 lemon

1.5 dl/¼ pint medium sherry
slices of cucumber

Put the wine to chill several hours in advance. Rub the lump sugar over the rind of the well-washed lemon until the sugar is yellow and full of zest. Put in a jug and crush the lumps. Add the strained lemon juice and stir to dissolve the sugar.

Add the sherry and chilled wine, and stir to blend. Decorate with slices of cucumber.
Makes 12-14 glasses

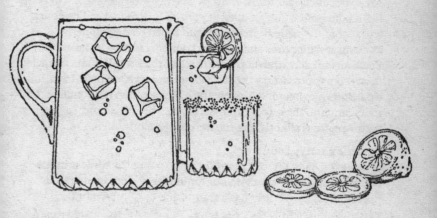

Claret cup

2 bottles claret
1.5 dl/¼ pint water
75 g/3 oz castor sugar
2 oranges

2 lemons
1 496-ml/17½-fl oz bottle soda
  water
sliced orange and sprigs of mint

Put the wine to chill well in advance. Measure the water into a saucepan, add the sugar and thinly pared rinds from the oranges and lemons. Stir over low heat to dissolve the sugar, then bring to the boil. Simmer for a few moments, then strain and leave until cold.

Squeeze the juice from the oranges and lemons and add to the cold syrup. When ready to serve, put a few ice cubes in the serving jug.

Pour in the syrup and the chilled wine and stir well to blend. Top up with the soda water, and float slices of orange and a sprig of mint. **Makes 14-16 glasses**

Using the freezer in June

Gather herbs on a warm sunny day. Chop them finely and freeze in ice-cube trays with a little water. Each cube will hold just enough for a sauce or to add to a prepared dish like a stew or a soup. Mint, parsley and chives are particularly useful but it should be remembered that they are best used in cooked dishes and are not suitable for a garnish.

Make delicious ice creams from fresh fruits – home-made ice cream has an unrivalled flavour and they are so easy to make. The easiest ice creams are made from frozen fruit fools. Use equal parts sweetened fruit purée and whipped double cream – gooseberry, blackcurrant and strawberry are three of the best. For an unusual dinner party dessert try the *fresh mint ice cream* (see page 163). It has a pale green colour and a lovely fresh flavour. Pop the container of ice cream into the refrigerator 30 minutes before serving so the texture softens slightly and the flavour develops.

Freezing dairy foods
Butter Unsalted butter keeps for up to 9 months. Freeze in the foil wrapping for 1–2 weeks, but for longer periods overwrap in polythene. Salted butter has a shorter life of about 6 months.

Milk Ordinary milk does not freeze but it's worth putting a carton of homogenized milk in the freezer before you go on holiday, for the day you return. Milk that is in waxed cartons can be put in just as it is and has a keeping life of about 1 month.

Cream Cream has a tendency to separate when frozen but it happens less with double cream. Remember to transfer the cream from the container in which you buy it to a new one which will allow the necessary 1-cm ($\frac{1}{2}$-in) headspace at the top of the carton. Frozen double cream will whip up when thawed, although not so thickly as fresh cream so it's better to use it for cooking purposes in ice creams and desserts. Lightly whipped cream can be piped out on to waxed paper in rosettes. Freeze uncovered until firm, then carefully pack in a rigid container. Use for decoration on summer desserts. Place on the dessert while still frozen, about 15 minutes before serving, as they thaw quickly. Do not keep cream more than 2–3 weeks.

Eggs It's not worthwhile freezing eggs unless you have a glut or some leftover whites or yolks from cooking. Whole eggs freeze provided they are cracked out into a container. Whisk lightly to blend yolks and whites and take care to mark the number of eggs on each container. Use in cooking for cakes, custard or scrambled eggs. Whites can be frozen separately and are ideal for meringues. Egg yolks are more difficult and should be mixed with $\frac{1}{2}$ teaspoon salt for each egg for use in savoury recipes, or 1 teaspoon sugar per yolk for dessert recipes. Label each container whether sweet or savoury and use accordingly. Thaw eggs in the unopened container and use as usual.

Cheese Freezing gives a crumbly texture to hard cheese and is not recommended. But it makes no difference to the flavour. Pieces of leftover cheese can be grated and kept in the freezer for sandwiches or salads. Any cheese from the freezer must be given ample time to come back to room temperature otherwise it lacks flavour. Store cheese not longer than 4–6 months. Cottage and cream cheeses are not suitable for freezing.

July

In *July* even the most stringent spender is tempted to buy quantities of delicious food. It's a month that is synonymous with the best of our home-grown fruits. Such lovely ingredients are best served in a simple fashion, which is fortunate, for warm weather inevitably dulls appetites. Keep main meals light, choosing from chicken, veal, salmon and summer shellfish including lobsters and prawns. Serve them with this month's garden peas, calabrese, courgettes and French beans.

Now is the peak of the strawberry season and there should be plenty of raspberries and red- and blackcurrants. Gooseberries are getting larger and riper and towards the end of the month the juicy red eating gooseberries will be in the shops. Possibly they will be rubbing shoulders with loganberries and the advance supplies of imported peaches soon to reach the market.

Courgette soup

Courgettes are plentiful this month and they make a very good soup. As a rule courgettes do not freeze well, but this soup is as good a method of storing a bumper crop of courgettes in the freezer as I know.

25 g/1 oz butter	450 g/1 lb courgettes
1 large onion, finely chopped	a scant litre/1½ pints chicken stock

Melt the butter in a large saucepan. Add the finely chopped onion and sauté gently for about 5 minutes until the onion is soft but not brown.

Trim and slice the courgettes, add to the pan and mix with the onion and butter. Stir in the chicken stock and bring up to the boil. Cover and simmer gently for 30 minutes. Draw off the heat and purée the liquid and vegetables from the pan in a blender. Return to the pan, check seasoning, reheat and serve.
Serves 4

Chilled parsley soup

For the best flavour, parsley must be very fresh. This is a good recipe to make if you grow parsley in the garden.

good bunch (about 100 g/4 oz) parsley	1 small onion
	25 g/1 oz butter
450 g/1 lb new potatoes	a scant litre/1½ pints chicken stock

3 dl/½ pint milk   1.5 dl/¼ pint single cream
salt and freshly milled pepper

Thoroughly wash the parsley then remove and discard the stems.
Chop the remainder coarsely. Scrape the potatoes and cut into large
dice. Peel and finely chop the onion.

Melt the butter in a large saucepan. Add the onion, cover with a lid
and fry gently without browning for a few moments until the onion
is soft. Add the potatoes and chopped parsley and fry for a further
few moments over low heat. Stir in the stock and the milk. Season
with salt and pepper and bring up to the boil. Cover with a lid and
simmer gently for 1 hour. Draw the pan off the heat and purée in a
blender.

Stir in the cream, check the seasoning and if necessary thin down
with a little extra stock. Chill well before serving.
Serves 6

Lettuce soup with chives

*One of the advantages of making your own soups is that they can be so
individual and different from the canned and packet varieties. If you
have lettuce growing in the garden this soup is a lovely one to serve and
cheap to make.*

25 g/1 oz butter   a scant litre/1½ pints chicken stock
1 medium-sized onion, peeled and   1 large head lettuce (see method)
  finely chopped   salt and freshly milled pepper
225 g/8 oz (1 large) potato   freshly chopped chives

Melt the butter in a saucepan and add the onion. Fry gently for
about 5 minutes or until the onion is soft and tender, but not brown.
Peel and dice the potato and add to the pan. Toss in the onion-
flavoured butter and then stir in the stock. Bring up to the boil,
lower the heat and simmer for about 15 minutes or until the potato
is quite tender.

Meanwhile separate the lettuce leaves, wash them and shred coarsely.
You can also use the coarser outer leaves of several lettuces which
are to be used for salad, or 2–3 smaller lettuces. Either way the
amount should be the equivalent of a good-sized lettuce.

Add the lettuce to the pan, bring back to the boil and then draw off

the heat. Ladle the liquid and vegetables a little at a time into a blender and purée. Pour into a bowl, check the seasoning and allow to cool. Chill until ready to serve. It might be necessary to thin the cold soup down with a little extra stock or cream to get the right consistency. Stir in the chopped chives and serve.
Serves 4-6

Prawn cocktail

For an alternative first course, spoon this delicious pink cocktail sauce over hard-boiled egg halves – rather like egg mayonnaise – and garnish with shredded lettuce.

225–350 g/8–12 oz prepared
  prawns

6 crisp lettuce leaves
paprika

for the cocktail sauce:

3 rounded tablespoons mayonnaise
3 tablespoons tomato ketchup
3 tablespoons double cream

1 teaspoon Worcestershire sauce
squeeze of lemon juice

Pick over the prawns and shred the lettuce leaves – the easiest way is to roll the leaves up together and then shred them across finely. Shake the lettuce to separate the pieces and place in a polythene bag with a sprinkling of water to keep fresh in the refrigerator.

Combine together the mayonnaise, tomato ketchup, cream and Worcestershire sauce for the dressing. Add a good squeeze of lemon juice – check flavour for sharpness. Add the prawns and set aside.

When ready to serve, place a little shredded lettuce in the base of six individual glasses. Spoon the sauce and prawns on top. Garnish with a sprinkling of paprika and serve with thinly sliced brown bread and butter.
Serves 6

Eggs with avocado mayonnaise

Avocados puréed in a blender make an unusual sauce which is green in colour and with a fresh flavour. Use it like mayonnaise, as a coating for eggs or as a dressing for tomato salad.

6 eggs

bunch watercress

for the dressing:

1 ripe avocado
1 egg
juice of ½ lemon

6 tablespoons oil
salt and freshly milled pepper

Hard-boil the six eggs and plunge immediately into cold water to prevent further cooking. Remove the shells and leave the eggs submerged in cold water until required.

To make the dressing, cut the avocado in half and remove the stone. Scoop out the flesh into the blender container. Add the egg and lemon juice, cover and blend to a purée. Measure the oil into a jug. Remove the centre cap from the blender top and gradually pour the oil into the mixture on low speed. Season to taste with salt and pepper.

Using a sharp knife, cut the eggs in half lengthways and arrange in pairs on serving plates. Spoon over the avocado dressing. Garnish with watercress and serve with thinly sliced brown bread and butter.
Serves 6

Roll-mop herrings

If you prepare herring roll-mops yourself you can control the amount of vinegar used. These are mild in flavour but the nicer for it. Roll-mops offer an ideal way of serving fish cold and they are handy too because they can and should be prepared in advance of serving.

4 herrings
salt and freshly milled pepper
4 tablespoons malt vinegar

1.5 dl/¼ pint water
bay leaf
crisp lettuce leaves and lemon

Wash the herrings and scrape away any loose scales with a knife. Leave the fin on the back of each fish but trim off the others with a pair of scissors. Cut off the head and tail from each herring. Slit down the belly, remove the roes and clean out the inside. Place the herrings cut side down on a working surface and press along the backbone to loosen. Turn the fish over and carefully pull away the bone. Rinse well.

Season the inside of each herring with salt and pepper. Roll up starting from the tail end and pack the herrings closely together in a baking dish. When rolled the fin (left on the back) opens out and looks pretty. Mix the vinegar and water and pour over the herrings;

the liquid should just cover the fish. Add the bay leaf and cover with a buttered paper and a lid. Place in the centre of a moderate oven (180°C., 350°F., Gas Mark 4) and bake for 45 minutes. Remove from the heat and allow to cool in the liquid. Drain and serve on crisp lettuce with a lemon wedge for garnish.

Serves 4

Scampi Newburg

Scampi is an expensive ingredient to start with, so it's worth making a nice accompanying sauce. This recipe is easy enough to make and the sauce has a delicious sherry flavour.

450 g/1 lb prepared scampi
50 g/2 oz butter
2–3 tablespoons medium-dry
  sherry
2 egg yolks

1 level tablespoon flour
3 dl/½ pint single cream
salt and freshly milled pepper
squeeze of lemon juice

If the scampi are frozen, allow them to thaw, discard any watery liquid and pat dry. Melt the butter in a frying pan, add the scampi and sauté gently for 2–3 minutes. The scampi flesh will firm up. Lift from the pan and keep hot. Add the sherry to the hot butter remaining in the pan and simmer for a few moments until reduced by about half.

Meanwhile blend the egg yolks and flour together in a small basin. Gradually stir in the cream. Pour this mixture into the frying pan and stir over moderate heat until the sauce has thickened and is just

simmering. Season well with salt and pepper and add a squeeze of lemon juice. Replace the scampi and cook gently for a few moments to heat through. Then draw off the heat. Serve with buttered rice.
Serves 4

Deep-fried king prawns

Frozen king prawns are an ideal item for the home freezer. The large succulent prawns are frozen in their shells but uncooked. They are as filling as scampi and a lot easier to peel.

1 450-g/1-lb packet headless king prawns

oil for deep-frying

for the batter:

50 g/2 oz plain flour
1 pinch salt
2 teaspoons olive oil

4 tablespoons water
1 egg white

Defrost the prawns for 1 hour. Peel off the shells, leaving the last section of tail and tail fins on.

Sieve the flour and salt for the batter into a small basin and hollow out the centre. Add the oil and water. Using a wooden spoon, mix from the centre outwards, gradually drawing in the flour from around the sides of the bowl. Beat well to get a smooth batter. Whisk the egg white until stiff and, using a metal spoon, fold into the batter.

When ready to fry, dip the prawns by the tail ends into the batter. Allow excess batter to drip away and add the prawns a few at a time to the hot oil. Deep-fry for 2–3 minutes or until golden brown. Drain and tip out on to absorbent kitchen paper. Keep the fried prawns hot in the oven, uncovered so the batter remains crisp, while frying the rest. Serve with wedges of lemon and tartare sauce.
Serves 4

Gammon with raisin sauce

Sweet and sour flavours go well with rich meats and this unusual raisin sauce makes a wonderful accompaniment for grilled rashers of gammon.

| 4 gammon rashers | oil |

for the raisin sauce:

2 tablespoons seedless raisins	1 level tablespoon cornflour
3 dl/½ pint cider	2 tablespoons water
25 g/1 oz brown sugar	1 tablespoon wine vinegar
pinch salt	15 g/½ oz butter

Soak the gammon rashers in cold water for 2 hours to draw out surplus salt. Drain and pat dry. Trim off the rind and rub a little oil over the lean meat. Place under a hot grill for about 2 minutes each side to seal. Then reduce the heat and cook gently for 4 minutes on each side.

Meanwhile put the raisins in a saucepan with the cider. Add the sugar and salt and stir in the cornflour which has been blended with the water. Stir until boiling, then cook for a few minutes until the sauce clears and thickens slightly. Add the vinegar and butter, stir until blended and then serve with the gammon.
Serves 4

Chicken livers in red wine

Chicken livers are easy to buy now that they are packed separately and sold frozen in most supermarkets. Allow frozen livers to thaw completely before making this recipe.

675 g/1½ lb chicken livers	1 slightly rounded tablespoon flour
100 g/4 oz butter	3 dl/½ pint red wine
1 small onion	salt and freshly milled pepper
2 level teaspoons dried mixed herbs	

Trim and separate out the chicken livers. Melt half the butter in a frying pan. Add the chicken livers and fry gently for 2–3 minutes, turning to seal them on all sides. Lift from the pan and keep hot.

Add the remaining butter and the finely chopped onion to the hot pan. Fry gently until the onion is tender. Replace the chicken livers in the pan, add the herbs and sprinkle with the flour. Stir to blend the flour with the butter, then gradually stir in the wine and bring up to a simmer, stirring all the time to get a smooth sauce. Simmer for 2–3 minutes, then season to taste with salt and pepper. Serve with rice.
Serves 4

Fresh salmon

In summer months salmon is more often served cold. For a dinner party this is very much the easiest way of coping with it. There is a method used in Scotland which never fails – the resulting salmon is moist and pink and cooked perfectly every time. The method remains the same for a piece of salmon of any size and there is no need to wrap in muslin or foil; once the fish has cooled it will be firm and easy to lift out of the pan.

Fill a saucepan with sufficient lightly salted water to cover the piece of fish – it is advisable to put the piece of fish in the pan to measure this and then take it out again. Some cooks like to add 1 tablespoon vinegar – but it's optional. Bring the water up to the boil and then add the piece of salmon. When the water reboils, boil it hard for 2 minutes exactly. Then draw the pan off the heat, particularly if over an electric hot plate.

Cover with a tight-fitting lid and leave for 12 hours or until quite cold. At this stage I usually transfer the pan to the larder, and it's best to do it overnight before serving. The bigger the piece of salmon the more water required and the larger the pan. In this way the method adapts itself to any size of fish. The fish continues to cook in the water as it cools and it stays beautifully moist.

Veal with cream and mushroom sauce

Veal is a delicately flavoured meat and one that should be cooked and served very simply. Ask the butcher to beat the escalopes out thinly and take care to use small closed mushrooms that will not discolour the sauce.

4 veal escalopes

for the marinade:

2 tablespoons olive oil	freshly milled black pepper
2 tablespoons lemon juice	few crushed parsley stalks
1 small clove garlic, crushed and chopped	

for the sauce:

175 g/6 oz button mushrooms	2 tablespoons sherry
1 medium-sized onion	salt and freshly milled pepper
50 g/2 oz butter	1.5 dl/¼ pint double cream

Trim the escalopes neatly and arrange in a shallow plate or dish. Mix together all the ingredients for the marinade and pour over the veal. Leave to marinate for about 30 minutes.

Meanwhile trim and slice the mushrooms for the sauce and peel and finely chop the onion. Melt the butter in a frying pan and add the mushrooms and onion. Fry over very gentle heat for 5 minutes until the onion is quite soft. Lift the vegetables out of the pan and keep warm, leaving the flavoured butter in the pan to fry the veal. Drain the veal escalopes from the marinade, allowing surplus marinade to drain from the meat. Add to the hot butter and fry gently for about 4–5 minutes on each side. Lift the veal from the pan on to a hot serving plate and keep warm.

Measure the sherry into the frying pan and heat briskly, stirring until almost evaporated. Replace the cooked onion and mushroom in the pan, season with salt and pepper and stir in the cream. Stir until almost boiling, then draw the pan off the heat. Pour the sauce over the veal and serve.
Serves 4

Pepper steak

Serve pepper steak with a green salad which is cool and crisp in contrast. Take care not to be over-generous with the quantity of peppercorns used, the flavour should be pleasantly hot but not overpowering. Peppercorns are hard to crush but don't be tempted to use a peppermill which makes the mixture too fine.

4 fillet steaks	50 g/2 oz butter
2 tablespoons whole black peppercorns	1 tablespoon oil

Wipe the meat and trim neatly. Crush the peppercorns in a basin using the end of a rolling pin, with a pestle and mortar, or on a board under a heavy weight.

Using the fingers, press the crushed peppercorns into the surface of the meat on both sides. Heat the butter and oil in a frying pan and when frothing add the steaks. Cook fairly quickly for the first few moments and turn the steak – the initial hot frying seals the peppercorns on to the surface of the meat. Lower the heat and cook

the steaks for the required amount of time, allowing 8–10 minutes for rare to medium-done. Turn the meat for even cooking, then lift from the pan and serve with any buttery juices poured over.
Serves 4

Chicken with pineapple and almonds

This recipe is surprisingly quick to prepare and has a pleasant sweet-sour flavour. Choose a good-sized frying pan, for the whole dish is cooked in the one utensil.

1 medium-sized chicken, about 1–1.25 kg/2½–3 lb	4 tablespoons pineapple juice
seasoned flour	1 tablespoon soy sauce
65 g/2½ oz butter	1 tablespoon clear honey
2 young carrots	25 g/1 oz brown sugar
1 small green pepper	4 tablespoons vinegar
2 rounded tablespoons shredded pineapple	2 level tablespoons cornflour
4 spring onions	3 dl/½ pint chicken stock
	seasoning to taste
	25 g/1 oz blanched almonds

Cut away all the flesh from the chicken and put the bones to simmer with about 6 dl (1 pint) water for the stock. Cut the chicken flesh into fork-sized pieces, toss in seasoned flour and fry gently in 50 g (2 oz) of the butter until tender. Dish up and keep warm while preparing the sauce.

Scrape the carrot and shred into wafer-thin slices. Add to the frying pan with the deseeded and shredded green pepper, the shredded pineapple and cut-up spring onions. Stir in the pineapple juice, soy sauce, honey, sugar and vinegar. Simmer for 3 minutes, then add the cornflour blended with the chicken stock. Stir until boiling, when the sauce will become clear and slightly thickened. Check the seasoning and pour over the chicken. Scatter with the almonds browned in the remaining butter and serve with rice.
Serves 4

Baked chicken with courgettes

Joints of chicken liberally spread with parsley butter are oven-roasted, with courgettes added to the pan. Small new potatoes scrubbed and left in their skins are very good used instead of or in addition to the courgettes. This is an easy-to-make summer recipe that is perfect for lunch.

4 chicken joints	1 tablespoon finely chopped parsley
salt and freshly milled pepper	juice of ½ lemon
50–75 g/2–3 oz butter	450 g/1 lb courgettes

Place the chicken pieces in a buttered shallow roasting tin or baking dish. Choose one big enough to take both chicken and vegetables. Season the chicken with the salt and freshly milled pepper. Cream the butter until soft, then beat in the chopped parsley and lemon juice. Spread the parsley butter generously over the chicken joints. Place in the centre of a moderate oven (180°C., 350°F., Gas Mark 4) and bake for 1 hour.

Meanwhile trim either end of the courgettes, wash and slice thickly. Add to a pan of boiling salted water, bring back to the boil and simmer for 2–3 minutes to blanch the slices, then drain well. (If new potatoes are used, make sure to select small potatoes which will cook quickly, and blanch as for the courgettes.) Add the courgettes to the chicken after about 15 minutes of the baking time. Turn the courgettes in the parsley butter which will have begun to melt around the sides of the baking dish. Baste the chicken joints and replace in the oven to complete cooking time. Baste chicken and courgettes occasionally.

Serve the chicken with the vegetables, butter and juices from the pan.
Serves 4

Barbecued pork spareribs

Spareribs of pork have been a popular feature at American barbecues and outdoor eating for many years. Supermarkets are now selling fresh pork ribs, just the right 'bony' cut for this kind of recipe. Larger quantities of meat are required because there is a lot of waste. Barbecued pork spareribs are messy to eat but delicious with a salad and French bread on a hot summer evening.

675 g/1½ lb pork ribs, cut in pieces	salt

for the barbecue sauce:

1 tablespoon oil	1 small onion, finely chopped

4 tablespoons tomato ketchup	1 teaspoon made mustard
2 tablespoons vinegar	1 tablespoon Worcestershire sauce
1 tablespoon soft brown sugar	

Cut between the flesh of each pork rib bone so that individual pieces of meat are obtained and can be held in the fingers to eat after cooking. Sprinkle the meat with salt and place in a shallow roasting tin. Place in the centre of a moderately hot oven (200°C., 400°F., Gas Mark 6) and roast for 30 minutes.

Meanwhile prepare the barbecue sauce. Heat the oil in a saucepan and add the onion. Fry gently until the onion is soft but not brown. Mix together the tomato ketchup, vinegar, sugar, mustard and Worcestershire sauce in a basin. Add this to the onion in the saucepan and bring up to the boil stirring well. Remove the sauce from the heat.

Lower the oven heat to moderate (180°C., 350°F., Gas Mark 4) and pour away any fat in the pan. Pour the barbecue sauce over the pork ribs and replace in the oven. Continue to roast the meat at the lower temperature for a further 1 hour. Baste often with the sauce. Towards the end the rib bones will become rather crisp and brown round the edges.

Serve the pork ribs with any sauce spooned from the roasting tin. Provide napkins and when cool enough to handle nibble the spicy meat off the bones.
Serves 2-3

Mangetout peas

Mangetout are tender young pods picked before the peas inside begin to swell. Although a relative newcomer to our vegetable market, they are already very popular. They are easy to grow too and if you have them in the garden they should be ready to eat this month. The pods should be barely cooked so they are still a little crisp and, as the name implies, they are eaten whole.

| 450 g/1 lb mangetout | 15 g/½ oz butter |

Wash and top and tail the pods. Add to plenty of boiling salted water and cook quickly for 6–8 minutes or until just tender. Drain

and return to the hot pan, adding the butter. Toss and serve.
Serves 4

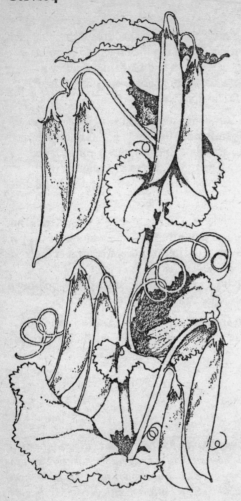

Old-fashioned egg salad

*Choose an old-fashioned crisp Webb's Wonderful or a Cos lettuce for
this salad. Either makes a change from the more usual cabbage lettuce.
Simmer the eggs until firm-set but not hard-boiled, so that when cut
they are moist and not rubbery. Plunge the eggs into cold water*

immediately they are ready, to prevent over-cooking. This is the kind of salad to serve with cold sliced ham.

6 eggs

1 Webb's Wonderful or Cos lettuce

1 onion, finely chopped

1 tablespoon finely chopped parsley

2 tablespoons grated Cheddar cheese

for the dressing:

salt and freshly milled pepper

2 tablespoons vinegar

4 tablespoons olive oil

1 teaspoon Worcestershire sauce

Add the eggs to the simmering water, reboil and cook for 5 minutes until firm-set, but not hard-boiled. Drain and cover immediately with cold water. When cool peel away the shells and leave the eggs submerged in cold water until required.

Separate the lettuce into leaves and wash thoroughly. Tear away any coarse stems and tear large leaves in two. Arrange the leaves in the base of a salad bowl. Halve the eggs and arrange over the lettuce in layers with the onion.

Place a seasoning of salt and pepper in a mixing basin. Add the vinegar and stir to dissolve the salt, then add the oil and Worcestershire sauce. Mix well and pour over the salad. Sprinkle with chopped parsley and cheese and serve.

Serves 6

Spanish rice salad

Cold rice salads which include a selection of colourful ingredients are simple to prepare and are easy to make up in quantity for buffet supper parties. Mix the rice while hot with some of the dressing so that as it cools the grains absorb some of the flavour and the rice remains separate and loose.

100 g/4 oz long-grain rice

4–5 tablespoons oil and vinegar dressing

225 g/8 oz firm ripe tomatoes

2–3 stalks celery

1 green pepper

4–6 black olives

Cook the rice in boiling salted water for 8–10 minutes or until tender. Drain well and place in a bowl. To the hot rice, add about 3 tablespoons of the oil and vinegar dressing. Toss to glaze all the grains of rice and set aside until cold.

Scald the tomatoes and peel away the skins. Cut the tomatoes in quarters. Wash and finely shred the celery. Deseed and finely shred the green pepper. Add to the salad with the stoned black olives and the remainder of the dressing. Toss to mix.

Serve with cold chicken, beef or ham. This is particularly good with *cold chicken in lemon sauce* (see page 210).
Serves 4-6

Avocado dressing

The pretty pale green colour and delicate flavour of this dressing make it an unusual and very worthy accompaniment for cold poached salmon or salmon trout. It makes a pleasant change from mayonnaise.

1 ripe avocado
3–4 tablespoons prepared oil and
  vinegar dressing

1 carton soured cream
salt and freshly milled pepper

Halve the avocado, remove the stone and scoop out the flesh into a basin. Take care to scoop out the very green part of the flesh next to the skin which contributes largely to the colour of the mixture.

Using a fork, mash the avocado flesh with the oil and vinegar

dressing until smooth. Stir in the soured cream and season with salt
and pepper. Spoon into a serving dish, cover tightly with cellophane
wrap to exclude the air and chill until ready to serve.
Serves 4-6

Courgettes with tomatoes

*Courgettes stewed gently with tomatoes and onion can be served cold as
an hors-d'oeuvre or hot as a vegetable. The mixture is particularly nice
with veal, chicken or lamb recipes.*

450 g/1 lb courgettes
2 medium-sized onions
2 tablespoons oil
25 g/1 oz butter

1 clove garlic, crushed
450 g/1 lb tomatoes
salt and freshly milled pepper

Wash the courgettes and trim the ends. Slice across about 0.5 cm
($\frac{1}{4}$ in) thick. Sprinkle with salt and place in a colander. Leave for 1
hour until the excess moisture has drained out, then shake in a cloth
to dry them. Peel and slice the onions.

Heat the oil and butter in a frying pan and add the onions. Sauté
gently for a few moments to soften the onion and then add the
crushed garlic. Add the courgettes, cover the pan with a lid and
cook gently for 10 minutes, shaking the pan occasionally. Scald the
tomatoes and peel away the skins. Slice and add to the courgettes.
Continue to cook, uncovered, for a further 10 minutes or until the
courgettes are quite tender and much of the liquid from the tomatoes
has evaporated. Season with salt and pepper and serve.
Serves 4

Raspberry mousse

*Use fresh raspberries in summer or fruit from the garden which has
been frozen in winter. If the raspberries have been frozen with sugar it
is not usually necessary to add any more.*

450 g/1 lb fresh raspberries
2 tablespoons castor sugar
4 tablespoons water
1 level tablespoon powdered
  gelatine

3 dl/$\frac{1}{2}$ pint double cream
2 egg whites

Pick over fresh raspberries and place in a mixing basin. Sprinkle with the sugar. Separate frozen raspberries and set aside until thawed.

Measure the water into a small saucepan and sprinkle over the gelatine. Set aside to soak for 5 minutes. Place over a low heat and warm until the gelatine has dissolved, then draw the pan off the heat.

Sieve the raspberries along with the juices formed, or pass through a Mouli food mill. Stir in the cream. Slowly pour in the liquid gelatine, whisking all the time. Continue the whisking for a further few minutes until the mixture begins to thicken. Then in a separate basin whisk the egg whites until thick and fold into the raspberry mixture. Pour into a pretty serving dish and chill until firm before serving.
Serves 6

Strawberries in raspberry syrup

Few fruit flavours combine so well as those of strawberries and raspberries. This is one of the most delicious ways of serving strawberries.

450 g/1 lb fresh strawberries

for the raspberry syrup:

450 g/1 lb raspberries   juice of ½ lemon
100 g/4 oz castor sugar

Wash and hull the strawberries leaving them whole. Place in a serving dish and chill while preparing the sauce.

Place the raspberries in a saucepan. Add half the sugar and heat very gently for about 5 minutes, crushing the fruit a little to make the juice run. When the fruit is soft, rub through a sieve to make a purée and discard the pips. Add the remaining sugar and the strained lemon juice. Pour over the strawberries and toss to coat the fruit well. Serve chilled.
Serves 6

Sponge flan

You need a special sponge flan tin for baking these. It really is worthwhile buying one of the new silicone-lined tins so that the sponges turn out every time without sticking in the centre.

2 large eggs
85 g/3 oz castor sugar

70 g/2½ oz plain flour
25 g/1 oz melted butter

Well butter a 20-cm (8-in) sponge flan tin. Sprinkle with a mixture of equal quantities of flour and castor sugar – 1 tablespoon of each should be sufficient. Shake the mixture over the tin to coat evenly, then tap out the surplus. (This preparation is not necessary with a silicone-lined tin.)

Choose a mixing basin that fits neatly over a medium-sized saucepan. Crack in the eggs and add the sugar. Half fill the saucepan with water and bring to the boil, take off the heat and move it to table level – at this height it is less tiring to whisk. Place the bowl over the saucepan and beat the mixture until thick and light – this takes about 8–10 minutes. Remove the bowl from the heat and whisk for a further few minutes to cool the mixture a little. Sift the flour over the surface and, using a metal spoon, carefully fold the flour into the mixture. When the flour is half folded in, add the melted butter and blend the ingredients gently but thoroughly.

Pour into the prepared tin and spread evenly. Place in the centre of a moderately hot oven (190°C., 375°F., Gas Mark 5) and bake for 18–20 minutes. Turn out and leave until cold.

Fill with fresh soft fruits like raspberries or strawberries and top with ice cream; or spoon over almost setting jelly – dissolve half a raspberry or strawberry jelly in 1.5 dl (¼ pint) boiling water and make up to 3 dl (½ pint) with ice cubes. When the mixture shows signs of thickening pour over the fruit to glaze and chill until set firm.

In winter, fill with drained canned fruits and thicken the juice to spoon over as a glaze. To 1.5 dl (¼ pint) fruit juice allow 1 rounded teaspoon arrowroot. Blend in a saucepan and then set over the heat. Bring just up to the boil stirring all the time. Use as required.
Makes one 20-cm (8-in) sponge flan

VARIATION
To bake a single sponge layer Well butter a 20-cm (8-in) sandwich tin. Sprinkle with a mixture of equal quantities of flour and sugar – 1 tablespoon of each should be sufficient. Shake the mixture evenly over the tin to coat and then tap out the surplus. Prepare the mixture as above and then pour into the prepared tin. Place in the centre of a moderately hot oven (190°C., 375°F., Gas Mark 5) and bake for 20 minutes. Turn out and allow to cool. Use as a base for baked Alaska, or split and fill with fresh cream and raspberries.

Redcurrant and raspberry crumble

Redcurrants and raspberries combine very well and make a good contrast to a sweet, crunchy topping of crumble.

225 g/8 oz redcurrants	75 g/3 oz castor sugar
225 g/8 oz raspberries	1 tablespoon water

for the shortbread crumble:

100 g/4 oz plain flour	50 g/2 oz castor sugar
75 g/3 oz butter	little icing sugar

Strip the redcurrants from the stalks using the prongs of a fork. Hull the raspberries and combine the fruits. Place in the base of a 1-litre (2-pint) baking or pie dish. Sprinkle with the sugar and add the water. Set aside while preparing the crumble topping.

Sift the flour into a mixing basin, add the butter cut into pieces and rub into the flour. Add the sugar and continue rubbing in until the mixture clings together in large crumbs. Spoon evenly over the fruit mixture and pack down lightly. Place in the centre of a moderate oven (180°C., 350°F., Gas Mark 4) and bake for 45 minutes. Dust with icing sugar and serve hot with cream.
Serves 4-6

Summer fruit compote

Any combination of summer fruits can be used in a compote. Stoned cherries should be simmered with the gooseberries and currants. Strawberries should be added along with the raspberries. When proportions of fruit used vary from those given here the sugar added should be adjusted according to the proportion of sharp-flavoured fruits included.

450 g/1 lb dessert gooseberries
100–175 g/4–6 oz (1 punnet)
  redcurrants or blackcurrants

175 g/6 oz castor sugar
100–175 g/4–6 oz (1 punnet)
  loganberries or raspberries

Top and tail the gooseberries and strip the redcurrants from the stems. Wash the fruits well and place in a saucepan. Add the sugar and place the pan over low heat. Bring slowly to the boil. It is important that the fruit remains whole, to give the finished dessert a more attractive appearance, so refrain from stirring but shake the pan occasionally to mix the fruits and help the sugar dissolve. Simmer very gently, covered with a lid, for about 5 minutes.

Draw the pan off the heat and add the loganberries or raspberries. These are added at a later stage since they require hardly any cooking at all. Allow the fruit to cool, then serve warm with cream.
Serves 4-6

Mint jelly

Mint jelly has a far better flavour if a proportion of vinegar is included as part of the liquid in the recipe. Pot the jelly in small jars that can be used up at one time when opened.

1.25 kg/3 lb cooking apples
6 dl/1 pint water
1 bunch well-washed mint
6 dl/1 pint vinegar

granulated or preserving sugar (see
  method)
few drops green colouring

Wash the apples and cut up without peeling. Place them in a large preserving pan, add the water and about half the mint tied in a bunch. Place over moderate heat and bring to the boil. Simmer gently until the fruit is quite soft – press the apples with a potato masher occasionally to pulp them down really well. Add the vinegar and bring up to the boil. Simmer for 5 minutes. Then ladle the fruit juice into a scalded jelly bag and allow to drip for several hours.

Measure the juice back into the preserving pan and for every 6 dl (1 pint) of juice add 475 g (1 lb) sugar. Stir over low heat to dissolve the sugar, then bring up to the boil. Boil rapidly for a set – about 15 minutes. Remove from the heat and skim. Add about 3–4 tablespoons finely chopped mint and a few drops green colouring. Stir through the jelly, then ladle or pour into small jars. Cover with waxed paper circles when hot and seal when cold.
Fills 8 225-g (8-oz) jars

Raspberry jam

Raspberries usually crop very well and if you grow your own fruit you are likely to have plenty to spare for jam. Some people dislike the pips in raspberry jam and to make a seedless preserve, strain the jam when the sugar has dissolved but before you bring it up to the boil.

1.75 kg/4 lb raspberries   1.75 kg/4 lb granulated or
                                                          preserving sugar

Place the hulled raspberries in a preserving pan and heat gently to draw the juice. It's a good idea to crush a few near the base of the pan to start the juice off. Simmer for 5 minutes until the fruit is tender.

Add the sugar and allow to dissolve over low heat. Bring up to the boil and boil rapidly for 8–10 minutes when the setting stage should have been reached. Draw off the heat, skin and ladle or pour into jars. Cover with waxed paper circles when hot and seal when cold.
Makes 2¾–3 kg (6–7 lb).

Redcurrant and raspberry jelly

Redcurrants and raspberries combine to make a clear bright red jelly preserve that has a lovely flavour and is marvellous as a spread for tea-time.

900 g/2 lb redcurrants   granulated or preserving sugar (see
900 g/2 lb raspberries   method)
a generous litre/2 pints water (see
  method)

Wash the redcurrants gently but leave the stalks on – there is no need to string them. Place in a preserving pan with the raspberries. Add the water; there should be sufficient just to come level with the top of the fruit in the pan. Bring up to the boil and simmer gently for 1 hour to extract all the juice. Ladle the fruit and liquid into a scalded jelly bag and leave to drip for several hours.

Ladle the juice back into the preserving pan and for every 6 dl (1 pint) juice add 475 g (1 lb) sugar. Stir over low heat to dissolve the sugar and then bring up to the boil. Boil briskly for a set – about 10 minutes. Draw off the heat and skim. Ladle or pour the jelly into jars and cover with waxed paper circles. Seal when cold.
Makes 2.25 kg (5 lb)

Green gooseberry jam

A good colour in gooseberry jam comes from using green gooseberries and boiling fast for a set after the sugar has dissolved. Lengthy boiling darkens the colour of jam but acid unripe fruit should reach setting point fairly quickly. For extra flavour tie a few heads of elderflowers in muslin and cook with the gooseberries. Remove before adding the sugar.

1.25 kg/3 lb green gooseberries   1.25 kg/3 lb granulated or
5.5 dl/1 pint water   preserving sugar

Top and tail the gooseberries using scissors and place in a preserving pan with the water. Bring them slowly to the boil, crushing the juice out of the berries with the back of a spoon. Simmer gently until the skins are quite tender – about 20–30 minutes.

Add the sugar and stir over low heat until the sugar has dissolved. Bring up to the boil and cook rapidly for a set – about 10 minutes. Draw off the heat and skim. Ladle or pour the jam into jars. Cover with waxed paper circles when hot and seal when cold.
Makes 2·75 kg (6 lb)

Strawberry jam

Acid, slightly under-ripe strawberries are the best to use for jam especially if you include one or two with a little green on them. The kind of strawberries you pick towards the end of the season, when the berries are not ripening very well any more, are ideal.

1.75 kg/4 lb strawberries	1.75 kg/4 lb granulated or preserving sugar

Hull the strawberries and put them into a preserving pan. Crush a few of the berries near the base and set the pan over low heat to draw the juices.

Add the sugar and stir gently over low heat until dissolved. Bring up to the boil. Boil rapidly for a set – about 10 minutes. Draw the pan off the heat and skim. Leave to stand for about 15–20 minutes so that the berries will be evenly dispersed. Ladle or pour into jars. Cover with waxed paper circles when hot and seal when cold.
Makes 2·75-3 kg (6–7 lb)

Jam-making
Summer is the best time for jam-making – there are so many soft fruits to choose from. For good jams and jellies the fruit used should be sound and slightly under-ripe. Over-ripe fruit does not make good jam. Some fruits have a better pectin level than others; fruits like blackcurrants, green gooseberries and redcurrants are excellent to combine with other fruits. Green gooseberries make delicious jam with strawberries, redcurrants with raspberries and blackcurrants with rhubarb.

Choice of sugar Choose preserving crystals or granulated sugar for best results and least scum on the jam. Brown sugar is not recommended;

it alters the flavour and colour of the finished jam and produces quantities of scum on the surface.

Choice of pan Copper or brass preserving pans are excellent, they heat quickly and evenly, but cleaning must be scrupulously carried out in case poisonous copper salts are left in the pan. Modern aluminium or stainless steel pans are good and easy to clean. Unlike brass or copper pans they can be safely used for acid pickles and chutneys as well as for jams and jellies. A preserving pan is essential to allow fast boiling which gives a good colour and set. For a small quantity of jam a saucepan can be used.

Making the jam All fruits need softening before the sugar is added. Soft fruits like strawberries and raspberries require no added water, it is only necessary to crush a few berries in the base of the pan. Add the remaining berries and heat gently to draw out sufficient juice to dissolve the sugar. Tough-skinned fruits such as gooseberries, black-currants and damsons must be stewed in water until quite tender before adding any sugar. Sugar added too soon is the cause of tough fruit in the finished preserve.

The sugar must be completely dissolved before the jam is brought to the boil. Failure to do so often causes the preserve to re-crystallize in the jars. When the sugar has dissolved, the jam should be boiled really briskly until setting point is reached. Remember that jam tends to froth up a great deal while it is boiling, so choose a large enough pan to allow for this. A small knob of butter stirred in just before bringing the jam to the boil helps to reduce frothing.

Testing for a set There are various ways of deciding when your jam has reached setting point. With a jam thermometer you can use the 'temperature test' – most jams set between 103°C. (218°F.) and 104°C. (220°F.); or you can use the 'saucer' test and for this you must have a cold saucer for a really quick result. Draw the preserving pan off the heat – this is important, otherwise you may boil the jam past setting point whilst waiting for the result of the test spot. Allow a few small drops of jam to fall on the saucer and leave until cold. Then push gently with the finger tip. If the jam has reached setting point you will see a wrinkled skin appear in front of your finger. If there is no sign of this, return the pan to the heat and bring back to a brisk boil. Recheck the jam at 5-minute intervals until the test is positive.

Potting the jam Most jams are potted quickly. Cool for a few moments to allow the scum to firm up and push it to the side of the pan so that it can easily be removed. Ladle the jam into jars and put on waxed discs immediately. Then cover the jars with a clean cloth to exclude any dust and leave until cold. Finally cover with transparent cellophane covers and labels. The exceptions are strawberry or cherry jam which are potted when half cold to prevent separation of the fruit.

Using the freezer in July

Fruits make lovely summer desserts and you'll find you can serve them in a variety of ways. The *sponge flan* (see page 189) freezes very well, like all cake mixtures. Make two or three and freeze them unfilled. An hour's thawing at room temperature and they are ready to fill and serve. Single sponge layers can be used as a base for baked Alaska. Layers split and filled with fresh raspberries and sweetened whipped cream can be kept as an excellent standby sweet in the freezer. Dust with icing sugar and serve as a dessert. Frozen ready-baked flan cases made using a *rich flan crust* (see May, page 140) are marvellous for all summer open fruit flans. Bake following instructions and freeze over-wrapped in a freezer bag when quite cold.

Freezing summer fruits
The method you use for freezing summer fruits can be important from the point of view of using them later in the year. If you are smart enough now, you can freeze fruits in season at this minute and use them to make 'summer' recipes in winter.

Freeze fruit in quantities you are likely to use in a recipe, or serve at any one time. Packs of 225 g (8 oz) or 450 g (1 lb) fruit and 3-dl ($\frac{1}{2}$-pint) cartons of purée are the most useful. Prepare all fruits for freezing just as you would for using normally. Fruit can be frozen in a dry pack – that is with no sugar added – with sugar or in a syrup. The method you choose depends on the fruit and the way you wish to serve it later on.

Dry pack With this method no sugar is added; it is a satisfactory way for fruits which can be prepared without breaking or ones which do not discolour during preparation, like gooseberries, rhubarb, loganberries, raspberries and black- or redcurrants. Freeze the prepared fruits just as they are in polythene bags. It's a good idea to mix together in packages fruits like raspberries and red-currants.

Use the fruits while still frozen in fruit compotes. You can combine several fruits together with sugar to sweeten – simmer gently just until the fruits are tender. For pies, crumble or cobbler, allow the fruit to thaw just until you can separate the pieces to place them in a pie dish. Add sugar to sweeten and then follow your own recipe.

Sugar pack This is a method to use when you want to serve fruit as a dessert straight from the freezer. Sugar sprinkled over the fruit draws out fruit juices and forms a sugar glaze. During freezing the glaze protects the fruit and is a very good method for soft, juicy berries like raspberries, loganberries and strawberries. The fruit can either be sprinkled with sugar in a basin and left to stand at room temperature until the sugar goes into solution, or the fruit can be packed in layers with the sugar in waxed containers and allowed to stand until the juices run. Use approximately 100–175 g (4–6 oz) sugar for every 450 g (1 lb) fruit.

These fruits should be allowed to thaw in the refrigerator and be served chilled. A 450-g (1-lb) pack takes 6–8 hours to thaw and should be left unopened. Turn the pack while thawing to keep the juices flowing over the berries inside. Serve them on their own or with ice cream or another dessert.

Syrup pack This method should be used for fruits which discolour quickly, like apricots, peaches and cherries. Strawberries and blackcurrants are also good frozen this way. The syrup to be used should be made in advance and allowed to become quite cold. The strength of the syrup is determined by the tartness of the fruit. A medium syrup for stone fruit can be made by dissolving 450 g (1 lb) sugar in a generous litre (2 pints) water to make about 1.5 litres (2½ pints) syrup. A heavy syrup for soft fruits should be made using 900 g (2 lb) sugar and a generous litre (2 pints) water to make 1¾ litres (3 pints) syrup. Prepare sufficient syrup, allowing 5.5 dl (1 pint) syrup for every 900 g (2 lb) fruit to be frozen. Freeze the fruits in waxed cartons leaving 1 cm (½ in) headspace. Place a piece of crumpled kitchen foil between the fruit and the container lid to keep the fruit submerged.

These fruits should be thawed in the refrigerator and can be served with a little brandy or kirsch added to the syrup. They can be used as the basis for a fruit salad, or in a trifle to soak the sponge cake base.

August

Despite holiday spirits, *August* is a sharp reminder of autumn. Early varieties of cookers and dessert apples, as well as plums, green grapes, damsons and cultivated blackberries appear, in sombre contrast to the most colourful fruits of last month. Blackcurrants and raspberries are still plentiful and imported peaches, pineapples, and small seedless sultana grapes are a good buy.

Vegetables give scope for new ideas this month with the first baby marrows, sweetcorn, which has all too short a season, and the beginning of the runner beans. Tomatoes and cucumbers are plentiful and cheap so now is a good time to use them to make any sweet pickles or preserves.

Blender beetroot soup

Make this soup in a blender to get a really smooth mixture. Chill well before serving.

3 medium-sized cooked beetroot
2 298-g/10½-oz cans beef
 consommé

1 carton soured cream
salt and freshly milled pepper

Peel the beetroot and slice into the goblet of the blender. Add the beef consommé, two-thirds of the soured cream and a seasoning of salt and pepper. Cover and blend until smooth.

Pour into soup cups and chill. Serve with the remaining soured cream spooned on top.
Serves 4-6

Tomatoes stuffed with cream cheese and caviar

Use a soft cream cheese for these. The 'caviar' becomes squashed and turns the mixture grey if stirred into a mixture that is too firm. The red of the tomato cases and the contrasting white and black of the filling makes this a pretty first course.

8 ripe medium-sized tomatoes
175–225 g/6–8 oz fresh cream
 cheese

squeeze of lemon juice
1 tablespoon caviar-style lumpfish
 roe

Scald the tomatoes and peel away the skins. Cut a slice off the top of each and, using a teaspoon, scoop out the seeds. Sprinkle with salt and turn the tomato cups upside down to drain.

Using a wooden spoon blend together the cream cheese and lemon juice, then using a tablespoon fold in the caviar. Pile the cheese mixture into the tomato cups and replace the lids. If preferred they can be topped with additional caviar. Serve with thinly sliced brown bread and butter.

Serves 4

Chilled marrow soup

Marrow soup should have a pleasant taste, so avoid buying marrows that are too large – apart from the surplus of seeds in the centre, the flesh definitely lacks flavour.

1 medium-sized marrow	3 dl/½ pint milk
40 g/1½ oz butter	6 dl/1 pint chicken stock
salt and freshly milled pepper	1 level tablespoon flour

Peel the marrow and cut in half lengthways. Scoop out centre seeds, cut the marrow flesh into chunks and place in a saucepan. Cover with cold salted water and bring to the boil. Draw the pan off the heat and drain the marrow flesh. This initial blanching helps to preserve any natural green colour in the marrow flesh.

Melt 25 g (1 oz) of the butter in a large saucepan, add the marrow flesh and a good seasoning of salt and freshly milled pepper. Cover with a lid and simmer very gently for about 10–15 minutes or until the marrow is quite tender. Stir in the milk and chicken stock and bring up to the boil. Draw the pan off the heat and rub the marrow and liquid through a sieve or use a blender to make a purée. Return the purée to the pan and reheat gently.

Cream the remaining butter with the flour to make a *beurre manié*. Add in pieces to the hot soup and stir until the small lumps of mixture have melted into the soup. Bring to the boil, stirring all the time. Simmer for 1 minute, then draw the pan off the heat. Cool, stirring occasionally to prevent a skin forming, then chill until ready to serve.

Serves 6

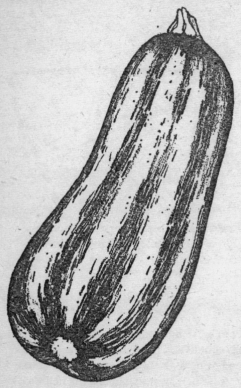

Consommé mousse

Chill this mixture in consommé cups or ramekin dishes and serve with a spoon. The texture is very light, rather like a mousse, but it must be served like a soup.

2 298-g/10½-oz cans beef consommé

350 g/12 oz cream cheese
2 level teaspoons curry powder

Put the ingredients, in the order given, into a blender and purée until smooth. Alternatively whisk by hand until smooth. Pour the mixture into individual small soufflé or ramekin dishes. The mixture can be poured into one large serving dish, in which case the mousse should be spooned into individual dishes for serving. Chill the mixture for several hours.

Serve garnished with a little caviar (use caviar-style lumpfish roe), which looks most attractive and tastes delicious. Or use chopped chives or parsley.
Serves 6

Peaches in curry sauce

This is a lovely way to serve fresh peaches as a first course. At other times of the year use canned white peaches and use peach syrup in place of the stock in the recipe. Omit the sweet chutney or jam from the sauce.

6 fresh peaches   few crisp lettuce leaves

for the curry sauce:
1 tablespoon oil   juice of ½ lemon
1 small onion   1 rounded tablespoon sweet
1 level tablespoon curry powder   chutney or jam
1.5 dl/¼ pint chicken stock or water 1.5 dl/¼ pint double cream
1 rounded teaspoon concentrated
  tomato purée

Where fresh peaches are to be used, prepare the curry sauce in advance, leaving the preparation of the peaches until nearer serving time.

Measure the oil into a saucepan, add the finely chopped onion and cook gently for a few minutes until the onion is soft but not brown. Stir in the curry powder and cook for a few moments then add the stock, tomato purée, lemon juice and chutney or jam. Bring up to the boil and simmer gently for 5 minutes to concentrate the flavour. Strain into a basin and leave until quite cold.

Lightly whip the cream and whisk in the curry sauce. Scald the fresh peaches in boiling water for 30 seconds and then peel away the skins. Halve and remove the stones. Arrange the peach halves in pairs on crisp lettuce. Spoon over the curry sauce and serve.
Serves 6

Spaghetti carbonara

Quick like most spaghetti recipes and easy, because the same pan is used throughout, spaghetti carbonara makes a light lunch or supper dish. Serve it with the white wine remaining in the bottle after making the recipe.

100–175 g/4–6 oz spaghetti
4 rashers lean bacon
freshly milled pepper
1.5 dl/¼ pint dry white wine

1 egg yolk
4–5 tablespoons double cream
grated Parmesan cheese for
  serving

Add the spaghetti to a saucepan of boiling salted water, reboil and simmer until just tender – quick-cooking spaghetti will take just 6 minutes. Drain in a colander.

Return the saucepan to the heat and add the trimmed and chopped bacon rashers. Lightly fry the bacon until just beginning to crisp, then sprinkle with freshly milled pepper and add the wine. Return the spaghetti to the pan and reheat gently; the spaghetti will absorb all the wine. When well heated through, add the egg yolk blended with the cream. Draw the pan off the heat and using two forks toss the spaghetti in the mixture. The heat of the pan will be quite sufficient to thicken the sauce.

Serve with a sprinkling of grated Parmesan cheese over the top and serve with a bowl of grated cheese separately.

Serves 2-3

Grilled salmon steaks

Individual steaks or cutlets of salmon are good for grilling and it's an ideal way to cook salmon for a small number. A pat of herb butter melting over the top as they are served is all the garnish needed.

4 salmon steaks, 2–2.5 cm/¾–1 in thick	little flour
	50 g/2 oz butter

for the parsley butter:

75 g/3 oz butter	salt and freshly milled pepper
squeeze of lemon juice	1 tablespoon finely chopped parsley

Prepare the parsley butter well in advance of grilling the salmon steaks so that the mixture sets in a firm shape. Cream the butter and gradually work in a squeeze of lemon juice to sharpen the flavour. Add a seasoning of salt and pepper and the parsley. Beat well to mix, then spoon the mixture into the centre of a small square of foil. Roll the butter up in the foil and twist the ends like a cracker so that the butter is pressed into a thick roll. Chill until quite firm.

Rinse the salmon steaks, season and dust lightly with flour. Place the butter for grilling under gentle heat in the grill pan. The minute it stops foaming but before it turns colour, put in the salmon steaks, then smartly turn them over so that both sides are butter-coated. The first side should be grilled for 3 minutes, then turn the fish and cook the second side for a further 7 minutes.

Dust the steaks with a little more flour, baste well with the buttery pan juices and brown under a slightly hotter grill for about 1 minute more. Once cooked, the flesh is firm and will shrink slightly from the bone.

Lift the salmon steaks from the grill pan, top with a slice of the parsley butter and serve at once.
Serves 4

Quick pizza

No lengthy yeast dough to make for this recipe: a savoury scone mixture provides the base for the pizza topping. Serve warm from the oven with a crisp salad.

225 g/8 oz self-raising flour	25 g/1 oz butter
1 level teaspoon baking powder	50 g/2 oz finely grated hard cheese
½ level teaspoon salt	1.5 dl/¼ pint milk

for the topping:

2 tablespoons oil	pinch oregano or marjoram
1 medium-sized onion, finely chopped	salt and freshly milled pepper
	50 g/2 oz grated hard cheese
2 tablespoons concentrated tomato purée	anchovy fillets or stuffed olives

Sift the flour, baking powder and salt together. Rub in the butter and add the grated cheese. Stir in the milk and using a fork mix to a rough dough in the basin. Turn out on to a floured surface and knead lightly until smooth. Cover and rest in a cool place for 10 minutes while preparing the topping.

Heat the oil in a saucepan. Add the onion and fry gently for a few moments until softened but not brown. Stir in the tomato purée, the herbs and a seasoning of salt and pepper. Cook for a moment and then draw off the heat.

Roll out the prepared scone dough to a circle of about 23 cm (9 in) in diameter. Slide on to a greased baking tray. Spread the tomato mixture over the surface right to the edges. Sprinkle gently with the grated cheese and top with a lattice-work of anchovy fillets or garnish with a few sliced olives. Place in the centre of a hot oven (220°C., 425°F., Gas Mark 7) and bake for 20–25 minutes or until well risen. Cut into wedges and serve warm.

Cuts into 6 portions

Sandwich fillings

Sandwiches can be made in advance. Wrap in greaseproof paper and then over-wrap in foil or place in a polythene bag. A damp lettuce leaf placed on top of the stack of sandwiches before wrapping will keep them moist and can be discarded afterwards. Refrigerate the sandwiches until required.

Use sliced bread or a day-old loaf for sandwiches. If the loaf is very fresh, store in the refrigerator for a few hours before cutting. When you have a large number of sandwiches to prepare it really is worth-while and much more economical to soften the butter to be used by beating 2 teaspoons hot water into every 100 g (4 oz) butter – beat in by hand or with a mixer. The butter will go to a creamy consistency that is easy to spread thinly and does not harden.

Line up the bread slices in pairs on your working surface, pairing the slices that were next to each other in the loaf, so that the sandwich edges will match. Butter all slices to the very edge – this keeps the bread moist and prevents the filling from soaking through. Spread filling on alternate slices; be generous, but do not over-fill.

Cheese, apple and walnut

100 g/4 oz Cheddar cheese
2 dessert apples

squeeze of lemon juice
50 g/2 oz walnuts

Coarsely grate the cheese. Peel, core and grate the apples and toss in a little lemon juice. Coarsely chop the walnuts and mix all together. Use to fill six sandwiches.

Cream cheese and prawns

2 85-g/3-oz packets cream cheese
1–2 tablespoons cream
salt and freshly milled pepper

100 g/4 oz peeled prawns
squeeze of lemon juice

Beat the cream cheese until soft, adding a little cream or milk. Season with salt and pepper. Chop the prawns and stir into the mixture. Add a squeeze of lemon juice to taste. Use to fill six sandwiches.

Egg and watercress

6 eggs
25 g/1 oz butter

salt and pepper
1 bunch watercress

Hard-boil the eggs and shell them. While still hot put the eggs in a basin with the butter. Season with salt and pepper and using a knife chop the eggs coarsely. The heat from the eggs melts the butter which blends in and makes a firm filling that does not fall out of the sandwiches. Use with the washed watercress to fill six sandwiches.

Date, apple and lettuce

1 box dessert dates
2 dessert apples

1 tablespoon salad cream
3–4 leaves lettuce

Stone the dates and chop coarsely. Peel and chop the apples and mix with the salad cream. Shred the lettuce finely. Mix all the ingredients together and use to fill six sandwiches.

VARIATIONS
Other fillings that taste particularly good include thin slices of salami and lettuce; liver pâté and lettuce; sliced cold roast beef with a little creamed horseradish; flaked canned salmon moistened with salad cream and slices of cucumber; sardines mashed with lemon juice and lettuce; or slices of ham spread with mustard and topped with a slice of cheese.

Piperade

Tomato, onion and green pepper flavour this omelette. If you like the traditional taste of garlic, rub a crushed clove round the inside of the basin to be used for mixing the eggs.

4 eggs
salt and freshly milled pepper
2 tomatoes
1 medium-sized onion

1 medium-sized green pepper
1–2 tablespoons oil
25 g/1 oz butter

Crack the eggs into a basin and whisk thoroughly with a fork. Add a seasoning of salt and pepper and set aside while preparing the vegetables.

Scald the tomatoes and peel away the skins. Halve, deseed and slice the tomatoes. Peel and slice the onion and deseed and shred the green pepper. Heat the oil in a frying pan and add the onion and green pepper. Fry gently until both are soft but not brown. Add the tomato flesh and cook gently until the vegetables are quite soft. Draw off the heat and add the cooked vegetables to the egg mixture.

Heat the butter in a clean frying pan. When frothing pour in the omelette mixture. Stir for a moment then allow the omelette to cook gently until brown on the underside and set but still moist on top. Loosen the omelette, slide on to a plate and put back into the pan reversed to cook the second side. Serve with a salad and brown bread and butter.
Serves 2

Fried chicken with peperonata

The chicken in this recipe is served with a delicious spicy tomato and green pepper sauce. The sauce goes well with chicken but it can be cooked separately and served with steak or chops.

4 chicken joints
25 g/1 oz butter
2 tablespoons olive oil
2 medium-sized onions, peeled and sliced
1 clove garlic, crushed and finely chopped

2–3 green peppers
450 g/1 lb tomatoes
2 level teaspoons castor sugar
1 level teaspoon paprika
salt and freshly milled pepper
bay leaf
few black or green olives

Wipe the chicken joints and trim neatly. Melt the butter and oil in a large frying pan. Add the chicken joints and fry gently for about 15 minutes, turning to brown on both sides.

Meanwhile, prepare the onion and garlic, halve, deseed and shred the peppers. Scald the tomatoes and peel away the skins. Slice the tomatoes, then add along with the prepared vegetables to the chicken. Sprinkle with the sugar, paprika and a seasoning of salt and pepper. Add the bay leaf and cover with a lid. Simmer gently for a further hour; no liquid is needed as sufficient will come from the tomatoes.

About 5 minutes before serving add the olives, then check seasoning and serve the chicken joints with the rich vegetable sauce that will have cooked around them.
Serves 4

Grouse

In season August 12th–December 10th. Has a very distinctive flavour. Needs to hang 4–6 days depending on age. Allow one bird per serving. Roast young birds, but cook older ones in a casserole as they can be tough.

To roast, place a nut of butter inside each trussed bird and tie fatty bacon rashers over the breast. Set each bird on a slice of toast and roast in a hot oven (220°C., 425°F., Gas Mark 7) for about 25–30 minutes according to size. Remove bacon rashers towards end of cooking time. Dredge breast with flour, baste and return to oven to brown. Serve on the toast on which it was cooked – sometimes the lightly fried liver of the grouse is spread on the toast before roasting.

Chicken mayonnaise

Chicken salad is too nice to make only when there are leftover pieces from a roast bird. Select the pieces you like – leg or breast portions – and cook them specially. Cold chicken has a lovely flavour and a salad is an ideal way of serving it in hot weather.

4 chicken joints
25 g/1 oz butter
1 cucumber

salt and freshly milled pepper
2 hard-boiled eggs
chopped chives

for the dressing:

1.5 dl/¼ pint double cream
3 rounded tablespoons mayonnaise

1 tablespoon lemon juice
1 teaspoon made mustard

Wipe the chicken joints, spread a little of the butter on each joint, arrange in a roasting tin and cover with a buttered paper. Place in the centre of a moderate oven (180°C., 350°F., Gas Mark 4) and bake for 1 hour or until tender. Remove from the oven and allow the joints to cool.

Meanwhile, peel the cucumber and cut in half lengthways. Remove the centre seeds and then dice the flesh. Place in a saucepan, cover with cold water and bring up to the boil. Draw off the heat, drain and allow to cool. This blanching removes indigestible juices and improves the colour of the cucumber. Combine the chicken and cucumber in a basin, season well with salt and pepper and toss to mix.

For the dressing, blend the cream, mayonnaise, strained lemon juice and mustard. Check taste, adding more mustard if liked – for the best flavour use English mustard. Pour the dressing over the chicken and cucumber and toss well. Pile the salad on to a serving platter, garnish with slices of hard-boiled egg and sprinkle with finely chopped chives. Serve with brown bread and butter.

Serves 4

Cold chicken with lemon sauce

Chicken flesh keeps deliciously moist if the bird is allowed to cool in the liquor after cooking. This is a very summery recipe and one that is easy to make in advance. Serve it with a cold rice salad made colourful with the addition of tomatoes, cucumber and cooked peas – see page 185.

1 chicken, about 1.5–1.75 kg/
  3½–4 lb dressed weight

1 whole onion, peeled
bay leaf

for the sauce:

25 g/1 oz butter
1 rounded tablespoon flour
3 dl/½ pint chicken stock (see
  method)
salt and freshly milled pepper

juice and finely grated rind of
  1 lemon
2 egg yolks
3 dl/½ pint single cream

Wipe the chicken and place in the largest pan you have. Add the onion and bay leaf and cover with cold salted water. Cover with a lid and bring slowly to the boil. Simmer for 1 hour then draw off the heat and allow the chicken to cool in the liquid, preferably overnight. When cold discard the chicken skin and bones and cut the flesh into neat pieces. Arrange on a serving plate.

Remove any fat from the chicken stock and measure out 3 dl/½ pint. Melt the butter for the sauce in a saucepan over low heat. Stir in the flour and cook gently for 1 minute. Gradually add the stock and bring to the boil, stirring all the time for a smooth sauce. Simmer gently for 2–3 minutes. Season with salt and pepper and stir in the strained lemon juice and grated rind.

Place the egg yolks in a small basin and blend with the cream. Mix well and stir into the hot sauce. Stir over low heat for a few moments, but on no account allow the sauce to boil. Draw off the heat and recheck flavour. Pour into a basin and allow to cool, stirring occasionally to prevent a skin forming. The sauce will thicken considerably on cooling. Spoon the cold sauce over the chicken several hours in advance of serving. Then cover and keep in a cool place.
Serves 6

Chicken in barbecue sauce

Chicken takes the flavour of spice ingredients very well. Serve this recipe with a mound of plain boiled rice cooked with a slice of lemon to keep it nice and white.

1 oven-ready chicken, about
  1.75 kg/4 lb, jointed into 6

for the barbecue sauce:
1 onion
1 tablespoon oil
1 level teaspoon salt
freshly milled pepper
4 level tablespoons soft brown sugar
1 level tablespoon cornflour

50 g/2 oz butter
½ lemon, thinly sliced

2 teaspoons made mustard
1 teaspoon Worcestershire sauce
juice of ½ lemon
1 71-g/2½-oz can concentrated
  tomato purée
3 dl/½ pint water

Trim the chicken pieces neatly. Heat the butter in a frying pan, add the chicken and fry gently to brown. Lift the chicken from the pan and arrange in a casserole with the slices of lemon.

Peel and finely chop the onion. Heat the oil in a saucepan, add the onion and cook gently for a few moments until the onion is tender. Measure the remaining ingredients for the sauce into a basin. Blend well and then add to the onion in the pan. Stir to mix, bring up to the boil and simmer for 5 minutes. Draw the pan off the heat and pour the sauce over the chicken joints.

Cover the casserole and place in the centre of a moderate oven (180°C., 350°F., Gas Mark 4) and cook for 1 hour. Spoon the chicken and sauce into a hot serving dish before you take it to the table.
Serves 6

Veal and ham plate pie

Use a flat ovenware or enamel plate for this pie. The pastry crust underneath the pie is not easy to cook completely if a deep pie dish is used. Serve veal and ham plate pie cold for supper or take it on a picnic outing. Serve with fresh tomatoes or a coleslaw salad.

225 g/8 oz shortcrust pastry	beaten egg to glaze

for the filling:

225 g/8 oz lean veal	pinch dried mixed herbs
225 g/8 oz lean gammon	1 heaped teaspoon chopped parsley
2 hard-boiled eggs	finely grated rind of ½ lemon
1 tablespoon oil	freshly milled black pepper
2 tablespoons stock	

Divide the pastry in half and roll one piece out to a circle large enough to line a 20-cm (8-in) greased pie plate. Set aside while preparing the filling.

Cut the veal into neat very small pieces. Trim the rind from the gammon and pass the gammon flesh through a mincer. Shell the eggs and cut each one in half lengthways. Mix the oil, stock, herbs, chopped parsley, lemon rind and a good seasoning of black pepper. Mix with the chopped veal and leave to soak for 30 minutes. Then add the minced gammon and mix well.

Spread half the filling over the pastry. Top with the eggs, placing them cut side down. Cover with the remaining filling. Roll out the remaining pastry to a circle large enough to cover the pie. Damp the pie pastry edges and cover with the pastry top. Seal the edges together and trim neatly. Use any trimming to decorate the pie, then cut a cross in the pie centre and turn in the corners to make a reasonably sized hole in the centre. Glaze the pie with beaten egg.

Place in the centre of a moderately hot oven (200°C., 400°F., Gas Mark 6) and bake for 30 minutes. Then reduce the oven heat to 180°C., 350°F., Gas Mark 4 and bake for a further 30–40 minutes to cook the filling. Leave the pie until quite cold. To make a little jellied stock (which is used to fill any space between the filling and the pastry top in a cold pie) dissolve 1 level teaspoon powdered gelatine in half a teacup chicken stock, made using a cube. Allow to cool until beginning to thicken and then pour into the pie through the hole in the centre. Use the knife blade to lift the pastry crust a little and encourage the jelly to flow underneath. Keep the pie in a cool place until ready to serve.
Serves 4-6

Onions à la Grecque

These sweet and sour onions in a well-flavoured dressing can be served as part of an hors-d'oeuvre or on their own as an accompaniment to cold meats.

450 g/1 lb small button onions
1.5 dl/¼ pint water
4 tablespoons dry white wine or wine vinegar
25 g/1 oz sugar
2 tablespoons oil

juice of ½ lemon
1 tablespoon concentrated tomato purée
salt and freshly milled pepper
1 tablespoon seedless raisins
freshly chopped parsley

Peel the onions, leaving them whole. Cover with fresh cold water and bring to the boil. Simmer for 5 minutes to blanch and then drain. Return the onions to the pan and add the remaining ingredients except the parsley. Bring up to the boil, then cover and simmer gently for 25 minutes or until the onions are tender.

Using a perforated spoon lift out the onions and place in a serving dish. Boil the liquid in the pan to reduce and concentrate the

flavour. Taste and check seasoning. Pour over the onions and set aside until quite cold. Sprinkle with chopped parsley and serve.
Serves 4-6

Hot breads for salad meals

Slices of crisp, buttery herb-flavoured breads combine deliciously with summer meals, particularly cold foods. Serve hot breads for a barbecue or outdoor meal and flavour them with herbs, garlic or savoury cheese.

Slice two Vienna loaves into diagonal slices, leaving the bottom crust whole. Spread both sides of each slice with any of the following flavoured butters; any butter left over may be spread over the top of the loaves. Wrap each loaf in aluminium foil and heat through in a moderately hot oven (200°C., 400°F., Gas Mark 6) for 15–20 minutes. Serve at once; keep wrapped in the foil to hold the heat.
Serves 6

Herb butter

100 g/4 oz butter	1 tablespoon finely chopped parsley
2 teaspoons lemon juice	1 level teaspoon dried mixed herbs

Cream the butter and lemon juice together, then add the parsley and mixed herbs. Blend well and use as above.

Garlic butter

100 g/4 oz butter	1 clove garlic
2 teaspoons hot water	salt (see method)
1 tablespoon finely chopped parsley	

Cream the butter until soft with the hot water. Beat in the chopped parsley and the clove of garlic which has been peeled and mashed to a purée with a little salt. Use as above.

Savoury butter

100 g/4 oz butter	100 g/4 oz Cheddar cheese, grated
2 teaspoons hot water	1 tablespoon finely chopped parsley

Cream together the butter and hot water. Beat in the grated cheese and chopped parsley and use as above.

Cauliflower in curry dressing

The slightly nutty flavour of cauliflower comes through very well when served cold as a salad. A dressing of soured cream with a touch of curry powder gives just the right amount of piquancy to the dish.

1 head cauliflower	freshly chopped parsley

for the dressing:

1 carton soured cream	1 level teaspoon curry powder
½ level teaspoon castor sugar	squeeze of lemon juice

Break the head of cauliflower into small sprigs and rinse in cold water. Add to a pan of boiling salted water and simmer for about 8–10 minutes or until barely tender. Drain the sprigs of cauliflower and place in a serving bowl.

Blend the soured cream, sugar, curry powder and lemon juice to taste in a small basin. Pour over the cauliflower sprigs while they are still warm. Toss gently in the dressing and then set aside until quite cold. Sprinkle with chopped parsley and serve.

Serves 4

Summer tomato salad

Tomatoes for salad should be ripe but firm enough to slice thinly without squashing. This dressing is a change from the usual oil and vinegar mixture and has a pleasant piquant flavour. For gourmet freshness, prepare not more than 1 hour before serving.

450 g/1 lb firm tomatoes	few drops Worcestershire sauce
1 level tablespoon castor sugar	finely chopped fresh parsley and
salt and freshly milled pepper	mint
juice of 2 lemons	

Place the tomatoes in a large bowl, pour over boiling water and allow to stand for 1 minute. Drain and peel away the skins. Slice the tomatoes and arrange on a large shallow serving dish. Sprinkle with the sugar, a seasoning of salt and pepper, the strained lemon juice, Worcestershire sauce and plenty of washed finely chopped parsley

and mint. Leave to marinate for 30 minutes. Then toss and serve.
Serves 4

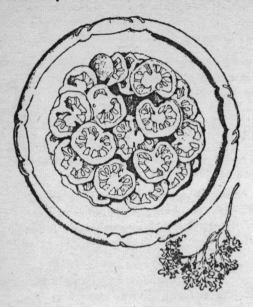

Corn on the cob

What a tremendous increase in popularity this vegetable has enjoyed in recent years. Where whole fresh cobs are cooked they can be served as a first course.

4 heads corn on the cob

75–100 g/3–4 oz butter for serving
salt

Remove the outer or green husks and silks from the cobs and trim the stalk ends level. Add the heads to boiling water; either use a large saucepan if cooking four at one time or use a large frying pan with 2.5 cm (1 in) boiling water and cover with a lid. Simmer for 15 minutes, turning the heads over in the water if necessary for even cooking.

Drain and serve hot with melted butter for pouring over and salt for sprinkling. Salt should not be added until after cooking to keep the corn tender.
Serves 4

216

Peaches ambrosia

Fresh peaches in an orange- and lemon-flavoured syrup – so easy and they taste like ambrosia. When you choose your fresh peaches remember that the pink blush on the skin is no test of ripeness – look for a change in colour from pale green to yellow around the stalk end.

6 peaches
175 g/6 oz castor sugar
3 dl/½ pint water

thinly pared rind of 1 orange
thinly pared rind and juice of
  1 lemon

Cut the peaches in half following the natural line in the skin. Separate the two halves and remove the centre stones. Blanch the peach halves for 30 seconds in boiling water and peel away the skins. Arrange the peach halves in a serving dish.

Measure the sugar and water into a saucepan. Add the pared rind from the orange and lemon and bring slowly to the boil. Simmer for 5 minutes then remove from the heat and add the lemon juice. Pour the syrup over the peaches. Cool and then chill until ready to serve.
Serves 6

Iced grapes

The idea of covering fresh fruit with whipped cream and then caramelizing the top with sugar like a crème brûlée did the rounds as a popular dinner party dessert a few years ago. Among the many different fruits used as the base were peaches soaked in brandy, fresh raspberries and mixed soft summer fruits. A contrast of green and black grapes is perhaps the most effective and certainly one that can be made all year round.

450 g/1 lb mixed green and black
  grapes
6 dl/1 pint double cream

3 rounded tablespoons demerara
  sugar

Peel, halve and deseed the grapes, then arrange over the base of a serving dish. Since the final dessert is put under a hot grill for a few minutes, choose a heatproof glass or china dish. Whisk the cream until thick, spoon over the grapes to cover and spread level. Set aside to chill thoroughly for several hours until the cream is firm.

Sprinkle the sugar over the top evenly, then place under a preheated hot grill. Grill just long enough for the sugar to melt, turning the dish round so that the surface is caramelized all over. Replace at once in the refrigerator and chill again so that the sugar topping becomes quite crisp before serving.

Serves 8

Blackcurrant ice cream

This ice cream has a marvellous fresh fruity flavour and a rich colour. It is a recipe that could be served for dessert at the smartest dinner party, yet the mixture is quickly prepared and does not need stirring during freezing.

450 g/1 lb blackcurrants	juice of ½ lemon
225 g/8 oz icing sugar	3 dl/½ pint double cream

Rinse the blackcurrants, then using a fork strip the berries from the stems. Crush the berries in a nylon sieve using a wooden spoon and retain the juices in a basin. Add the sieved icing sugar and the lemon juice and mix well. Beat the cream until thick and fold into the blackcurrant mixture.

Pour the ice cream into two large refrigerator ice trays and place in the frozen food compartment. Alternatively pour into one large polythene freezer box or into one or two waxed cartons, allowing at least 1 cm (½ in) headspace. Cover and place in the freezer. Freeze for several hours until firm.

Serves 6

Raspberry pudding

An old-fashioned recipe that's worth making when there are plenty of raspberries available.

450 g/1 lb raspberries	100 g/4 oz dry white breadcrumbs
100 g/4 oz castor sugar	3 eggs
25 g/1 oz butter	icing sugar

Hull and wash the raspberries and place in a saucepan along with the sugar. Warm gently over low heat, crushing a few of the berries until the juice begins to run. Continue to heat gently until the fruit is quite soft and a purée is formed. Draw off the heat and pass through a sieve. Add the warmed butter and stir in the breadcrumbs.

Stir in the eggs and mix well. Pour the mixture into a well-buttered

1-litre (2-pint) baking dish. Place in the centre of a moderate oven (180°C., 350°F., Gas Mark 4) and bake for 1 hour. Allow to cool. Dust the top with icing sugar and serve warm or cold with single cream.
Serves 6

Blackcurrant fool

One unbeaten egg white added to the cream before whisking does increase the volume of the cream. This results in a lighter, not so rich blackcurrant fool which some may prefer.

450 g/1 lb blackcurrants
2 tablespoons water
100 g/4 oz castor sugar

3 dl/½ pint double cream
sponge fingers for serving

Wash the blackcurrants and remove any leaves, but there is no need to strip the berries from the stems. Place the fruit in a large saucepan and add the water. Cover with a lid and simmer over low heat for 10 minutes or until the fruit is soft. Draw the pan off the heat and stir in the sugar. Rub the fruit and juices through a sieve, preferably a nylon sieve, into a mixing basin to make a purée. Discard all seeds, skins and stalks left in the sieve. Set the purée aside to cool.

Whip the cream until thick in a large mixing basin, then fold the fruit purée into the cream. Pour into a glass serving dish and chill for several hours before serving. Serve the blackcurrant fool with soft sponge fingers.
Serves 4-6

Fresh lemonade

Fresh home-made lemonade is a refreshing summer drink. Lemonade is a generic name for all long, thirst-quenching drinks with a taste of lemon juice. Bottled lemonade is always sparkling – this is a still lemonade. Choose large juicy lemons.

3 lemons
100 g/4 oz castor sugar

a scant litre/1½ pints water

Scrub the lemons, halve and squeeze out the juice. Reserve the lemon juice and place the lemon halves in a basin along with the sugar. Measure the water into a kettle or saucepan and bring up to the boil. Pour over the lemons and sugar and stir to dissolve the sugar. Leave until cold.

Strain the lemonade into a jug, add the lemon juice and chill well before serving. Pour into ice-filled tumblers and serve.
Makes 6 glasses

Lemonade syrup for drinks

Holiday time is a thirsty time for children. Make up a concentrated lemonade syrup and keep it in a cold larder or refrigerator ready to dilute with water for a refreshing lemon drink. Tartaric acid, often used in the preparation of lemon drinks, is available from chemists. Made up in quantity this is also ideal for the drinks stall at a garden fête.

2 lemons
675 g/1½ lb castor sugar

25 g/1 oz tartaric acid
a generous litre/ 2 pints water

Scrub the lemons and cut in half. Squeeze out the juice and set aside. Place the rinds in a large basin and add the sugar and tartaric acid. Pour on the boiling water and stir to dissolve the sugar. Leave until cold.

As the rinds soften, press occasionally with a wooden spoon to extract all the flavour. When cold, squeeze out and discard the lemon rinds. Add the lemon juice. Strain and pour into bottles – this mixture makes sufficient to fill about two large lemonade bottles. Cover and store in a cool place. The syrup will keep for about 2 weeks.

To use, dilute one part of syrup with two parts of water and add ice if liked.
Makes 36 glasses

Coffee syrup

Make this syrup with freshly ground or instant coffee. If using fresh coffee choose a medium-ground Kenya blend for the best flavour. Store the ready-made syrup in the refrigerator. With chilled milk, you can make iced coffee instantly.

175 g/6 oz ground coffee
6 dl/1 pint boiling water

175 g/6 oz granulated sugar

Measure the coffee into a saucepan. Pour in the boiling water and stir well. Return to the heat for about 1 minute until the coffee just comes to the boil. Draw off the heat, cover and leave to infuse for 6–8 minutes.

Strain through muslin or a fine strainer and return the coffee to the pan. Add the sugar. Stir over low heat to dissolve the sugar, then boil without stirring for 2 minutes. Remove from the heat and allow to cool. Pour into a bottle, cover and store in a cool place.

To use, measure 2–3 tablespoons syrup into a tall glass and top up with milk. Stir well before serving.
Makes about 7 dl (1¼ pints) syrup

VARIATION
To make the syrup with instant coffee, measure 225 g (8 oz) sugar and 4 heaped tablespoons instant coffee into a saucepan. Stir in 3 dl (½ pint) boiling water. Stir until the sugar has dissolved, then boil for 2 minutes without stirring. Draw off the heat and allow to cool. Bottle and store in a cool place.
Makes 4 dl (¾ pint) syrup

Home-made lemonade
On a really hot day make a cool, fresh lemon drink with the sharp tangy flavour of the whole fruit. Blender lemonade is best made on a larger machine – usually free-standing and with a 1-litre (1½-pint) capacity.

Cut 2 whole lemons into chunky pieces including skin and pips. Place in the blender container. Add 4 rounded tablespoons castor sugar and a scant 0.5 litre (1 pint) cold water. If the blender is marked with the capacity up the sides, then fill to the 1-litre (1½-pint) level.

Cover and blend on high speed until the lemons are chopped up. Then strain into ice-filled tumblers. Makes enough for 3.

Sweet pickled peaches

Peaches take spicy sweet pickle flavours very well indeed. A sweet pickled fruit like this should be served with cold meat, particularly ham, gammon or pork. Make some now for Christmas.

1.75 kg/4 lb fresh peaches
900 g/2 lb granulated sugar
6 dl/1 pint distilled malt vinegar
2 teaspoons whole cloves

2 teaspoons whole allspice
3 sticks cinnamon, each about
  5 cm/2 in long
1 piece root ginger

Dip the peaches, a few at a time, into a pan of boiling water. Leave for about 30 seconds, then lift out with a perforated spoon and place immediately in a bowl of cold water. Peel away the skins, halve the fruit and remove the stones.

Measure the sugar and vinegar into a large saucepan and add the crushed cloves and allspice, the sticks of cinnamon and bruised ginger loosely tied in a muslin bag. Stir over low heat until the sugar has dissolved, then bring up to the boil. Add the peaches to the spiced, sweetened vinegar and simmer gently until the fruit is tender. Drain the fruit from the liquid and remove the bag of spices.

Replace the saucepan of vinegar over the heat and boil quickly until reduced to a thin, honey-like syrup. Meanwhile pack the peaches neatly into clean warm jars. Draw the boiling syrup off the heat and fill each jar with enough syrup to cover the fruit. Cover with a plastic top, or with a circle of greaseproof paper and then a square of cotton dipped in melted paraffin wax. Label and store for several months before using.

Makes 1¾ kg (4 lb)

Bottled fruit salad

Bottling is considered rather old-fashioned these days, but it is a form of preservation that is particularly good for fruits and should not be entirely forgotten. Try bottling a variety of fruits to make a fruit salad which can be served straight from the jar during winter months. Any mixture of fruits can be used, but avoid dark-skinned fruits which are inclined to colour all the others and bananas which tend to ferment.

1.25 kg/3 lb plums, preferably
  Victoria
675 g/1½ lb small seedless green
  grapes

12 ripe peaches
1.25 kg/3 lb ripe pears

for the syrup:
1.75 litres/2 pints water

1 kg/2¼ lb granulated sugar

Prepare the sugar syrup first, before preparing the fruit. Measure the water into a saucepan, add the sugar and stir over low heat until the sugar has dissolved. Bring up to the boil, simmer for 2 minutes and draw off the heat.

Wash the plums, remove the stalks, then halve the fruit and remove the stones. Wash the grapes and remove any stalks – halve and deseed if using large grapes. Plunge the peaches into boiling water for 30 seconds, drain and place in cold water. Peel away the skins, halve the fruit and remove the stones. Keep submerged in cold water until required. Halve, core, quarter and peel the pears and keep submerged in cold water to prevent discolouration.

Pack a selection of the fruit in each of six clean jars. Stand the jars about 5 cm (2 in) apart on a baking tray lined with folded newspaper. Bring the syrup up to the boil and fill each jar to the brim with the hot syrup. Cover with the lids or rubber rings and lids, according to the type used. Place in the centre of a slow oven (150°C., 300°F., Gas Mark 2) and process for 1 hour 10 minutes. Remove the jars from the oven; using an oven cloth to protect the fingers press down the lid on each one and seal or put on the screw caps and screw down tightly. Leave until quite cold. Test the seal before storing.
Fills approximately 6 1-kg (2-lb) jars

Using the freezer in August

Cool summer drinks are always in demand on hot days. If you have a freezer keep a good collection of ice cubes handy. To prevent them from sticking together when stored in a bag either use the rubber ice-cube trays from which the cubes can be pressed without running under cold water, or turn out the ice cubes and arrange on a flat tin or tray. Space them apart, so they do not touch. Replace in the freezer, uncovered, for long enough for the outside surfaces of the cubes to freeze dry. Tip the ice cubes into a bag and they will stay separate. Tie the ice bag closed and keep in the freezer, adding more cubes when necessary.

Decorative ice cubes are pretty. Take a tip and make these cubes with water that has been boiled and allowed to cool. Boiled water freezes clear whereas tap water freezes cloudy. At this time of year tiny mint sprigs, fresh raspberries or strawberries, grapes or segments of orange or lemon can be set in the ice-cube trays. Afterwards you can see the garnish through the ice quite clearly. Slices of fresh orange or lemon can be frozen – a good way to make use of any leftover cut fruits, and a helpful bit of advance preparation for a party. Open-freeze the slices on a flat tray until firm, then tip into a bag. Frozen orange and lemon slices flavour and cool drinks at the same time.

Freezing autumn fruits and vegetables Late maturing vegetables and fruits from the trees and hedgerow are autumn's contribution to the freezer. These need more careful preparation than early summer varieties but nevertheless considerably add to the variety and flavour of winter recipes.

Runner beans Top and tail and string the beans. Beans finely shredded tend to become limp; better to cut the beans in chunks of about 2.5 cm (1 in). Blanch beans for 2 minutes for chunks, and for 1 minute for shredded. Open-freeze on a tray until firm, then tip into a polythene bag for storage.

Cauliflower Cauliflower is best frozen in sprigs; separate the head into even-sized flowerets. Wash and soak in salt water then blanch for 3 minutes with lemon juice added to the blanching water to help keep the colour. Cool then open freeze until firm and pack in rigid containers.

Green peppers Freeze peppers sliced for soups or stews. Wash carefully then remove seeds and membrane. Blanch sliced peppers for 2 minutes.

Mushrooms Cultivated mushrooms are best for freezing and must be very fresh and white. Leave button mushrooms whole, wipe the head with a cloth. Larger mushrooms can be sliced. Pack them dry but for short-term storage only.

Tomatoes Tomatoes frozen are not good for salads, but if available cheaply or from the garden scald and skin them and freeze whole. Use in casseroles, stews or soups – they are too watery to fry.

Sweetcorn This should be quite fresh and firm. Remove the leaves and silk threads. Blanch similar-sized cobs together allowing 5 minutes for a small cob and up to 8 minutes for larger ones. Cool and dry then pack in pairs. Thaw for several hours in the refrigerator before cooking.

Peaches Peaches lose their firm texture but are useful for adding to fruit salad. Scald in boiling water for 30 seconds to remove skins. Then halve and remove stones. Freeze in a syrup to prevent discolouration, using 450 g (1 lb) sugar dissolved in a generous litre (2 pints) water. Freeze in rigid containers. Thaw in the unopened container. These are even better if a tablespoon of brandy is added before serving. Use in trifles or for serving with ice cream.

Cranberries Should be firm and glossy. Sort through the fruit and discard any soft berries. Wash and pack dry, unsweetened, or for a purée stew in a very little water and then add 225 g (8 oz) sugar for 6 dl (1 pint) fruit purée. Freeze in rigid containers.

Apples Peel, core and then slice apples into acidulated water. Freeze in dry packs, without blanching, for using in recipes like stewed apple compote or apple crumble. Label dessert and cooking apples for identification afterwards and to make sure they are used in recipes that suit the apple. Use dry-pack apple slices from frozen. Apple slices can also be frozen with sugar using 225 g (8 oz) sugar for every 900 g (2 lb) apple slices. These are useful for using in pies when the apples are already sweetened. Thaw until the fruit can be broken apart before spooning into the pie dish. Cooking apples can be reduced to a purée, in which case pulp down apple slices using 2–3 tablespoons water for every 900 g (2 lb) apples. Sweeten to taste, using about 175–225 g (6–8 oz) sugar. Use for apple sauce – freeze in small containers of quantities likely to be used at one time. Thaw in the refrigerator and the purée is ready to serve as an accompaniment to roast pork.

Blackberries Blackberries freeze perfectly. They can be picked, rinsed and put straight in the freezer without the addition of sugar. Store in polythene bags. Use for jams or jellies, fruit mousse or compotes. Blackberries can be frozen with sugar using 225 g (8 oz) sugar for every 900 g (2 lb) fruit. For pies, apple slices and black-berries can be combined in proportions of 675 g (1½ lb) apple slices and 225 g (8 oz) blackberries for each pie. Sweeten as above.

Plums and damsons The skins of stone fruits such as these toughen on storage and the stones affect the flavour unless removed. Damsons can only be stored in purée form whereas plums cut in half, stones removed and popped in a polythene bag for short storage can be used in jams and jellies. Otherwise they can be prepared and frozen in a sugar syrup made using 450 g (1 lb) sugar dissolved in a generous litre (2 pints) water. Use these in fruit cobbler, crumble or other cooked recipes.

September

From a culinary point of view, *September* brings a change. This is the last month when we can enjoy eating out-of-doors, but there is plenty of work to be done in the kitchen. Now is the time to preserve and bottle the fruits of autumn and to prepare traditional chutneys.

Game is back with the exception of pheasant, and white fish improve as the cold weather approaches. Autumn vegetables like onions, marrow, sweet peppers and aubergines combine to make interesting cooked vegetable dishes and give unusual flavours when added to casseroles. There are many varieties of home-grown apples and pears to choose from and an abundance of plums and damsons which will make lovely autumn puddings. Baskets should be looked out, for soon the wild blackberries in the hedgerow will be ready for picking.

Pears vinaigrette

Mint gives the essential flavour to the dressing served over these pears. Take care to chop mint with a stainless steel knife to preserve the colour and add just before serving for the freshest taste.

4 ripe dessert pears

for the dressing:

salt and freshly milled black pepper
 1 teaspoon castor sugar
juice of 1 lemon
4 tablespoons salad oil

1 rounded tablespoon finely
  chopped mixed parsley and mint
4 crisp lettuce leaves for serving

Choose ripe dessert pears such as Comice or Williams. Measure a good seasoning of salt and pepper and the sugar for the dressing into a bowl. Add the strained lemon juice and stir in the oil. The chopped parsley and mint are added just before spooning the dressing over the pears.

Peel the pears, cut in half and remove the core with a teaspoon. Arrange on a salad plate with crisp lettuce leaves and immediately spoon over the dressing. Serve with brown bread and butter.
Serves 4

Mozzarella cheese salad

Mozzarella cheese from Italy has a smooth texture and is absolutely white in colour. It's a cheese that can do with a little 'dressing up' and goes well with salad ingredients. Serve it with sliced tomato and cucumber to make a striking first course that is cool and fresh on a hot day.

1 mozzarella cheese	4 large tomatoes
½ cucumber	

for the dressing:

1 clove garlic	dried oregano
1.5 dl/¼ pint olive oil	4 tablespoons wine vinegar
salt and freshly milled pepper	

Remove the paper wrapping and slice the mozzarella cheese. Peel and thinly slice the cucumber; skin and slice the tomatoes.

Peel the garlic and leave to marinate in the oil for about 1 hour. When the oil has taken the flavour remove and discard the garlic. Place a seasoning of salt and pepper, the oregano and the vinegar in a basin, add the oil and mix well.

Arrange slices of mozzarella, cucumber and tomato in neat lines of contrasting colours on four serving plates. Spoon over the dressing. Serve with freshly milled pepper over the top.
Serves 4

Mushroom soup

Use large open mushrooms to get a good flavour in mushroom soup. If they are field-picked, wash them well first.

350 g/12 oz mushrooms	25 g/1 oz flour
1 medium-sized onion	6 dl/1 pint milk
50 g/2 oz butter	salt and freshly milled pepper
4 dl/¾ pint chicken stock	2–3 tablespoons cream
bay leaf	

Wash the mushrooms and peel them. Peel the onion. Put the mushrooms and onion through the mincer or chop finely. Melt half the butter in a large saucepan and add the mushroom mixture. Cover with a lid and cook gently for about 5 minutes until the juices from the mushrooms run and the onion is soft. Add the stock and the bay leaf. Bring up to the boil and simmer for a further 15–30 minutes. Draw off the heat and pass the liquid and vegetables through a sieve or purée in a blender.

Melt the remaining butter in the hot saucepan and stir in the flour.

Cook gently for 1 minute. Add the milk gradually stirring all the time to get a smooth thin sauce. Bring up to the boil and simmer for 2–3 minutes, then season with salt and freshly milled pepper. Stir in the mushroom purée and blend well. The soup should have a fairly thin consistency. Bring back up to the boil, then draw off the heat. Stir in the cream, check seasoning and serve.

Serves 6

Home-made tomato soup

Home-made tomato soup is not so sweet as the canned varieties. Serve this one with small dice of crisply fried bread sprinkled over the top.

50 g/2 oz butter	1 level teaspoon castor sugar
2 carrots	1 tablespoon concentrated tomato
1 large onion	purée
675 g/1½ lb ripe tomatoes	salt and freshly milled pepper
a scant litre/1½ pints chicken stock	1 rounded tablespoon flour
few bacon rinds	2–3 tablespoons single cream

Melt half the butter in a saucepan over low heat. Add the peeled and sliced carrots and onion and fry gently for 5 minutes until the onion is soft but not browned. Wash the tomatoes, cut in half and add to the pan. Cover with a lid and fry gently to soften the tomatoes and draw out the juice. Stir in the stock and add the bacon rinds for flavour, the sugar, tomato purée and a seasoning of salt and pepper. Bring up to the boil and simmer gently for about 1 hour or until the vegetables are quite soft.

Draw the pan off the heat and pass the soup through a 'Mouli' or sieve to make a purée. Discard the bacon rinds and tomato skins remaining behind. Return the soup to the pan. Blend the remaining butter and the flour on a plate to make a *beurre manié*. Add to the hot soup in pieces, stir until melted, then bring up to the boil and cook, stirring, until thickened. Check seasoning and stir in the cream before serving.

Serves 6

Oysters
Oysters are in season from September 1st–April 30th. Natives, that is Colchester, Whitstable or Helford oysters, are sold within this season.

Others sold outside the season are imported. Native oysters are sold and eaten by the dozen, nines or half dozen and since they are eaten raw they must be very fresh with the shells tightly closed. If you give your fishmonger sufficient warning he will open them for you. They will be packed with the deep shell underneath to retain the oyster liquor. Serve the oysters open in the shells with the liquor. Arrange them on a flat plate and pass lemon wedges and thinly sliced brown bread and butter.

Ceviche

In this unusual recipe the fish is marinated in lemon or lime juice and the acid of the juice actually makes the fish tender and turns the flesh white. Use fresh halibut, a fish with a firm-textured flesh and one that tastes good in cold recipes or salads.

450 g/1 lb fresh halibut
juice of 2 large lemons, about
  6 tablespoons
1 onion
225 g/8 oz tomatoes
1 green pepper

1 tablespoon freshly chopped
  parsley
4 tablespoons olive oil
2 tablespoons vinegar
salt and freshly milled pepper
dash of Tabasco sauce

Trim the fish, remove any skin and cut the raw fish into small neat pieces. Place in a bowl and pour over the strained lemon juice. Place the fish in the refrigerator and leave to marinate for 4–6 hours, turning the pieces from time to time.

Peel and chop the onion. Scald the tomatoes and peel away the skins. Halve, remove the seeds and chop the tomato flesh coarsely. Halve, deseed and chop the green pepper. Add the onion, tomato, green pepper and chopped parsley to the fish with the oil and vinegar, a seasoning of salt and pepper and a dash of Tabasco sauce.

Chill for several hours more, then check seasoning and flavour before serving.
Serves 4

Halibut with mornay sauce

A mornay sauce is not just a cheese sauce, it is a cheese sauce enriched with egg yolk and cream – a sauce worthy of the more expensive types of fish. The addition of egg yolk encourages the mixture to brown under the grill and makes the finished recipe look very appetizing.

4 halibut steaks, about
  100–175 g/4–6 oz each
salt

for the sauce:
25 g/1 oz butter
25 g/1 oz flour
3 dl/½ pint milk
salt and freshly milled pepper

juice of ½ lemon
2 tablespoons milk
15 g/½ oz butter

50–75 g/2–3 oz grated hard cheese
1 egg yolk
2 tablespoons cream

Rinse the fish and place the steaks in a well-buttered large baking dish. Season with salt and squeeze over the lemon juice. Add the milk and place a small nut of butter on each steak. Cover the dish with buttered paper, place in the centre of a moderate oven (180°C., 350°F., Gas Mark 4) and bake for 25–30 minutes, until the fish is white and flakes easily from the bone.

Meanwhile melt the butter for the sauce in a pan over low heat. Stir in the flour and cook gently for 1 minute. Gradually stir in the milk, beating in each addition well before adding the next. Bring up to the boil and simmer for 1–2 minutes. Season with salt and freshly milled pepper and add 50 g (2 oz) of the cheese. Stir until the cheese has melted. Drain the liquid from the cooked fish into the sauce.

Gently lift the skin away from the halibut steaks and lift the fish out on to a hot serving plate. Stir the blended egg yolk and cream into the sauce. Pour over the fish and top with the remaining grated cheese. Brown under a hot grill and serve.
Serves 4

Pizza omelette

Sturdy, pancake-like flat omelettes are the kind to go for when you're hungry. The quantities of additional ingredients can be much more generous than in the filling for a folded omelette. This omelette with a savoury tomato and cheese topping makes a filling lunch or supper snack.

4 eggs
salt and freshly milled pepper

1 tablespoon cold water
25 g/1 oz butter

for the topping:

25 g/1 oz butter
1 medium-sized onion, chopped
2 teaspoons concentrated tomato purée

pinch mixed herbs
3–4 lean bacon rashers
50 g/2 oz grated cheese

Crack the eggs into a basin, add the seasoning and water. Mix thoroughly with a fork and set aside while preparing the topping.

Melt the butter for the topping in a saucepan. Add the chopped onion, cover and cook gently for 4–5 minutes or until the onion is tender. Add the tomato purée and mixed herbs, cook for a moment and then draw off the heat. Trim and chop the bacon rashers. Fry in a dry pan until the fat runs and the bacon is cooked. Drain and reserve.

Place the butter in a 20- to 23-cm (8- to 9-in) heavy frying pan. When melted and bubbling pour in all the omelette mixture. Stir for a moment, drawing the omelette mixture in towards the centre of the pan. When set underneath, but still moist on top, draw the pan off the heat. Cover with the tomato and onion mixture. Then top with the bacon and sprinkle with the cheese.

Place the omelette under a hot grill just long enough for the cheese to melt and brown. Slide out of the pan on to a hot dish and serve.
Serves 2

Creamed fish

Serve creamed fish over hot fluffy rice, in crisp vol-au-vent cases or on slices of hot buttered toast. You can make the mixture even more special if you poach the fish in a little white wine and then use the wine along with milk to make the sauce.

450–675 g/1–1½ lb fresh haddock or cod fillet	25 g/1 oz flour
3 dl/½ pint milk	3 dl/½ pint fish cooking liquor (see method)
slice lemon	salt and freshly milled pepper
bay leaf	squeeze of lemon juice
few parsley stalks	1 egg yolk
few peppercorns	2 tablespoons single cream
40 g/1½ oz butter	

Cut the fish into pieces and place in a saucepan with the milk, slice of lemon, bay leaf, parsley stalks and peppercorns. Cover with a lid and simmer gently for about 15 minutes to cook the fish. Strain off the cooking liquor and reserve it for the sauce. Allow the fish to cool for a few moments, then carefully remove the skin and small bones and flake the flesh.

Melt the butter in a saucepan and stir in the flour. Cook over low heat for a few moments, then gradually stir in the reserved fish cooking liquor. Bring up to the boil, stirring well to make a smooth sauce. Simmer gently for 2–3 minutes. Add salt and pepper and lemon juice to taste.

Blend the egg yolk and cream together in a small basin. Add a little of the hot sauce, mix well and return to the saucepan. Stir to blend the sauce which should now be shiny and golden. Add the flaked fish, warm through gently and serve.

Serves 4

Haddock and egg mousse

This mousse looks best set in a shallow round mould about 20 cm (8 in) in diameter – a cake or baking tin is a good shape. When unmoulded the decoration shows up attractively. Otherwise, set the mixture in a white china soufflé dish and run the decoration over the surface.

450 g/1 lb smoked haddock fillet	6 dl/1 pint water
2 hard-boiled eggs	salt and a few peppercorns
1 onion, peeled and sliced	15 g/½ oz powdered gelatine
1 carrot, peeled and sliced	freshly milled pepper
few stalks parsley	juice of ½ lemon
bay leaf	3 dl/½ pint double cream

Cut the smoked haddock into pieces and slice the hard-boiled eggs. Set the eggs aside for the decoration of the mould. Place the onion, carrot, parsley stalks, bay leaf and water in a saucepan. Add a seasoning of salt and a few peppercorns. Bring up to the boil, cover with a lid and simmer gently for about 10 minutes. Add the pieces of haddock, re-cover and simmer gently for a further 10 minutes or until the haddock is cooked. Lift the pieces of haddock out of the pan and allow to cool. Then flake the flesh, removing all skin and any bones.

Boil up the fish liquid in the pan for a further 10 minutes to reduce and concentrate the flavour. Strain and measure out 3 dl ($\frac{1}{2}$ pint). Place the gelatine in a bowl and allow to soak for a few minutes with about 4 tablespoons of the fish liquid. Add the remainder and return to the saucepan. Stir over low heat just long enough to make certain the gelatine has dissolved.

Measure out 3 tablespoons of the gelatine liquid and dilute it by adding 2 tablespoons water. Set the rest of the jelly aside to cool. Pour about half of the diluted jelly into a 20-cm (8-in) cake tin or 1-litre ($1\frac{1}{2}$-pint) mould. Chill until the jelly has set. Arrange the egg slices flat in a circle over the jelly, add the remaining diluted jelly and chill until the decoration has set firm.

Mix the remainder of the gelatine – now cooled – with the flaked haddock. Add lemon juice and freshly milled pepper to taste. Lightly whip the cream and fold into the mixture. Taste and check seasoning. Pour into the decorated mould and chill until set firm. To serve, unmould on a plate, so that the jelly top with the egg slices is uppermost.
Serves 6

Wild duck In season from September 1st–February 17th. Needs hanging 1–3 days. Allow one bird for two people – wild duck are quite small.

To roast, spread the trussed bird with softened butter. Cook in a hot oven (220°C., 425°F., Gas Mark 7), basting frequently, for 25–30 minutes. Do not overcook.

Partridge In season September 1st–January 31st. Needs hanging 1–3 days. Allow one bird per person, larger birds could serve two. Young birds can be roasted; cook older birds in a casserole.

To roast, smear the trussed birds with butter and tie fat bacon rashers over the breast. Cook in a moderately hot oven (200°C., 400°F., Gas Mark 6) for 30 minutes. Towards the end of the cooking time remove the bacon rashers. Dredge the breast with flour, baste and return to the oven to brown.

Blender liver pâté

This mixture is easy to prepare and makes a rich, smooth-textured pâté. Serve it sliced with hot toast; any left over makes a good sandwich filling.

5 streaky bacon rashers
450 g/1 lb chicken livers
1 egg
1 slice white bread
1 level teaspoon dried mixed herbs

1 level teaspoon salt
freshly milled pepper
2 tablespoons dry sherry
1.5 dl/¼ pint double cream

Grease a small (18- by 10- by 5-cm, 7- by 4- by 2-in) loaf tin or a 1-litre (1½-pint) baking dish, line with the trimmed bacon rashers and set aside.

Trim the chicken livers and place in the blender goblet. Add the egg, the slice of bread, broken in pieces, the herbs, salt, a seasoning of pepper and the sherry. Cover and blend until smooth. Then stir in the double cream.

Pour the mixture into the prepared baking dish. Fold in any overlapping pieces of bacon and cover with a buttered paper or foil. Set in a roasting tin with 2.5 cm (1 in) water. Place in the centre of a very moderate oven (160°C., 325°F., Gas Mark 3) and bake for 2 hours. Leave until cold. Turn out and serve.

Serves 6

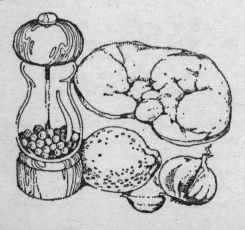

Veal with bacon and mushroom salad

A marinade can be used to give extra flavour to a delicate meat like veal. The egg marinade used here serves two purposes, to flavour the meat and coat it ready for cooking.

4 veal escalopes
50–75 g/2–3 oz fresh white
  breadcrumbs

50–75 g/2–3 oz butter
½ lemon

for the marinade:

1 large egg, lightly mixed
1 tablespoon oil

little finely grated lemon rind
freshly milled black pepper

for the salad:

225 g/8 oz button mushrooms
8 lean bacon rashers
4–5 tablespoons prepared French
  dressing

crisp lettuce leaves for serving

Place the veal in a shallow dish. Combine the ingredients for the marinade and pour over the escalopes. Leave for 30 minutes, turning the meat occasionally. When ready to cook, lift the meat from the marinade and coat both sides in the white breadcrumbs. Pat the coating on firmly and add the escalopes to the hot butter in the frying pan. Fry gently for 6–8 minutes, turning once, then lift from the pan on to a hot serving dish. Add a squeeze of lemon juice to the hot butter in the pan and pour over the escalopes.

Meanwhile trim and slice the mushrooms. Trim and chop the bacon rashers and fry until crisp. Drain the bacon from the fat in the pan and add it to the mushrooms in a basin. Add the French dressing and toss well to mix. Line a serving bowl with a few crisp lettuce leaves and pile the salad in the centre. Season well with freshly milled pepper and serve along with the veal.
Serves 4

Braised steak with onion rice

Braising is a good method of cooking cuts of steak that are not tender enough to grill. You get plenty of good gravy in this recipe, which blends well with the onion-flavoured rice.

a generous kg/2½ lb lean braising
  steak
seasoned flour
25 g/1 oz butter
2 medium-sized onions, peeled and
  finely chopped
2 bacon rashers
225 g/8 oz small mushrooms

1 clove garlic
3 dl/½ pint stock
1.5 dl/¼ pint red wine
1 rounded teaspoon cornflour
1 tablespoon cold water
4 medium-sized tomatoes
salt and freshly milled pepper

for the onion rice:

25 g/1 oz butter
1 onion, peeled and sliced

225 g/8 oz long-grain rice
6 dl/1 pint stock

Trim the steak and cut the meat into six neat pieces. Dip in
seasoned flour and then add to the hot melted butter in a wide
saucepan or shallow frying pan. Fry quickly to brown on both sides
then lift the meat from the pan. Add the onions and the trimmed
and chopped bacon rashers to the hot fat. Fry gently for 5 minutes
to soften the onions.

Meanwhile, trim and slice the mushrooms. Remove the outer
papery coating and chop the garlic finely. Add the mushrooms and
chopped garlic to the pan and fry for a few moments. Replace the
meat on the bed of vegetables and add the stock and wine. Cover
with a close-fitting lid and simmer gently for 1½–2 hours.

Towards the end of the cooking time prepare the onion rice. Melt
the butter in a saucepan, add the onion and cook gently until soft
and golden brown. Add the washed rice and toss well in the butter
and onion. Add the stock and stir until boiling, then cover and cook
very gently until the stock is absorbed and the rice is tender – this
takes about 20 minutes.

Lift the cooked meat from the pan and keep hot. Blend the cornflour
with the water and stir into the liquor in the pan. Stir until boiling.
Skin, halve and deseed the tomatoes, then chop the flesh and add to
the sauce. Simmer for a moment to heat through and check the
seasoning.

Spoon the rice on to a hot serving dish. Place the meat neatly on
top, spoon the sauce over and serve.

Serves 6

Meat sauce for pasta

Serve this meat sauce with spaghetti or ribbon noodles. It can be mixed in, in which case turn the pasta in the sauce with two forks, never stirring, or pass the sauce separately.

2 tablespoons oil
1 medium-sized onion
1 clove garlic
450 g/1 lb lean minced beef
2 level tablespoons flour
1 level teaspoon salt
freshly milled pepper

1 425-g/15-oz can peeled tomatoes
1 71-g/2½-oz can concentrated
  tomato purée
pinch dried mixed herbs
4 dl/¾ pint stock
1.5 dl/¼ pint red wine

Heat the oil in a medium-sized saucepan. Peel and finely chop the onion, peel the garlic and crush with a little salt. Add the onion to the hot oil, cover and cook gently for about 5 minutes until the onion is soft but not brown. Stir in the minced beef and the crushed garlic. Continue to fry gently for a moment to seal the meat.

Stir the flour, salt, pepper, tomatoes and juice from the can, tomato purée and mixed herbs into the meat mixture. Add the stock and red wine. Bring to the boil. Lower the heat and simmer gently for 40–45 minutes. Stir occasionally to prevent the sauce sticking and add a little extra stock if necessary. The final consistency should not be too thick. Check seasoning and use as required.
Makes 6 dl (1 pint) sauce

Lasagne verdi

Lasagne makes an inexpensive buffet supper dish. Plan the preparation of the recipe to suit your timetable. The tomato sauce can be made the day before. On the morning of the party assemble the lasagne, then cover and refrigerate until ready to heat through.

2 tablespoons oil
1 medium-sized onion
450 g/1 lb lean minced beef
1 clove garlic
1 level teaspoon salt
freshly milled pepper
1 397-g/14-oz can peeled tomatoes

tomato sauce (see next recipe)
225 g/8 oz lasagne with spinach
2 227-g/8-oz cartons cottage cheese
1 egg
50–75 g/2–3 oz grated Parmesan
  cheese

Heat the oil in a saucepan and add the peeled and finely chopped onion and the meat. Fry gently until the meat loses its red colour, then drain off the fat. Peel the garlic clove, crush with a little salt to a purée and add to the pan along with the salt and pepper. Stir in the contents of the can of tomatoes, break the tomatoes up with a fork and then add the tomato sauce. Bring up to a simmer. Cook gently, stirring occasionally, for about 1 hour until the meat is cooked and you have a fairly thick meat sauce.

Bring a large pan of salted water with 1 tablespoon oil added up to a brisk boil. Add the lasagne pieces, one at a time. Boil for about 15 minutes (or according to packet directions) until the lasagne is tender. Drain in a colander and separate out the pieces to cool. Meanwhile sieve the cottage cheese and mix with the egg. Have the Parmesan cheese handy.

To assemble the lasagne, spoon a little of the meat sauce into the base of a large shallow baking dish. Cover with a layer of lasagne, spoon over a layer of cottage cheese and sprinkle with Parmesan. Repeat the layers, ending with a layer of meat sauce. Finally sprinkle with Parmesan cheese.

Heat through in a moderate oven (180°C., 350°F., Gas Mark 4) for 30–40 minutes, allowing an extra 10–15 minutes if the lasagne has been refrigerated. For easier cutting allow the lasagne to stand for 10 minutes after removing from the oven.
Serves 6

Tomato sauce for lasagne

Tomato sauce is a necessary part of many pasta recipes. A few bacon rinds added with the bouquet garni gives extra flavour, or a tablespoon of concentrated tomato purée added with the stock.

450 g/1 lb tomatoes	salt and freshly milled pepper
1 carrot	3 dl/½ pint stock
1 onion	bouquet garni
25 g/1 oz butter	1 level tablespoon cornflour
1 level teaspoon castor sugar	3 tablespoons cold water

Scald the tomatoes in boiling water for a few seconds, then plunge into cold water to loosen the skins. Peel away the skins, halve the tomatoes and scoop out the seeds. Chop the tomato flesh roughly. Scrape and chop the carrot and peel and chop the onion.

Sauté the onion and carrot in the melted butter for 5–6 minutes. Add the chopped tomatoes and sauté for a further 5–6 minutes to draw the juices. Stir in the sugar, a seasoning of salt and pepper, the stock and the bouquet garni. Cover the pan with a lid and simmer for 30–40 minutes or until the vegetables are soft.

Remove the bouquet garni and press the sauce and vegetables through a sieve. Stir in the cornflour blended with the water. Return to the heat and stir until boiling. Check seasoning before using.

Makes 3 dl ($\frac{1}{2}$ pint) sauce

Chicken with tomatoes and sweet peppers

Tomatoes along with onions and green sweet peppers make a tasty and colourful combination of vegetables for a casserole. Only a little stock is required in this recipe since much of the juice needed will come from the tomatoes during cooking.

4 chicken joints
seasoned flour
50 g/2 oz butter
3 medium-sized onions
2 large green peppers

350 g/12 oz tomatoes
salt and freshly milled pepper
1 teaspoon castor sugar
1.5 dl/$\frac{1}{4}$ pint chicken stock

Trim the chicken joints neatly and dip both sides in seasoned flour. Add to the hot butter melted in a frying pan. Fry the chicken joints gently, turning to brown on both sides. Then lift from the pan and place in a casserole.

Peel and slice the onions and halve, deseed and shred the green peppers. Add these to the hot butter remaining in the frying pan. Cover and fry gently for about 10 minutes to soften them.

Meanwhile skin the tomatoes, then halve them and scoop out the seeds. Chop the tomato flesh up coarsely and add to the chicken joints along with the softened onion and green peppers. Season with salt and pepper and add the sugar. Add the stock. Cover the casserole with a lid, place in the centre of a moderate oven (180°C., 350°F., Gas Mark 4) and cook for 1 hour. Serve the chicken joints with the cooked vegetables and juices from the casserole.

Serves 4

Marrow in parsley sauce

Marrow is a difficult vegetable to cook satisfactorily; the secret is to blanch it first in boiling water and then finish cooking in a casserole.

1 medium-sized marrow   25 g/1 oz butter
salt and freshly milled pepper

for the sauce:

25 g/1 oz butter   salt and freshly milled pepper
1 level tablespoon flour   1 tablespoon chopped parsley
2 dl/⅓ pint (1 teacup) milk

Peel, halve and deseed the marrow. Cut the flesh into chunks and place in a saucepan. Cover with cold salted water and bring to the boil. Draw off the heat and drain. Place the marrow flesh in a casserole along with a seasoning of salt and pepper and the melted butter. Cover with a lid, place in the centre of a moderate oven (180°C., 350°F., Gas Mark 4) and bake for 25–30 minutes, until tender.

Meanwhile, melt the butter for the sauce over low heat. Stir in the flour and cook gently for 1 minute. Gradually stir in the milk, beating well to get a smooth sauce. Bring up to the boil, season, add the chopped parsley and simmer for 2–3 minutes.

When the marrow is cooked and ready to serve, drain away any liquid in the casserole. Pour over the sauce and serve.
Serves 4

Rice with almonds and raisins

Flaked almonds give recipes a delicious crunchy texture. This mixture of rice cooked in chicken stock with browned onions and almonds added is delicious served hot with fried chicken or pork chops.

175 g/6 oz long-grain rice   1 medium-sized onion
4 dl/¾ pint chicken stock (see   25 g/1 oz flaked almonds
  method)   1 tablespoon seedless raisins
25 g/1 oz butter   chopped parsley

Butter the inside of a medium-sized saucepan and measure in the rice and chicken stock. Use well-seasoned home-made chicken stock or a chicken bouillon cube. Bring to the boil, then lower the heat until the water is just simmering. Cover with a lid and leave the rice to cook gently for 15 minutes, without removing the lid. The rice grains will swell up and absorb all the stock. Draw the pan off the heat and leave to stand, still covered with the lid, for a further 5–10 minutes while preparing the remainder of the recipe.

Melt the butter in a good-sized 20- to 23-cm (8- to 9-in) frying pan. Add the peeled and finely chopped onion and fry gently, covered with a lid, until the onion is tender but not brown. Add the flaked almonds, raise the heat and fry more quickly to brown both the onion and almonds.

Add the raisins. Stir up the cooked rice with a fork and tip into the frying pan. Stir and toss the rice, onion, almonds and raisins together. Sprinkle with chopped parsley and serve hot.
Serves 4

Fried onions and green peppers

Fried onions on their own are sometimes rather dull, but the addition of green pepper makes them much more interesting. Both green peppers and onions take about the same time to cook, the flavours are very compatible and the colour contrast extremely attractive.

2–3 medium-sized onions   25 g/1 oz butter
1 large or 2 small green peppers

Peel and slice the onions. Remove the stalks from the peppers, halve and discard the seeds. Shred the peppers fairly thinly.

Heat the butter in a frying pan and add the onions and peppers. Cover with a lid and fry gently, stirring occasionally, for about 10 minutes until the onions and peppers have softened.

Serve at once. They are particularly nice with fried or grilled steaks or chops.
Serves 4

Mushrooms in garlic butter

Garlic blends well with mushrooms to give them a delicious flavour. Prepared in this way they make an attractive garnish for steak or chops. For a milder garlic taste, simply rub round the inside of the frying pan with a crushed garlic clove before adding the butter for frying.

225 g/8 oz small button mushrooms   50 g/2 oz butter
1–2 cloves garlic   1 tablespoon chopped parsley
salt

Wipe the mushrooms, trim any stalks level with the caps and slice the mushrooms thinly. Peel the garlic cloves and, using the blade of a knife, mash the garlic to a purée with a little salt. Beat the garlic into the butter.

Melt the garlic butter in a frying pan and when hot add the mushrooms. Fry gently for 2–3 minutes, tossing the mushrooms in the butter. Sprinkle with extra salt to taste and add the chopped parsley.
Serves 4

Blackberry and apple trifle

Fruit trifles can be made at any time of the year, using cooked and sweetened fruits that are in season. Canned fruits could also be used. Spoon in sufficient juice to soak the sponge cake base.

450 g/1 lb dessert apples
225 g/8 oz blackberries
4 tablespoons water

100–175 g/4–6 oz castor sugar
4 trifle sponge cakes

for the custard topping:
2 level tablespoons cornflour
6 dl/1 pint milk
4 egg yolks
50 g/2 oz castor sugar

few drops vanilla essence
toasted flaked almonds for
 decoration

Peel, core and slice the apples. Pick over the blackberries. Place the apple slices and the water in a saucepan and cook gently over low heat until the apples are half cooked. Add the sugar and blackberries and cook until the fruit is tender and juices have formed. Draw off the heat. Break the trifle sponge cakes into the base of a glass serving dish and spoon over the fruit and sufficient juice to soak the sponge cakes. Set aside while preparing the custard.

Custard for trifle made using a little cornflour helps to economize on the number of eggs required. The milk is thickened slightly first and then used to make the custard in the usual way. Measure the cornflour into a small basin. Add about 1.5 dl (¼ pint) of the milk and stir to blend well. Pour the remaining milk into a saucepan and heat until almost boiling. Stir a little hot milk into the cornflour, mix well and return to the milk saucepan. Stir until thickened and boiling, then draw off the heat.

Crack the egg yolks into a large basin, add the sugar and stir well to mix. Stir in the hot milk mixture and blend thoroughly. Rinse out the milk saucepan and strain the custard back into the pan. Stir constantly over low heat until the custard has thickened, but do not allow to boil. Stir in the vanilla essence.

Draw off the heat and dip the base of the pan in cold water to prevent overcooking. Stir occasionally until cool and then pour over the fruit and sponge base. Leave until quite cold, then chill for several hours. Sprinkle with toasted flaked almonds and serve with single cream.
Serves 6

Glacé fruit ice cream

Home-made ice cream is a special treat, but if it's going to be worth making it must be just a little different from the kind you buy in the shops. One of the easiest to make is a vanilla-flavoured ice cream, spiked with chopped glacé fruits.

1 tablespoon seedless raisins
1 tablespoon rum
1 tablespoon finely chopped glacé cherries
1 tablespoon finely chopped angelica

1 170-ml/6-fl oz carton double cream
40 g/1½ oz sifted icing sugar
few drops vanilla essence
2 egg whites

Soak the raisins in the rum overnight and have the glacé cherries and angelica ready chopped. The red, green and brown give the ice cream a delightful contrast in colours. Lightly whip the double cream until just beginning to thicken, then whisk in the icing sugar and a few drops of vanilla essence. Fold in the egg whites, stiffly beaten, the rum-soaked raisins and any rum they didn't soak up and the chopped glacé fruits.

Pour the mixture into a plastic freezer container, cover and freeze. As the mixture becomes icy round the sides during the first stages of freezing, stir the sides into the centre with a fork. This is necessary to disperse evenly the glacé fruits, which tend to sink to the bottom of the soft, newly made mixture. After one stir the mixture can be left for several hours or until frozen firm.

Serve straight from the freezer using a spoon or scoop dipped in cold water. The ice cream needs no other embellishment – it tastes marvellous just on its own.

Serves 4-6

Plums baked in the oven

Plums baked in the oven are less likely to break up than stewed plums. The sugar, lemon juice and water form a delicious syrup during the cooking. Serve these with cream, vanilla ice cream or with a baked egg custard.

450 g/1 lb plums
100 g/4 oz castor sugar

juice of ½ lemon
2 tablespoons water

Wipe the plums and place in a casserole dish. If preferred they can be halved and stoned before cooking. Sprinkle with the sugar and add the lemon juice and water. Cover with a lid, place in the centre of a very moderate oven (160°C., 325°F., Gas Mark 3) and bake for 30–40 minutes. The fruit should be tender but still keep its shape. Serve warm or cold.

Serves 4

Blackberry and apple mousse

Blackberries and apples always go well together. This is a lovely autumn dessert that has the rich colour and flavour of the blackberries.

450 g/1 lb cooking apples
450 g/1 lb blackberries
1.5 dl/¼ pint water
100 g/4 oz castor sugar

juice of 1 lemon
15 g/½ oz powdered gelatine
2 egg whites

Peel and core the apples and slice into a saucepan. Add the washed blackberries, the water and 75 g (3 oz) of the sugar. Cover with a lid and simmer for about 15 minutes until the fruit is quite tender. Meanwhile, strain the lemon juice into a small basin, sprinkle in the gelatine and leave to soak.

When the fruit is cooked, draw off the heat. Add the soaked gelatine and stir until dissolved – the heat of the pan will be sufficient to do this. Rub the fruit and juice through a sieve into a mixing basin to make a purée; discard any pips from the blackberries remaining in the sieve. Set the fruit purée aside until cold and beginning to thicken.

Quickly whisk the egg whites until stiff, add the remaining sugar and beat again just to blend. Fold into the fruit purée, pour the mixture into a serving dish and chill until set firm.
Serves 6

Sloe gin

Made in September, sloe gin will be ready for Christmas. Rinse or wipe the sloes and remove the stalks. Discard any damaged or unsound fruit and prick the sloes with a silver fork.

Using 100 g (4 oz) castor sugar for 450 g (1 lb) sloes, pack alternate layers of sloes and sugar in a wide-necked screw-topped jar. Pour 1 bottle gin over, cover and screw up tightly. Store for three months, in a cool dark place, turning the jar occasionally.

Strain and pour into clean dry bottles. Stopper with clean corks, sterilized for 10 minutes in boiling water. Brush over the tops of the corks with melted paraffin wax if the bottles are to be kept for any length of time.

Macédoine of fruits

Autumn fruits like peaches, plums and pears make a pretty fruit salad and at this time of year you might find some Chinese gooseberries on sale. Buy just one and peel away the brown skin, then slice the bright green flesh in with the other fruits – the colour effect is quite startling.

2 dessert apples
2 dessert pears
2 ripe peaches

225 g/8 oz green grapes
225 g/8 oz dessert plums

for the syrup:

100 g/4 oz castor sugar
1.5 dl/¼ pint water

juice of ½ lemon

Make the sugar syrup first and allow to cool before preparing the fruit. The lemon juice added helps keep any white fruits attractive in appearance. Measure the sugar and water into a small saucepan. Stir over low heat to dissolve the sugar and then bring to the boil. Simmer for 2 minutes, then draw off the heat and add the strained lemon juice. Pour into a serving bowl and allow to cool.

Peel, quarter and slice the apples and add to the syrup. Peel and halve the pears, then scoop out the core with a teaspoon. Slice the pears and add to the bowl. Dip peaches in boiling water for 30 seconds, then plunge immediately into cold water. Peel away the skin and slice the flesh, then add to the other prepared fruits along with the halved and deseeded grapes. Halve, stone and slice the plums and add too. Mix the fruits well in the syrup and leave to chill for several hours before serving. Serve with single cream.
Serves 6

Green tomato chutney

Lack of sunshine during summer months invariably leaves many green tomatoes on outdoor plants. Some will ripen if brought indoors and placed in a warm dark place, like a drawer or a cupboard. Others can be made into chutney.

1.75 kg/4 lb green tomatoes
450 g/1 lb cooking apples
450 g/1 lb onions
225 g/8 oz sultanas
1 level tablespoon salt

1 level teaspoon mustard seed
1 level teaspoon ground ginger
¼ level teaspoon cayenne pepper
6 dl/1 pint malt vinegar
450 g/1 lb soft brown sugar

Wipe the tomatoes and cut away any bruised or bad parts, then slice the fruit into a preserving pan. Peel, core and finely chop the apples. Peel and finely chop the onions – because vinegar has a hardening effect on onion, it is advisable to soften the chopped onion by simmering in boiling water for 5 minutes. Drain and add to the pan of ingredients. Chop the sultanas and add too. Add the salt, mustard seed, ginger, cayenne pepper and half the vinegar to the pan. Cover with a lid and cook gently, stirring occasionally, for 1–2 hours or until the ingredients are very soft and pulpy. Dissolve the sugar in the remaining vinegar and add to the cooked mixture.

Stirring thoroughly, bring the contents up to the boil, then cook gently without a lid until the mixture is thick and no free vinegar remains in the pan. Pour at once into hot jars and fill to within 1 cm ($\frac{1}{2}$ in) of the tops. Cover and seal.

Store chutney for a few months before using, to allow the flavours to develop.

Makes about 3.5 kg (8 lb)

Apple jelly marmalade

A fine-shred orange marmalade using apple jelly as a base, this makes a delicious preserve. Makes good use of windfall apples too.

1.75 kg/4 lb cooking apples	juice of 1 large lemon
3–4 sweet oranges	granulated sugar (see method)

Wipe and quarter the apples. Cut away any bad parts and place in a preserving pan. Wipe and peel the oranges and, reserving the peel, cut the orange flesh up and add to the apples. Add the lemon juice and enough cold water to cover the apples. Bring up to the boil, then simmer for 1–1$\frac{1}{2}$ hours until very soft. Mash or squash the fruit to a good pulp. Strain the pulp and juice through a scalded jelly bag.

Cut the white pith away from inside the reserved peel. Cut the peel into neat strips and then shred very finely. Discard any uneven bits; these could be added to the apples while simmering. Put the shredded peel in a saucepan and add water to cover generously. Simmer gently, covered with a lid, until the peel is quite soft and tender – about 1$\frac{1}{2}$ hours. Then strain and reserve the peel. Meanwhile measure the strained juice from the apples back into the preserving pan – there should be about 2.25 litres (4 pints).

Add 450 g (1 lb) sugar for each 5.5 dl (1 pint) juice. Stir over low heat to dissolve the sugar, then boil briskly for 15 minutes, skimming well to clear the jelly. Add the cooked shredded peel and continue boiling for a set – about 5 minutes more. When a set is obtained draw off the heat. Cool for about 30 minutes, stir the jelly to distribute the

peel evenly and pour into clean dry pots. Cover when hot and seal
when cold.
Makes about 3.5 kg (8 lb)

Apple chutney

*Chutney enthusiasts will enjoy this apple chutney which uses golden
syrup as part of the sugar in the recipe.*

2.75 kg/6 lb cooking apples
900 g/2 lb onions
3 dl/½ pint water
2 level tablespoons cooking salt
40 g/1½ oz ground ginger

15 g/½ oz ground cinnamon
¼ level teaspoon cayenne pepper
a generous litre/2 pints malt vinegar
900 g/2 lb soft brown sugar
450 g/1 lb golden syrup

Peel, core and chop the apples and peel and chop the onions. Place
in a large stainless steel or aluminium saucepan with the water and
simmer for 20 minutes. Because vinegar tends to toughen onion it is
advisable to soften any quantity of onion in a chutney recipe by
simmering in water before the remaining ingredients are added.

Add the salt, ginger, cinnamon and cayenne pepper and half the
vinegar. Continue to simmer the ingredients until quite soft.

Add the sugar, syrup and remaining vinegar and simmer gently until
the mixture is quite thick. When ready there should be no free
vinegar in the pan. Bottle the chutney while hot in clean warm jars.
Makes 3.5 kg (8 lb)

Apple ginger

*If you have lots of windfall apples, use them to make apple ginger, a
kind of apple jam delicately flavoured with ginger and lemon. Root
ginger is available from a chemist; give the pieces a hearty whack with a
rolling pin to bruise and split them so they will adequately flavour the
preserve.*

1.25 kg/3 lb apples
5.5 dl/1 pint water
25 g/1 oz bruised root ginger
 uice and grated rind of 2 lemons

1.25 kg/3 lb granulated or
 preserving sugar
100 g/4 oz crystallized ginger

Peel, core and cut up the apples and place in a preserving pan. Tie
the cores and peel loosely in a muslin bag along with the root ginger

and add to the pan with the water, lemon juice and grated lemon rind. Bring up to the boil, then lower the heat and simmer gently until the apples are tender but not mushy. Remove the muslin bag, pressing out all the juices.

Add the sugar and the chopped-up crystallized ginger. Stir over low heat until the sugar has dissolved, then bring up to the boil and cook rapidly until setting point is reached – about 15 minutes. Draw off the heat and ladle into jars. Cover with waxed paper circles when hot and seal when cold. Keep for three months before using.
Makes 2.25 kg (5 lb)

Spiced pears

You can keep your spiced pears in any glass or stone storage jar or pretty china pot that has an airtight lid. They can be served at the table straight from the jar if the container is a pretty one. Spiced pears go well with cold meats, especially pork, ham or gammon.

900 g/2 lb firm cooking pears
450 g/1 lb sugar
3 dl/½ pint malt vinegar
8 whole cloves

2 level teaspoons whole allspice
25 g/1 oz cinnamon stick, broken up

Peel and core the pears and cut in quarters – keep them in acidulated water while preparing to preserve the colour.

Measure the sugar and vinegar into a saucepan and add the spices tied in muslin. Stir over low heat to dissolve the sugar, add the pears and bring to the boil. Simmer gently until the pears are tender but still whole, then draw off the heat. With a perforated spoon lift the pears out of the syrup and pack into a 900-g (2-lb) jar.

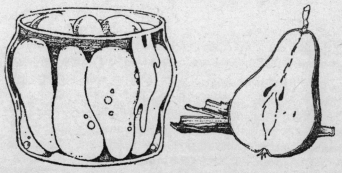

Remove the muslin bag of spices and return the saucepan of syrup to the heat. Boil gently until the syrup is quite thick, then pour into the jar to cover the pears. Seal airtight and store for a month or so before using. The jar can be opened as the pears are required and used so long as the lid is replaced each time.

Makes 900 g (2 lb)

Using the freezer in September

Do not plan on storing casseroles of cooked meat for a long time. Most of these contain fat which tends to become rancid and spices which change flavour. In general freeze only as much as you can use up within a month. You will find the *chicken with tomatoes and sweet peppers* (see page 241) is the kind of casserole dish that freezes well. Prepare recipes like this as for serving immediately, but cooking time should be shortened by 30 minutes to allow for additional cooking during reheating. Cool a cooked casserole quickly – setting the dish in iced water helps. Wash out the casserole and then line with foil – easiest if the foil is moulded over the outside of the casserole first. Leave enough extra foil at the top for a good seal. Return the contents to the casserole and chill in the refrigerator. Then freeze in the container. When solid, dip the casserole in cold water for a moment, loosen and lift out the frozen contents. Wrap and freeze.

To use, unwrap the frozen stew and place in the original casserole. Reheat without a lid in a moderate oven (180°C., 350°F., Gas Mark 4) – it will take about 1–1½ hours according to the size. Stir occasionally to break up and speed thawing. Heat until it is beginning to bubble in the centre.

Although cooked dishes are usually reheated from frozen, recipes can be thawed and then reheating times are considerably shorter. Take the dish out of the freezer and thaw overnight. Reheat for 30–40 minutes in a moderate oven (180°C., 350°F., Gas Mark 4).

Lasagne verdi (see page 239) can be made up and put in the freezer ready for serving. Assemble it in foil containers which have lids to fit. They can then be transferred directly to the oven for reheating. Cover with the top foil side inwards to make an airtight lid over the contents and on the cardboard side write the contents. Place in the freezer. Thaw overnight, reheat for 1 hour.

The *meat sauce for pasta* (see page 239) is a useful sauce to keep in the freezer for quick spaghetti dishes, and the *tomato sauce for lasagne* (see page 240) also freezes well.

Freezing meat

It may be a considerable saving to buy part of, or a whole carcass of an animal for your freezer. You may prefer to deal with a wholesale specialist butcher, or through your local retail butcher – many provide such a service. If the meat is delivered ready-frozen, it is simply a matter of transferring it to your freezer. If the meat is supplied fresh there are certain points to bear in mind.

Only foods totalling no more than 10 per cent of the capacity of the freezer should be frozen at any one time, that is within 24 hours. Too much fresh food in the cabinet of the freezer raises the temperature to the detriment of the contents already there. This means that a bulk order of beef weighing more than 45 kg (100 lb) could take 2–3 days to freeze. You should consider whether you have room in your refrigerator to store the meat ready for freezing the next day.

The order of freezing depends on the perishability of the cuts. Small cuts like stewing steak or mince, and all offal, should be frozen first. Follow with slightly larger cuts such as chops and steaks. Finish with the larger roasting joints. Freeze meat in quantities you are likely to use at one time, and remember to separate chops with waxed paper or foil for easy removal.

Wrap all meat carefully, using correct moisture-vapour-proof freezer bags. The air in a freezer is very dry. It will absorb moisture from uncovered or badly wrapped foods, and will result in dehydration and a change of flavour known as 'freezer burn'. The quicker the freezing, the less the 'drip' or juices that will run from the thawed joint. So use the 'fast freeze' cabinet if you have one.

Thawing times for meat
Thaw meat slowly, preferably in the refrigerator. Then cook as fresh meat.

	Refrigerator	Room temperature
Joints under 1.25 kg/3 lb	9–12 hours	3–6 hours
Joints over 1.25 kg/3 lb	12–20 hours	6–9 hours
Steaks and chops	5–6 hours	2–4 hours

October

Even when the *October* sun shines out of blue skies, there is a chill in the air. This is a month for walks in the wood and tea by the fire. The pheasant season opens on the first of the month and means all game is back in season ready to become a feature of dinner party menus.

This month sees the end of autumn vegetables and brings back leeks, red cabbage, celery, and the first Brussels sprouts. There is a good supply of onions and there should be some sprouting broccoli from the garden. October provides the finest selection of apples and pears at any time of year, so use them in delicious pies and tarts and remember that the later-maturing apples picked around now are the best keepers. Country greengrocers may have a supply of quinces towards the end of the month. They will certainly have fresh cobnuts and the start of the new season's supply of walnuts and chestnuts.

Cream of sweetcorn soup

Sweetcorn makes a satisfying soup and is infinitely better when puréed in a blender to get a really good creamy consistency.

2 312-g/11-oz cans sweetcorn
4 dl/¾ pint chicken stock
25 g/1 oz butter
1 small onion
1 level tablespoon flour

6 dl/1 pint milk
1 level teaspoon salt
2–3 tablespoons single cream
chopped parsley to garnish

Drain the liquid from the cans of sweetcorn and empty the corn into a saucepan. Add the stock and simmer gently for about 20 minutes or until the corn is very tender. Draw off the heat and either pass the liquid and corn through a vegetable mill or purée in a blender.

In a saucepan melt the butter over low heat. Peel and finely chop the onion, add to the pan. Cover and cook gently for about 5 minutes or until the onion is tender but not brown. Stir in the flour, then gradually add the milk, corn purée and salt. Bring up to the boil, stirring well, and simmer for 2–3 minutes. Draw off the heat and stir in the cream. Sprinkle with chopped parsley and serve.
Serves 6

Melon with French dressing

The firm flesh and slightly sweet flavour of a ripe honeydew melon combine very well with French dressing. Make this recipe more elaborate by adding a few prepared prawns – the contrast of colours is very pretty.

1 ripe honeydew melon
5–6 tablespoons prepared French
  dressing

4 crisp lettuce leaves
lemon slices

Cut the melon in half, scoop out the seeds, and then cut again into quarters. Either use a small round vegetable cutter and scoop out balls of the melon flesh, or slice the flesh from the skin and dice. Place the melon flesh in a mixing basin, add the prepared dressing and toss well. Leave to marinate until ready to serve.

Wash the lettuce leaves, remove stalks and then roll the leaves up together in a bundle. Shred across thinly with a sharp knife. Loosen the shredded lettuce and place in the base of four individual glasses.

When ready to serve, toss the melon again and spoon the flesh and dressing in the basin over the lettuce. Garnish the glasses with a slice of lemon.
Serves 4

Mixed vegetable soup

Use whatever vegetable you have to hand for this warming soup. Potatoes, carrots, onions, leeks and celery should form the main part with a little parsnip or turnip if liked.

450–675 g/1–1½ lb mixed
  vegetables
40 g/1½ oz butter
1 level teaspoon sugar
a generous litre/2 pints stock
bouquet garni of parsley stalks,
  sprig of thyme, bay leaf and a few
  bacon rinds tied in a bundle

1.5 dl/¼ pint milk
2 level tablespoons flour
salt and freshly milled pepper
chopped parsley

Prepare the vegetables and cut them up small. Melt the butter in a large saucepan. Add the vegetables and sugar and cook them gently for 5–6 minutes. Stir in the stock and add the bouquet garni. Bring up to the boil, simmer for 2 minutes and then skim. Cover the pan with a lid and simmer gently for about 40–50 minutes or until the vegetables are quite tender.

Remove the bouquet garni and pass the vegetables and liquid

through a soup mill or purée in an electric blender. Return the soup to the saucepan. Measure the milk into a basin and sift the flour over the top. Whisk well to mix thoroughly and then add the blend to the soup. Stir until boiling, then cook gently for 2–3 minutes. Check the seasoning with salt and pepper.

Scatter a little chopped parsley over the top and serve with diced toasted or fried bread.
Serves 6

Spinach soup

Spinach soup has a good flavour and a pretty green colour. It tastes even better the second day. For a special occasion, stir a spoonful of unwhipped double cream into the centre of each serving – it makes a pretty colour contrast.

450 g/1 lb fresh spinach
1 clove garlic
4 dl/¾ pint milk
small bay leaf
1 small onion, peeled and stuck
  with a clove

40 g/1½ oz butter
25 g/1 oz flour
6 dl/1 pint chicken stock
salt and freshly milled pepper
pinch nutmeg (optional)
2 tablespoons cream

Wash the spinach in plenty of cold water and tear out the large mid-rib. Peel and finely chop the garlic. Place the milk in a saucepan, add the bay leaf and the onion stuck with a clove and bring just to the boil. Draw off the heat and leave to infuse for 10 minutes.

Meanwhile melt 25 g (1 oz) of the butter in a saucepan and stir in the flour. Cook gently for a moment, then gradually stir in the hot infused milk. Bring up to the boil, stirring well to get a smooth sauce.

Sauté the prepared spinach along with the peeled and finely chopped garlic in the remaining 15 g (½ oz) butter. Cover the pan with a lid and cook gently until the spinach is quite soft. Stir the hot prepared sauce into the spinach. Heat both together for about 5 minutes, then draw off the heat and pass the soup through a vegetable mill or purée in a blender.

Return the soup to the saucepan and stir in the stock, thinning the vegetable mixture down to the right consistency. Add salt and pepper to taste and flavour with nutmeg. Reheat gently. Stir in the cream just before serving.
Serves 4-6

Goujons of sole with seafood sauce

Plump fillets of sole are cut into thin strips, breadcrumbed and fried to a delicious crispness for this recipe. But sole is an expensive fish, so serve this as a first course instead of a main dish. As a change from the more usual tartare sauce, offer a delicious tangy seafood sauce.

4 good-sized fillets of sole	2 teaspoons oil
seasoned flour	toasted breadcrumbs for coating
1 egg	salt

for the seafood sauce:

2 tablespoons mayonnaise	dash of Worcestershire sauce
2 tablespoons tomato ketchup	juice of ½ lemon
1 tablespoon cream	

Ask the fishmonger to skin the sole fillets and remove them from the bone. Rinse and pat dry. Halve each fillet, making a slanting cut right across – the same angle as you would cut a French loaf. Then cut each half into three or four narrow strips or *goujons*.

Toss the pieces of fish in seasoned flour, then shake in a sieve to get rid of the surplus flour. Lightly mix the egg and oil in a shallow plate. Dip the fish pieces first in the beaten egg, then roll in toasted breadcrumbs. Shake away loose crumbs and pat the coating on firmly. At this stage the fish can be chilled until ready to serve.

Fry the goujons in hot deep fat until crisp and golden – about 2–3 minutes. Drain thoroughly on absorbent kitchen paper. Sprinkle with salt and serve with the seafood sauce. To make this, blend all the ingredients together adding sufficient lemon juice to make a piquant flavour.

Serves 4

Sole Colbert

Choose small sole or dabs for deep-frying and have the skin removed from both sides of the fish. Make the parsley butter well in advance, so that it is firm and easy to cut in attractive slices for serving.

4 small sole	toasted breadcrumbs
seasoned flour	oil for deep-frying
lightly beaten egg	lemon slices

for the parsley butter:

100 g/4 oz butter	salt and pepper
1 tablespoon lemon juice	1 tablespoon finely chopped parsley

Slit down the centre of the back of each fish and, using a sharp knife, scrape the flesh away from the bone to loosen the fillets, but leave a small portion attached to the bone just at the head and the tail end. Cut through the backbone at either end but do not try to remove it. Gently replace the fillets quite flat. Dip the whole fish in seasoned flour then in lightly beaten egg and lastly the breadcrumbs, patting the coating on firmly. Set aside until ready to fry.

Cream the butter and gradually work in the lemon juice. Add the seasoning and parsley. Roll the butter up in a square of greaseproof paper and twist the ends like a cracker so that the butter is pressed into a thick roll. Chill until quite firm.

When ready to serve, prepare the oil for deep-frying. If a deep-frying pan is unavailable or the pan is too small for the size of the fish, fry the sole in a frying pan with 2.5 cm (1 in) hot oil. Heat the oil until very hot and fry the fish to a golden brown on both sides. Drain, carefully detach the backbone and discard it. Fry each sole in turn keeping the cooked ones hot. Fill the cavity in each sole with a slice of the parsley butter and a slice of lemon and serve.
Serves 4

Tuna fish pâté

Simply prepared mixtures of fish like this recipe can be served as a first course, or used as a spread on toast for a snack, as a sandwich filling or a topping on cocktail canapés.

1 198-g/7-oz can tuna fish	few black peppercorns
milk (see method)	40 g/1½ oz butter
blade of mace	1 level tablespoon flour
small bay leaf	2 tablespoons single cream
sprig parsley	juice of ½ lemon

Drain the liquor from the can of tuna fish and make up to 1.5 dl (¼ pint) with milk. Place in a saucepan and add the mace, bay leaf, parsley and peppercorns. Heat through until almost boiling, then draw off the heat. Leave to infuse for 15 minutes, then strain.

Melt the butter in a small saucepan and stir in the flour. Cook gently for a few minutes then gradually stir in the flavoured milk, beating well to get a smooth sauce. Bring up to the boil and cook for 1–2 minutes, then draw off the heat.

Tip the tuna fish into a bowl and mash well with a fork. Add the prepared sauce, the cream and lemon juice and beat very thoroughly to mix. Check seasoning with salt and pepper. Spoon into a small dish and leave in a cool place to firm up. Serve with hot thinly sliced toast and butter.

Serves 4

Herrings with apple salad

Sweet apples and soured cream make a perfect foil for any slightly vinegary flavour in pickled or roll-mop herrings. Serve this salad with a green salad and thin slices of buttered rye bread.

1 medium-sized onion	1 carton soured cream
2 dessert apples	salt and freshly milled pepper
juice of ½ lemon	4 pickled herrings

Peel the onion leaving it whole. Slice into rings and place in a mixing basin. Cover with boiling water and allow to soak for 2 minutes. Drain and chill.

Peel and core the apple and dice into a basin. Sprinkle with the lemon juice and toss the apple pieces. Add the onion rings, the soured cream and a seasoning of salt and pepper. Toss the ingredients to mix.

Drain the herrings from any liquor and open out. Arrange the herrings flat on individual serving dishes with the flesh side uppermost. Spoon the apple and onion and soured cream mixture over the top and serve.

Serves 4

Cheese and bacon tart

Savoury tarts or flans are economical and really quite easy to make. A variety of fillings can be used, but cheese and bacon is always one of the most popular. Serve warm with a coleslaw salad.

100 g/4 oz shortcrust pastry

for the filling:

100 g/4 oz lean bacon rashers	3 dl/½ pint milk
50 g/2 oz hard cheese, grated	salt and freshly milled pepper
3 eggs	

Roll out the pastry and use to line a 20-cm (8-in) round tart tin, a shallow sponge cake tin or a flan ring set on a baking tray. Trim the edges and set aside while preparing the filling.

Trim the bacon rinds from the rashers and cut the bacon into strips. Fry in a dry pan until the fat runs and the bacon is tender, then drain and sprinkle over the base of the pastry case. Add half the grated cheese.

Whisk together the eggs and milk and season well with salt and freshly milled pepper. Strain into a jug and then pour into the pie shell. Sprinkle with the remaining cheese.

Place just above the centre in a moderately hot oven (190°C., 375°F., Gas Mark 5) and bake for 40–45 minutes or until golden brown. Serve warm with salad.
Serves 4

Cheese soufflé omelette

A dish that really lives up to its name, the soufflé omelette combines the speed of a frying-pan omelette with the fluffy melt-in-the-mouth texture of a conventional soufflé. A soufflé omelette makes an excellent light luncheon dish.

3 large eggs
1 tablespoon tepid water
salt and freshly milled pepper

2 tablespoons grated Parmesan cheese
15 g/½ oz butter

Separate the eggs, placing the yolks together in a large basin and the whites in a second smaller basin. Add the water, a seasoning of salt and pepper and the cheese to the yolks. Using a wooden spoon, stir the egg yolk mixture until blended and creamy. Stiffly beat the egg whites and, using a metal spoon, fold them into the egg yolk mixture.

Melt the butter in a frying pan. When frothing, pour in the egg mixture and immediately lower the heat. Cook very gently – far more so than for a conventional omelette. After about 5 minutes the underside should be browned – lift the edges with a palette knife and have a look – and the omelette will have started to rise in the pan. Remove from the heat and place under the grill. Cook gently for a further 3–4 minutes until the soufflé is well risen and golden brown on the top. Cut through the centre and fold it in half. Turn out on to a plate and serve.

Cheese and chives soufflé omelette This makes a marvellous luncheon dish for slimmers. Follow the recipe above but add a 113-g (4-oz) carton plain cottage cheese to the egg yolks instead of the Parmesan. Add a pinch of mustard and 2 teaspoons chopped chives. Don't fold the omelette in half when cooked – slide it out on to a plate and serve cut in wedges with a salad.

Serves 2

Chicken with walnuts

Put the chicken carcass in a saucepan with a scant litre (1½ pints) water. Add a carrot, a small onion, a stick of celery, a few parsley stalks and a bay leaf. Simmer for about 1 hour and strain to make chicken stock for the recipe. The remaining stock can be used for soups.

1 oven-ready chicken, about 1.25 kg/3 lb, cut into joints
25 g/1 oz walnuts
2 tablespoons oil
1 small onion
seasoned flour
1.5 dl/¼ pint dry white wine or cider

1.5 dl/¼ pint chicken stock
salt and freshly milled pepper
pinch ground nutmeg or mace
1 level tablespoon cornflour
4 tablespoons cream
watercress

Trim the chicken joints neatly. Sauté the walnut halves in the oil for 3–4 minutes then lift out and set aside. Peel and chop the onion and add to the hot oil in the pan. Fry gently for a few moments until tender but not brown. Toss the chicken pieces in the seasoned flour and then add to the pan. Fry gently, turning the pieces of chicken occasionally, until they are brown on all sides.

Pour in the wine or cider and the chicken stock. Season with salt and pepper and the nutmeg or mace. Cover with a lid and cook gently for about 30–40 minutes or until the chicken pieces are quite tender.

Lift the chicken pieces from the pan on to a hot serving dish. Add the walnuts and keep hot. Blend the cornflour with 2 tablespoons water and stir into the chicken liquor in the pan. Stir until boiling and thickened. Check the seasoning and heat through for a moment.

Draw off the heat, stir in the cream and strain over the chicken. Serve with a garnish of watercress.

Serves 4

Braised venison

This is a good way to cook a piece of venison that you have had in the freezer. You can pour the marinade over the frozen meat and leave it to thaw overnight. Any juices from the venison run into the marinade and nothing is lost.

1–1.25 kg/2–3 lb haunch of venison

for the marinade:

1 onion	few parsley stalks
bay leaf	3 dl/½ pint red wine
4 black peppercorns	1 tablespoon oil
6 juniper berries	

for the braise:

25 g/1 oz dripping	1 orange
bed of vegetables including 1 onion, 2 carrots and few celery stalks	1 tablespoon redcurrant jelly
	salt and freshly milled pepper
	25 g/1 oz softened butter
3 dl/½ pint stock	25 g/1 oz flour

Place the venison in a deep dish. Peel the onion for the marinade and slice over the meat. Add the bay leaf, peppercorns, lightly crushed juniper berries and a few parsley stalks. Pour over the red wine and oil. Leave to marinate for 12 hours or overnight, turning the meat and basting from time to time. Drain and pat dry and reserve the marinade.

Melt the dripping in a large frying pan. Brown the venison on both sides in the hot fat and then remove from the pan. Add the peeled and thickly sliced onion, carrots and celery for the bed of vegetables. Fry for a moment in the hot fat and then transfer to the base of a large casserole. Strain in the reserved marinade. Add 2–3 pieces finely pared orange rind and sufficient stock just to cover the vegetables. Bring to a simmer then place the piece of venison on top. Cover the meat with a buttered paper and then a tight-fitting lid. Place in the centre of a very moderate oven (190°C., 325°F., Gas

Mark 3) and braise gently, allowing 30 minutes per 0.5 kg (1 lb) plus 30 minutes.

Lift the meat out, carve into slices and arrange in a hot serving dish. Meanwhile strain the stock from the braising pan into a saucepan. Add the strained juice of the orange, the redcurrant jelly and a seasoning of salt and pepper. Bring up to the boil, stirring to blend the ingredients. On a flat plate blend the butter with the flour to make a *beurre manié*. Add in pieces to the pan of gravy, stir until melted and blended and then bring up to the boil, stirring until thickened. Pour over the sliced venison. Heat through and serve.
Serves 6-8

Pheasant in cream sauce

Pheasants are usually roasted but it makes a change to braise or casserole them. They don't want elaborate treatment, just a simple recipe like this one.

1 large pheasant	3 dl/½ pint double cream
75 g/3 oz butter	juice of ½ lemon
1 onion	salt and freshly milled pepper

Have the pheasant cleaned and trussed ready for roasting. Heat the butter in a large flameproof casserole or large heavy saucepan. Add the pheasant to the hot butter and brown gently on all sides. Peel and slice the onion and add to the pan. Cover with a lid and cook very gently for 45 minutes.

Pour in the cream, stirring it round the sides of the casserole or saucepan, the strained lemon juice and a seasoning of salt and pepper. Replace the lid and cook for a further 15 minutes. Draw off the heat and lift the pheasant out on to a heated serving plate. Carve the legs from the pheasant first, then carve the breast into thin slices. Strain over the sauce and serve.
Serves 4

Beef stew with mustard dumplings

Dumplings have to be cooked in a traditional stew which is simmered over direct heat. Choose a pan big enough to allow room for the dumplings to be added later. This is a marvellous way of cooking a complete meal in a single pan.

675 g/1½ lb lean stewing steak
2 medium-sized onions
450 g/1 lb carrots
seasoned flour
25 g/1 oz dripping or white cooking
  fat

a scant litre/1½ pints stock or
  water
salt and freshly milled pepper

for the dumplings:

100 g/4 oz self-raising flour
pinch salt
1 level teaspoon mustard powder

50 g/2 oz shredded beef suet
½ level teaspoon dried mixed herbs
4 tablespoons water

Trim away any fat and cut the meat into neat pieces. Peel and slice
the onions and carrots. Toss the meat in seasoned flour and reserve
any extra flour for making the gravy later. Heat the fat in a frying
pan, add the meat and fry quickly to seal and brown on all sides.
Remove the meat from the pan and place in a medium-sized
saucepan with the prepared onions and carrots.

Add a tablespoon of the seasoned flour to the hot fat remaining in
the frying pan. If necessary add an extra nut of fat to absorb the
flour. Stir over the heat until the flour begins to brown – this gives
the colour to the gravy. Gradually stir in the hot stock. Stir well,
scraping up the bits from the pan, and bring up to the boil. Check
seasoning and strain over the meat and vegetables. Cover with a lid
and simmer gently for 2½–3 hours or until the meat is tender.
About 35 minutes before the end of the cooking time prepare the
dumplings. Sift the flour, salt and mustard into a basin. Add the suet
and mixed herbs and sprinkle in the water. Stir with a fork to a soft
scone-like dough. Turn out and divide the mixture into eight pieces.

With floured hands roll each one into a ball, coat lightly with flour
and set aside for 10 minutes before adding to the stew. Float the
dumplings on top of the almost cooked meat – do not submerge
them in the liquid. Cover and cook for the last 20 minutes of cooking
time. Serve the meat and vegetables with the gravy and dumplings.
Serves 4

Venison A roast cut of venison makes a lovely party dish and there is
no mystery about the cooking of it. Rub the flesh well with salt for extra
flavour and remember venison is a dry meat that lacks fat, so cover with
streaky bacon rashers.

Set in a covered roasting tin or in a traditional open tin with a 'tent' of kitchen foil over the top. Roast as for beef, allowing 20 minutes per 0.5 kg (1 lb) and 20 minutes extra.

Keep the venison hot and prepare a gravy made using the pan drippings with a little port or red wine added. Serve your venison on hot plates with gravy and rowan jelly.

Pheasant In season October 1st–February 1st. Should be well hung, for 7–10 days. A good pheasant will serve three or four people. The cock bird is larger than the hen, but the hen is fatter and the flesh more succulent. Roast young birds and casserole older birds.

To roast, cover the breast of the trussed bird with fat bacon rashers and baste with butter while cooking. Cook in a moderately hot oven (200°C., 400°F., Gas Mark 6) and roast for 45 minutes according to size. About 10 minutes before the end of the cooking time, remove the bacon rashers. Dredge the breast with flour, baste and return to the oven to brown.

Gammon with cider and apples

The bed of apples used for braising this bacon joint provides a delicious apple sauce to serve along with it. Choose a piece of bacon collar or a lean gammon joint with a good area of rind for glazing.

1 piece gammon or bacon, about 1 kg/2–2½ lb	bay leaf
675–900 g/1½–2 lb cooking apples	6 dl/1 pint dry cider
1 small onion, stuck with a clove	1 tablespoon sugar
	15 g/½ oz butter

for the topping:

1 teaspoon French mustard	few whole cloves
2–3 tablespoons demerara sugar	

Soak the gammon for several hours or overnight in cold water. Peel, core and quarter the apples and arrange over the base of a large saucepan. Add the onion stuck with the clove and the bay leaf. Set the piece of gammon on top of the apples and add the cider; it should be just sufficient to cover the apples. Cover the pan and bring up to the boil. Simmer gently allowing 30 minutes per 0.5 kg (1 lb).

Lift the gammon from the pan and, using a small sharp knife, strip away the rind. Score the fat in a criss-cross pattern. Spread with the mustard, then coat with the demerara sugar and finally stick in a few cloves. Set in a roasting tin, place in the centre of a moderately hot oven (200°C., 400°F., Gas Mark 6) and bake for 15–20 minutes, until glazed and brown.

Meanwhile strain off the cooking liquor, reserving the apples. Remove the onion and bay leaf and return the apples to the saucepan. Stir to break them up to a purée and add the sugar and butter. Heat gently, allowing any excess moisture to boil away. Serve the apple sauce with the sliced gammon.
Serves 6

Nuts

Cobnuts At this time of year look out for cobnuts with their greeny brown, lacy outer coating, and pass them round with the cheese tray at a dinner party, or serve with fruit. Cobnuts are always served fresh.

Almonds These add a delicious crunchiness to recipes. The shelled nuts have a brown skin which is easy enough to remove if the nuts are blanched in boiling water for 1–2 minutes. Hot almonds are soft and easier to flake or shred finely for recipes.

Hazelnuts These are almost exclusively used in baking and confectionery. They give recipes a lovely flavour, but are the very devil to use unless you have a blender or a Mouli grater to grind them up in. Hazelnuts should be spread out on a tray and popped in a hot oven for a few minutes. Tip the hot nuts into a teacloth and rub well together, when the feathery brown skins will flake off.

Walnuts Good in savoury recipes. Blend them with cream cheese, seasoning and chives for spreading on bread and butter. Use walnuts in a sauce to serve with chicken or add to a green salad. Use chopped walnuts instead of almonds in a cake recipe. The easiest way to chop walnuts coarsely is to snip them up with a pair of scissors.

Chestnuts Chestnuts are a nuisance to peel. The outer skin should be slit on the flat side and the nuts then simmered in boiling water for 10 minutes. Drain well and both the inner and outer skins should peel away quite easily. Prepare chestnuts in small quantities and wrap unpeeled ones in a teacloth so that they remain warm while you are peeling the rest. Once cooked chestnuts become floury and soft, and as such they lend themselves to such lovely recipes as chestnut soup and chestnut purée. Whole peeled chestnuts can be served with game, especially venison, and even added to a traditional beef stew.

Brazil nuts Brazils have the toughest outer coating but it hides what many people think is the most delicious eating nut of all. When fresh the brazil has a tender ivory smoothness and a rich flavour. The hard outer coating can easily be cracked if the nuts are blanched in boiling water for 3–4 minutes, then plunged into cold water for a moment. Make a pretty decoration for a trifle or mousse by shaving off slices of brazil, using a vegetable peeler. Eat brazil nuts plain, dipping the ends in salt.

Red cabbage with apple

The acid from cooking apples and lemon juice brings out an excellent colour in this delicious red cabbage recipe. Some like red cabbage a little sweet while others prefer a sharper flavour; the great thing is that you can alter the recipe to your taste as you cook it. Red cabbage reheats very well and can be cooked a day or more in advance of serving.

1 small red cabbage, about 675 g/1½ lb	2 large cooking apples
25 g/1 oz butter	salt and freshly milled pepper
1 medium-sized onion	1–2 tablespoons demerara sugar
	juice of ½ lemon

Quarter the cabbage and cut away the core. Pressing the cut surface firmly on the board, shred the cabbage across very finely. Wash in cold water. Melt the butter in a large saucepan and add the peeled and finely chopped onion. Cook gently for a few minutes until the onion softens, then pack the cabbage into the pan. Add sufficient boiling water to cover the base of the pan generously – about 2.5 cm (1 in) in depth.

Peel, core and cut up the apples and add. Season with salt and freshly milled pepper, then add the sugar and lemon juice. Stir to mix well. Cover with a lid and simmer gently for 3–4 hours. Red cabbage should be cooked slowly and for a long time. Keep the pan tightly covered; once the apples begin to pulp down no more water should be required. Stir occasionally and towards the end of the cooking time taste and add more sugar or lemon juice to your liking.

Serve hot with roast pork or duck, with grilled chops or any rich meat or game.
Serves 4

Braised celery with tomato

Whether you buy washed or unwashed celery see that the stalks are smooth and thick and that the base is fat. Any damaged or coarse stems should never be thrown away. They can be used to flavour soups and broths.

2 heads celery
25 g/1 oz butter
225 g/8 oz tomatoes

salt and freshly milled pepper
chicken stock (see method)
chopped parsley

Cut off the leafy tops and bases from each head of celery and wash thoroughly in cold water. Remove any coarse outer stems and trim the heads to an even size. This should include all the heart and some stem – cut each heart of celery in half. All discarded pieces of stem should be shredded coarsely and reserved. Blanch the celery hearts in boiling water for 10 minutes – this removes all bitter flavours.

Melt the butter in a large saucepan and add the shredded celery and washed sliced tomatoes. Season with salt and pepper, then place the blanched celery hearts on the top. Add just enough stock or water to cover the vegetables in the base of the pan. Cover and simmer very gently for one hour, until the celery hearts are quite tender.

Lift the hearts from the pan and place in a hot serving dish. Pass the cooking liquor and the soft parts of the vegetables – mainly tomatoes – through a sieve and return to the saucepan. Boil rapidly until reduced by half. Check the seasoning and pour over the celery hearts to glaze. Sprinkle with chopped parsley and serve.

Serves 4

German potato pancakes

Potato pancakes should be served with grilled bacon or fried eggs. They make an excellent supper dish.

450 g/1 lb potatoes	1 level teaspoon salt
1 onion	freshly milled pepper
2 eggs	2–3 tablespoons oil for frying
50 g/2 oz plain flour	

Peel the potatoes and onion, then grate both through the coarse side of a grater into a mixing basin. Add the eggs, flour, salt and pepper and using a wooden spoon mix the ingredients thoroughly.

Heat the oil in a frying pan and add the potato mixture in tablespoonfuls. Fry only three or four pancakes at a time and as the mixture is spooned in flatten them slightly. Fry over moderate heat until brown on the underside – about 5 minutes – then turn and brown on the second side. When cooked lift the pancakes from the pan and drain on absorbent paper. Add more oil as necessary and fry the remainder of the mixture.

Serve the pancakes hot as soon as they are made. This mixture makes about twelve and allows three per person.

Serves 4

Honey-glazed onions

These onions have the most delicious flavour – slightly sweet with honey, but spicy with lemon, Worcestershire sauce and vinegar. They would go well with roast pork, baked gammon or with any grilled foods.

450 g/1 lb small button onions	juice of ½ lemon
25 g/1 oz butter	½ teaspoon Worcestershire sauce
1 tablespoon clear honey	½ teaspoon wine vinegar
1 tablespoon sugar	salt and freshly milled pepper

Peel the onions, leaving them whole. Cover with fresh cold water and bring to the boil. Simmer for 5 minutes to blanch them and then drain.

Melt the butter in a saucepan and add the honey, sugar, lemon juice, Worcestershire sauce, vinegar and a seasoning of salt and pepper. Stir over low heat until the ingredients have blended. Add the onions. Cover with a lid and simmer gently for 25 minutes, or until the onions are tender. Shake the pan occasionally to turn the onions in the mixture and remove the lid towards the end of the cooking time to encourage them to glaze a golden colour. Serve the onions hot with all the juices from the pan.

Serves 4

Celery, leek and tomato salad

Leeks or large sprouts can be shredded raw to provide the green colour in a salad at this time of year. Mix with celery, tomatoes and watercress to make a colourful mixture.

1 small head celery	1 bunch watercress
2–3 leeks	1.5 dl/¼ pint oil and vinegar
4 tomatoes	dressing

Separate the stalks of celery and scrub well. Remove any strings from the larger stalks and slice the celery finely. Trim the base and excess green tops from the leeks, slit and wash thoroughly. Shred the leeks and add to the celery. Wash and slice the tomatoes and wash the watercress.

Mound the mixed leeks and celery in the centre of a flat serving dish. Arrange a ring of tomatoes around the edges and tuck the watercress heads under the tomatoes.

Serve the salad with the dressing separately, to spoon over as it is taken from the plate.
Serves 4

Apple pie

A little cornflour mixed with the sugar in this recipe slightly thickens the juices that run from the apple filling. It makes the pie easier to serve and gives it a pleasant texture.

225 g/8 oz shortcrust pastry	castor or icing sugar

for the filling:

675 g/1½ lb cooking apples	½ level teaspoon ground cinnamon
finely grated rind of ½ lemon	15 g/½ oz butter
100 g/4 oz soft brown sugar	1 tablespoon water
1 level tablespoon cornflour	

Divide the pastry in two portions making one slightly larger than the other. Set the larger piece aside for the top of the pie. Roll the remaining pastry out to a circle large enough to line a greased 20- to 23-cm (8- to 9-in) shallow pie plate.

Peel, core and slice the apples. Add the finely grated lemon rind. Mix together the sugar, cornflour and ground cinnamon. Arrange the apple slices in layers, sprinkling each with sugar and adding a few dots of butter. Finish off with a layer of apple slices. Sprinkle the water over the apples.

Damp the pastry rim. Roll out the reserved pastry to a circle large enough to cover the top. Cut a few slits in the pastry and cover the pie. Press the edges well together, trim and scallop the edges or mark with a fork. Place above centre in a moderately hot oven (190°C., 375°F., Gas Mark 5) and bake for 40–50 minutes. Dust with castor or icing sugar and serve hot or cold with cream or ice cream.
Serves 4-6

Pumpkin pie

Pumpkin has traditional associations with Hallowe'en. Fresh pumpkin can be bought by the pound; most greengrocers prefer to cut pumpkins at the weekend when they have several orders.

100 g/4 oz shortcrust pastry

for the filling:

900 g/2 lb fresh pumpkin
50 g/2 oz butter
100 g/4 oz castor sugar
½ level teaspoon salt
½ level teaspoon ground cinnamon

¼ level teaspoon ground nutmeg
¼ level teaspoon ground cloves
3 eggs, lightly beaten
1.5 dl/¼ pint single cream

Roll out the prepared pastry on a lightly floured working surface to a circle about 23 cm (9 in) in diameter. Line either a 20-cm (8-in) flan ring set on a baking tray or a 20-cm (8-in) buttered shallow pie plate. Trim the edges neatly and set aside in a cool place while preparing the filling.

Scoop out any centre seeds from the pieces of pumpkin and cut away the outer skin. Chop the pumpkin coarsely and place in a saucepan with butter. Set over low heat, cover with a lid and cook gently until the pumpkin is soft and reduced to a purée. Quite a lot of liquid will come out of the pumpkin flesh and towards the end of the cooking time it's a good idea to remove the lid to allow for a little evaporation. When quite soft, draw the pan off the heat and purée either by passing the mixture through a sieve or using a blender. Add the sugar, salt, cinnamon, nutmeg, cloves, eggs and cream and mix well. Pour the mixture into the prepared flan or pie dish. Place just above the centre in a moderately hot oven (200°C., 400°F., Gas Mark 6) and bake for 40 minutes or until the filling has set.

Allow to cool, then cut in wedges and serve with extra whipped cream flavoured with a pinch of nutmeg.
Serves 6

Pears with brown sugar and cream

Cold cream poured over a hot dessert, just before serving, is a marvellous combination. It's particularly good over hot baked fruits such as peaches, apricots, bananas or pears.

4 firm dessert pears   25 g/1 oz butter
2–3 tablespoons demerara sugar   1.5 dl/¼ pint double cream

Peel the pears, leaving them whole. Then slice in half lengthways and using a teaspoon scoop out the cores. Arrange the pears in a single layer in a buttered baking dish. Sprinkle liberally with the demerara sugar and add the butter cut in small pieces. Cover with a buttered paper, place above the centre of a moderately hot oven (200°C., 400°F., Gas Mark 6) and bake for 20 minutes or until the pears are tender.

Remove the dish from the heat, discard the buttered paper and pour the cold cream over the hot fruit. Serve at once from the dish.
Serves 4

Brandied apricots

Dried apricots prepared this way are delicious served with double cream – a simple dessert worthy of a special occasion. For an alternative use kirsch instead of brandy. Or omit either, use the juice of half a lemon and serve the apricots as a family dessert with vanilla ice cream.

225 g/8 oz dried apricots   2 tablespoons brandy
100 g/4 oz castor sugar

Rinse the apricots well in cold water, drain and place in a saucepan. Cover generously with boiling water. Place the lid on the pan and leave to soak for 4 hours.

Place the pan over the heat and bring up to a simmer. Cover and cook gently for about 40 minutes, or until the apricots are tender.

Draw the pan off the heat. Strain off the juice and place the apricots in a serving dish.

Measure out 1.5 dl ($\frac{1}{4}$ pint) of the apricot juice; if necessary make up with a little water. Return this to the saucepan and add the sugar. Stir over low heat until the sugar has dissolved. Remove from the heat and pour over the apricots. Cool, then add the brandy and chill for several hours until ready to serve. Serve with cream.
Serves 6

Iced coffee mousse

Coffee, brown sugar and brandy give this mousse a delicious flavour. It is a good dessert for a dinner party.

3 eggs
1.5 dl/$\frac{1}{4}$ pint strong black coffee (see method)
2 level teaspoons powdered gelatine

75 g/3 oz soft brown sugar
1 tablespoon brandy
1.5 dl/$\frac{1}{4}$ pint double cream

Separate the eggs and put the yolks and whites into separate basins. Measure the coffee into a small saucepan. If using instant coffee use 2–3 teaspoons to 1.5 dl ($\frac{1}{4}$ pint) boiling water and allow to cool. Sprinkle in the gelatine and set aside to soak for 5 minutes. Then stir over very low heat until dissolved, draw the pan off the heat and set aside while preparing the rest of the recipe.

Add the sugar to the egg yolks, then beat well with a whisk until thick and light in colour. Gradually whisk in the dissolved gelatine and continue beating until well blended. Stir in the brandy and set aside until cold and beginning to thicken.

Stiffly beat the egg whites and lightly whip the cream. Using a metal spoon, fold both into the coffee mixture. Pour the mousse into a serving dish and chill until set firm. Serve with a little extra single cream.
Serves 6

Scotch pancakes

Ideally these should be cooked on an old-fashioned iron girdle but a heavy cast-iron pan with a good flat base will do just as well. Thoroughly heating the pan is the first step towards success; test with a small spoonful of the mixture before making the pancakes in earnest.

225 g/8 oz plain flour
½ level teaspoon salt
2 level teaspoons cream of tartar
1 level teaspoon bicarbonate of
  soda

25 g/1 oz castor sugar
2 teaspoons golden syrup
1 large egg
a scant 2 dl/⅓ pint milk

Sift together the flour, salt, cream of tartar and bicarbonate of soda. Make a well in the centre and add the sugar, syrup and egg. Gradually add the milk, stirring from the centre of the bowl and slowly drawing in the flour from around the sides. Beat to a smooth, thick batter.

Have the girdle or frying pan well heated. Grease the surface with an oiled paper and drop dessertspoons of the batter mixture on to the hot surface. Cook only a few at a time spacing them well apart. When bubbles start to rise to the surface and the pancakes are brown on the underside, flip them over with a palette knife. Cook for a moment on the second side, then lift from the pan.

Cook the pancakes in batches, rubbing the pan with an oiled paper each time. As the pancakes are ready place between the folds of a clean teacloth. Serve warm with butter and jam.

Makes 2 dozen

Devil's food chocolate cake

Take care that the margarine used is at room temperature and so will blend easily with the other ingredients. Use the correct amount of sugar; the quantity listed is not a mistake.

225 g/8 oz plain flour
50 g/2 oz cocoa powder
1 level teaspoon bicarbonate of
  soda
¼ teaspoon salt

275 g/10 oz castor sugar
100 g/4 oz quick-creaming
  margarine
1.5 dl/¼ pint buttermilk
2 large eggs

Sift the flour, cocoa powder, bicarbonate of soda and salt into a mixing basin. Add the sugar and the margarine cut in pieces. Pour in the buttermilk and add the eggs. Stir with a wooden spoon just to blend the ingredients, then beat very thoroughly for 1 minute to get a smooth soft mixture.

Turn the mixture into two greased and lined 19- to 20-cm (7½- to 8-in) sandwich tins and spread level. Place in the centre of a moderate oven (180°C., 350°F., Gas Mark 4) and bake for 30 minutes. When baked the cakes will be well risen and springy to the touch. Cool in the tins and then turn out. Sandwich the layers with buttercream or with chocolate fudge frosting.
Makes two 19- to 20-cm (7½- to 8-in) layers

Fresh orange cake

A hot orange syrup spooned over the newly baked cake gives this recipe extra flavour and makes it deliciously moist. Serve it plain for tea, but for a party dessert cover the cake with whipped cream and decorate with segments of fresh orange.

175 g/6 oz self-raising flour
pinch salt
100 g/4 oz butter
100 g/4 oz castor sugar

finely grated rind of 1 large orange
2 large eggs
1–2 tablespoons milk to mix

for the orange syrup:
juice of 1 large orange

100 g/4 oz icing sugar

Sift the flour and salt on to a square of greaseproof paper and set aside. Cream the butter, sugar and finely grated orange rind until soft and light. Lightly mix the eggs and beat into the mixture a little at a time, adding a little of the flour along with the last few additions. Using a metal spoon, fold in the remaining flour and a little milk to make a soft dropping consistency.

Spoon the mixture into a greased and lined 20-cm (8-in) shallow

sandwich tin and spread level. Set in the centre of a moderate oven (180°C., 350°F., Gas Mark 4) and bake for 30 minutes or until risen and lightly brown. Remove the hot newly baked cake from the oven and leave in the tin.

Meanwhile put the strained orange juice in a saucepan and add the icing sugar. Set in a warm place or heat gently so that the sugar dissolves in the orange juice. Prick the hot cake layer all over with a fine skewer and spoon the hot orange syrup over the entire surface. It will appear at first that there is almost too much juice, but the cake will soak it all up. Leave until quite cold.

Loosen the sides and remove the cake carefully from the tin. Dust generously with icing sugar and serve.
Serves 6

Pastry-making for pies

Make pastry for fruit pies at least 30 minutes before rolling out; a relaxed pastry will shrink less in the heat of an oven. You can save time on preparation if you keep a supply of ready rubbed-in pastry in the refrigerator (see page 279). Just add water to make the pastry. Crumble toppings on fruit are quickest of all if you are really in a hurry. Add sugar to the rubbed-in pastry mix, sprinkle over the fruit and put to bake.

Layer the fresh fruit for a traditional pie with sugar to sweeten, about 75–100 g (3–4 oz) per 450 g (1 lb) of fruit, depending on the acidity. Finish with a layer of fruit – sugar next to the pastry crust makes it soft and sticky underneath. Use a pie funnel to hold the crust up when using soft canned or bottled fruit. Add only a small amount of liquid to pies, remembering that most of the juices will come from the fruit itself. Only

2–3 tablespoons of juice from canned or bottled fruit is necessary. The remaining fruit syrup can be thickened with a little cornflour and served as a sauce.

Set pies to bake in a hot oven – the richer the pastry the hotter the oven is the general rule. Once the pastry has browned, usually about 10–15 minutes, lower the heat for the filling to cook – about 20 minutes for soft fruit and up to 40 minutes for hard or stone fruits. Hot fruit pies are lovely served with chilled thick cream or vanilla ice cream.

Flapjack

Once baked and cooled, store flapjack in an airtight tin so that it remains nice and crisp.

50 g/2 oz butter	100 g/4 oz rolled oats
1 rounded tablespoon golden syrup	pinch salt
50 g/2 oz soft brown sugar	

Measure the butter, golden syrup and soft brown sugar into a saucepan. Set over low heat and stir occasionally until the butter has melted and the ingredients have blended. Draw the pan off the heat and add the rolled oats and a pinch of salt. Mix the ingredients together.

Spoon into a greased 18- to 20-cm (7- to 8-in) shallow sandwich tin and press level. Place in the centre of a moderate oven (180°C., 350°F., Gas Mark 4) and bake for 20–25 minutes. Remove from the heat and while hot mark the flapjack into eight neat divisions with a knife. Leave in the tin until cold, then remove from the tin and cut into pieces.
Makes 8 pieces

Shortcrust pastry mix

Your own pastry mix will save time when pastry is required. You simply do the rubbing in of fat to flour for shortcrust pastry in advance. Made in bulk and stored in a polythene bag in a cool place in the refrigerator, it will keep for about 4 weeks.

900 g/2 lb plain flour	225 g/8 oz white cooking fat
2 level teaspoons salt	225 g/8 oz butter or margarine

Sift the flour and salt into a large mixing basin. Blend the cooking fat and butter together. If both are at room temperature this is easily done with a palette knife on a flat plate. Add the fat to the flour and rub into the mixture. Cut through the mixture two or three times with a knife to remove any lumps of fat that might remain.

Spoon the mix into a polythene bag. Close and place in the refrigerator. To use the mix, just remember that the shortcrust pastry recipe has half as much fat as flour. In a recipe calling for 225 g (8 oz) flour and 100 g (4 oz) fat use 350 g (12 oz) mix. Use 175–250 g (6–9 oz) pastry mix to cover a 1-litre (1½-pint) pie dish and 350 g (12 oz) pastry mix for a plate pie with a top and bottom crust.

Measure the quantity required into a basin and, using a fork, stir in sufficient cold water – or water blended with 1 egg yolk for a rich shortcrust – to mix to a rough dough in the basin. Turn out on to a lightly floured working surface, knead for a moment and your pastry is ready to use.

Using the freezer in October

Get ahead with cooking sessions as October evenings draw in. Soups like *spinach soup, cream of sweetcorn soup* and *mixed vegetable soup* (see pages 256–8) all freeze well. Freeze in rigid containers leaving a 1-cm (½-in) headspace. Remove from the freezer, tip the contents into a saucepan when partly thawed and reheat gently, stirring until boiling. The *tuna fish pâté* (see page 260) can be made up in a foil container and frozen over-wrapped in polythene. Allow to thaw in the refrigerator overnight before serving. Storage time about 1 month. *Red cabbage with apple* (see page 269) is one of the best cooked vegetable recipes for the freezer. Freeze the cooked mixture in polythene bags. Reheat gently from frozen; it goes perfectly with game, roast pork or duck.

For children's teas you can make *Scotch pancakes* (see page 275) when you have a moment. They freeze perfectly. Pack flat in polythene bags in quantities for serving at one time. Allow to thaw at room temperature – about 1 hour. The *devil's food chocolate cake* (see page 277) with buttercream icing is also good for the freezer. Cut in portions and freeze uncovered until firm then pack in polythene bags. Slices can be taken out when required. Allow to thaw at room temperature.

Freezing game

All game must be hung before freezing – the length of time depends on individual taste. Pluck and clean birds and remove as much shot as possible. Then truss birds as for roasting to keep a neat shape. Old or badly shot birds can be made into casseroles or pâtés.

Pheasant Hang for 7–10 days according to the weather. A short spur at the back of the leg on a cock pheasant indicates a young bird. Hen birds should have a supple beak. Hold the full weight of the bird by the lower beak and if it doesn't bend or break it's last year's bird. Pack in polythene.

Wild duck and grouse Duck needs to hang for about 1–3 days and grouse for 4–6 days. Pack in polythene.

Rabbits and hares Rabbits should be hung for 24 hours but hares for up to 5 days. Skin and clean. Hare joints are bulky and it is best to make hare into a pâté or casserole before freezing.

Venison Hang usually for about 5 days and then skin, clean and cut up into joints. A piece of venison as a gift will already have been hung. Freeze good joints wrapped in polythene for roasting; other pieces can be made up into a casserole before freezing.

Pigeons These are useful frozen for casseroles.

All game should be thawed before cooking then roasting times are as for fresh birds. Thaw slowly overnight in the refrigerator and cook as soon as thawed.

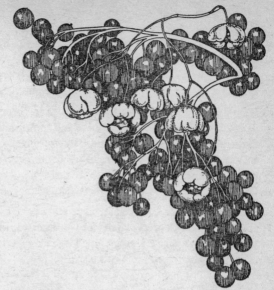

November

Although *November* brings cold weather and shorter evenings it has its compensations and provides a good supply of beef and pork, excellent game and a steadily improving selection of white fish. Winter greens have replaced salad vegetables and fine root vegetables are back for warming soups and stews. There are potatoes for baking and onions and parsnips to roast around the weekend joint.

Home-grown fruits consist only of apples and pears, but there is an increasing supply of imported fruits and some unusual ones among them, like bright red cranberries, attractive green Chinese gooseberries and fresh dates, all of which make lovely desserts. Towards the middle and end of the month, Christmas citrus fruit will begin to appear in the shops with juicy satsumas, clementines and tangerines.

It is as well to plan a little in advance and a good cook should be making elaborate culinary preparations for Christmas during the next four weeks. In an organized kitchen the Christmas pudding and cake should all be ready by the end of November.

Danish herrings

Before modern refrigeration techniques were developed herrings, when not eaten fresh, were preserved in casks between layers of salt. Salt herrings are very popular on the Continent and are available over here but usually at a Continental delicatessen counter. Quite frequently you can find Matjes herring fillets and these are especially good. The Danes serve them masked with sour cream and sprinkled with chives as part of a cold table, but they make a very good first course on their own.

4–6 salt herring fillets	1 tablespoon chopped chives
milk (see method)	pumpernickel or brown bread
1 carton soured cream	

Soak the herring fillets for several hours or overnight in milk to cover. Next day drain the fillets and place in a serving dish. Add the sour cream and chives and leave to marinate for 2–3 hours. Serve with slices of pumpernickel or brown bread and butter.

Serves 4

Anchovies in puff pastry

Serve these hot at a drinks or sherry party. You can get them ready for baking well in advance. Keep them in the refrigerator, then pop in the oven about 20 minutes before serving.

1 213-g/7½-oz packet frozen puff
  pastry

1 57-g/2-oz can anchovy fillets
lightly beaten egg

Allow the puff pastry to thaw for about 1 hour at room temperature. On a floured board roll the pastry to a rectangle about 20 cm (8 in) wide and 35 cm (14 in) long. Trim all the edges straight with a knife and then cut the pastry in half lengthways to make two strips. Brush one strip with lightly beaten egg.

Separate out the contents of the can of anchovy fillets and arrange the anchovies (unsoaked because they taste nice when a little salty) side by side down the pastry strip which has been brushed with egg. Cover with the second strip of pastry and press the edges well together to seal.

Using a sharp knife, cut across the strip to get about 24 thin fingers of puff pastry with anchovy inside. Brush the tops with a little beaten egg and arrange the strips of pastry on a baking tray rinsed with cold water. Place in the centre of a hot oven (220°C., 425°F., Gas Mark 7) and bake for 15 minutes or until risen and golden brown. Serve hot.
Makes 2 dozen

Pheasant soup

Game soup makes good use of the carcass left over from roast birds. This recipe can also be made using the carcass of wild duck, although the soup will need careful skimming to remove any fat.

3-4 rashers bacon
100 g/4 oz lamb's liver
50 g/3 oz butter
2 pheasant carcasses
2.25 litres/4 pints chicken stock
3 dl/½ pint dry white wine

salt and freshly milled pepper
pinch ground mace
bouquet garni
25 g/1 oz flour
2 tablespoons sherry

Dice the bacon, trim and cut up the liver. Melt 50 g (2 oz) of the butter in a large saucepan and lightly fry the bacon and liver. Add the pheasant carcasses, then pour in the stock and wine. Season with salt and pepper and add the mace and bouquet garni. Bring to the boil, skim the surface, then cover with a lid and simmer gently for 2 hours.

Strain the soup and return the stock to the pan. Pass the bits of meat from the carcass, the bacon and liver, along with a little of the stock, through a vegetable mill or purée in a blender. Add the purée to the soup along with the remaining butter, blended with the flour, which will slightly thicken the mixture. Bring back to the boil stirring all the time so that the soup thickens evenly. Taste for seasoning, add the sherry and serve.

Serves 6

Bacon and lentil soup

A small inexpensive bacon knuckle is marvellous for flavouring lentil soup. What little meat there is can be scraped off the bone and added too. Serve with a garnish of crisply fried bread.

175 g/6 oz lentils
1 small knuckle of bacon
15 g/½ oz butter
2 onions or leeks
1.5 litres/2½ pints water

bouquet garni
freshly milled pepper
1.5 dl/¼ pint milk
25 g/1 oz flour

Soak the lentils overnight in cold water to cover, then drain well. Soak the bacon knuckle separately in cold water to cover. Next day drain and pat dry. Scrape the skin well.

Melt the butter in a large saucepan. Peel and chop the onion or wash and finely shred the leeks. Add to the butter and fry gently for a few moments until soft but not brown. Stir in the soaked lentils and the water. Add the bacon knuckle, bouquet garni and a seasoning of pepper. Bring up to the boil, skim and cover with a lid. Simmer gently for 1½ hours. When the lentils are quite soft, draw the pan off the heat.

Remove the bacon knuckle. Pass the soup through a sieve or vegetable mill, or purée in an electric blender, and return to the pan. Pour the milk into a basin, sift the flour over the surface and whisk until smooth – there should be no lumps. Add to the soup and stir until boiling.

Remove the rind from the bacon knuckle and scrape the meat away

from the bone. Chop the meat coarsely and add to the soup. Taste
and season if required. Serve with a garnish of crisply fried bread.
Serves 4-6

Snails with garlic butter

*The strong flavour of garlic butter sometimes discourages people from
eating snails, so always check before you serve them. Edible snails are
specially bred, the finest being vineyard snails reared and fattened on
vine leaves. The average-sized can contains 24 snails with shells; allow
six snails per serving for four people. Any accompanying snail shells can
be washed and used again. After the first time, you can buy the cans of
snails without the additional shells.*

1 213-g/7½-oz can *escargots au
  naturel*, containing 24 snails with
  shells

for the garlic butter:
175 g/6 oz butter
3 cloves garlic
salt and freshly milled pepper

3 tablespoons finely chopped
  parsley

Wipe the snail shells and drain the snails from the can. Set aside
while preparing the garlic butter.

Cream the butter until soft. Peel the garlic and crush with a little
salt to a purée, using the blade of a knife. Add the garlic purée,
parsley and a seasoning of pepper to the butter and mix well.

Take each shell in turn and using a knife push a little of the garlic
butter into the shell. Push a snail right into the shell and finally seal
the entrance of the shell with more garlic butter. Keep refrigerated
until ready to serve.

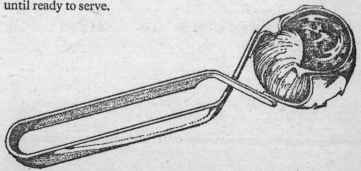

Place the prepared snails on fireproof snail plates allowing six snails per person, place in a hot oven (220°C., 425°F., Gas Mark 7) and heat through until the snails are hot and the butter is bubbling and beginning to brown.

Serve at once with hot French bread, which can be broken and used to mop up the melted butter on each plate.
Serves 4

Onion tart

The use of soured cream and caraway seeds gives this onion tart a delicious flavour. Serve warm as a first course or with a salad for a lunch dish.

100 g/4 oz shortcrust pastry

for the filling:

450 g/1 lb onions	3 large eggs
50 g/2 oz butter	1 carton soured cream
salt and freshly milled pepper	½ level teaspoon caraway seeds

Roll the pastry out on a floured working surface and use to line a 20-cm (8-in) tart or quiche tin with a loose base. Set aside in a cool place while preparing the filling.

Peel and slice the onions. Add to the melted butter in a saucepan. Cover and cook very gently for about 15–20 minutes or until the onions are soft. Remove the pan lid and fry a little more quickly for a few moments, this time to allow the onion to brown. Draw off the heat.

Lightly mix the eggs and soured cream and stir into the onions. Season well with salt and pepper and add the caraway seeds. Pour the filling into the pastry-lined case. Set above centre in a moderately hot oven (190°C., 375°F., Gas Mark 5) and bake for 40–45 minutes. Serve warm.
Serves 4-6

Sweetbreads in spinach sauce

Spinach gives colour and flavour to this sauce for lambs' sweetbreads. In a recipe such as this one, where part hot stock and part cold milk are used for mixing the sauce, always stir in the hot liquid first; it blends in more readily and smoothly.

675 g/1½ lb lambs' sweetbreads

4 dl/¾ pint chicken stock

for the spinach sauce:

450 g/1 lb fresh spinach
50 g/2 oz butter
25 g/1 oz flour
1.5 dl/¼ pint hot stock (see method)

1.5 dl/¼ pint milk
1–2 tablespoons cream
salt and freshly milled pepper
pinch nutmeg

Soak the sweetbreads for several hours in cold water, changing the water once or twice. This extracts the blood and helps keep the sweetbreads white. Rinse the sweetbreads and place in a saucepan. Cover with fresh cold salted water and bring up to the boil. Simmer for 5 minutes. Draw off the heat, drain the sweetbreads and when cool enough to handle, remove all the loose fat, tissue and skin. Replace in the saucepan and add chicken stock to cover. Bring to the boil, then simmer gently for 45 minutes or until the sweetbreads are tender.

Meanwhile, wash the spinach well and remove the coarse centre ribs from the leaves. When the sweetbreads are tender, drain and reserve the hot stock. Melt half the butter in a saucepan, stir in the flour and cook gently for a moment. Gradually beat in the hot stock and then the milk, stirring well all the time to get a smooth sauce. Bring up to the boil and simmer gently for 2–3 minutes.

Sauté the spinach in the remaining butter over a gentle heat for about 8–10 minutes, or until tender. Stir in the prepared sauce and heat the spinach and sauce together for about 5 minutes. Pass the mixture through a sieve or vegetable mill and return to the saucepan. Stir in the cream, season with salt, plenty of pepper and the nutmeg. Pour the sauce over the sweetbreads, reheat to serve.
Serves 4

Black pudding with apple sauce

On days when something inexpensive is required for lunch or supper take a look at your nearest delicatessen counter. Boudin noir, or black pudding as we call it, is good value for money. It should be sliced and then grilled or fried. It is spicy and is best served with something slightly sweet like apple sauce or red cabbage and plenty of sautéed potatoes.

2–3 black puddings, according to size
25 g/1 oz butter for frying

for the apple sauce:

450 g/1 lb cooking apples
2 tablespoons water

1 tablespoon castor sugar
15 g/½ oz butter

Remove any protective outer covering and cut the black puddings into 1-cm (½-in) thick slices. Set aside until ready to fry.

Meanwhile prepare the apple sauce. Peel, core and slice the apples. Place in a saucepan with the water. Cover and cook gently, stirring occasionally, until the apples become quite soft. Then stir with a wooden spoon to make a purée. Add the sugar and butter and keep hot.

Add the slices of black pudding to the hot melted butter in a frying pan. Fry gently for about 5 minutes, turning them occasionally to heat through. Serve hot with the apple sauce.

Serves 4

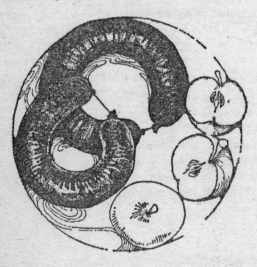

Stovies

Stovies are made using the leftover dripping and gravy from a roast. They are a regular Monday dish in many Scottish households. Chopped pieces of cooked meat, poultry or game can also be added.

450 g/1 lb potatoes
1 large onion
15–25 g/½–1 oz roast dripping

salt and freshly milled pepper
1.5 dl/¼ pint roast gravy or water
leftover cooked meat

Peel the potatoes and slice thickly. Peel and thinly slice the onion. Melt the dripping in a heavy frying pan, add the onion and fry for a few moments. Add the sliced potatoes and turn them in the hot fat. Season with salt and pepper and add any chopped meat. Pour over the gravy or water – there should be just enough to cover the base of the pan and prevent the stovies from sticking.

Cover with a lid and cook very gently for about 30 minutes. Strictly speaking stovies should not be stirred during cooking. Give the pan an occasional shake and keep the lid on. Stir only if the vegetables begin to stick. When cooked, stovies should be brown and slightly crisp underneath. Serve very hot.
Serves 4

Roasting joints

A good-sized joint of meat will always roast better than a small one. Meat that has a good covering of natural fat will retain more moisture and flavour. A lean joint of meat should be smeared with fat before roasting.

Beef Start beef in a hot oven (220°C., 425°F., Gas Mark 7) for 15 minutes then lower to 190°C., 375°F., Gas Mark 5 for the remaining time, allowing 15 minutes per 0.5 kg (1 lb) plus 15 minutes for a rare joint and 20 minutes per 0.5 kg (1 lb) plus 20 minutes for well done.

Lamb Roast lamb slowly. For a simple unstuffed joint, allow 30 minutes per 0.5 kg (1 lb), cooking the meat in a moderate oven (180°C., 350°F., Gas Mark 4). For stuffed joints allow 35 minutes per 0.5 kg (1 lb). A plain joint of lamb is greatly improved if the surface is rubbed all over with a cut clove of garlic. Dredge a little seasoned flour over the fatty part of the meat and rub it well in to get a crisp, golden finish.

Pork Pork needs a hot oven (220°C., 425°F., Gas Mark 7) for the first

20 minutes, then lower the heat to 190°C., 375°F., Gas Mark 5. Allow 35 minutes per 0.5 kg (1 lb) plus 35 minutes. For a crisp crackling make sure the joint has a good rind and that it is well scored. Rub with salt and roast *without* basting. Raise the heat for the last 15 minutes of the cooking time to crisp the crackling.

Take a chef's tip Instead of standing the meat on a trivet in the roasting tin stand it on a bed of vegetables – a carrot and an onion cut into 2–3 thick slices, a stalk of celery and a bay leaf. During the cooking the vegetables caramelize at the edges and give a wonderful colour and flavour to the gravy.

To make the gravy For a thin gravy, strain off all the fat from the roasting tin, leaving behind any flavouring vegetables or crispy brown bits. Add 6 dl (1 pint) stock or vegetable water. Stir and boil briskly till reduced by about half. Taste and correct the seasoning. Strain into a hot sauceboat. For a thick gravy, leave a tablespoon of fat in the tin, add a tablespoon of flour and blend well. Add the liquid and stir it in smoothly. Cook and stir for 2–3 minutes after boiling. Taste and correct the seasoning.

Meat patties

Savoury meat patties made using cold roast beef or lamb are delicious provided equal quantities of meat and potato are used and ingredients are well seasoned.

225 g/8 oz cold roast beef or lamb
225 g/8 oz cooked mashed potato
salt and freshly milled pepper
½ teaspoon Worcestershire sauce

1 egg
toasted breadcrumbs
50–100 g/2–4 oz white fat for frying

Trim away any fat and mince the meat. Mix the meat and the well-mashed potato very thoroughly. Season with salt, pepper and Worcestershire sauce. Separate the egg, adding the yolk to the mixture and reserving the white for coating the patties.

Turn the mixture out on to a clean working surface and divide equally into four or six portions. With lightly floured hands, shape each portion into a round patty. Lightly mix the egg white with a fork. Place the crumbs on a plate or square of greaseproof paper. Dip each patty first in the egg white to coat all sides, then roll in the toasted breadcrumbs. Pat the coating on firmly and set the patties aside until ready to fry.

Add to the hot fat, melted, in a frying pan. Fry for 3–5 minutes or until golden brown on both sides. Drain and serve.
Serves 4

Pot roast

This is the way to cook joints of meat like topside, fresh silverside or brisket, cuts that benefit from the gently moist method of cooking. If you use wine or cider the gravy will be rich and full of flavour. Choose a deep casserole with a tight-fitting lid that will keep in all the moisture.

1–1.25 kg/2⅓–3 lb topside of beef	1.5 dl/¼ pint red wine or cider
25 g/1 oz dripping or white cooking fat	bay leaf
2 carrots	stock or water (see method)
1 onion	1 level tablespoon cornflour
1 stalk celery	2 tablespoons water
1 leek	salt and freshly milled pepper

Add the meat to the hot dripping melted in a heavy fireproof casserole. Brown on both sides and then remove from the pan. Peel the carrots and slice in half lengthways. Peel the onion and slice thickly, cut up the celery and wash and halve the leek. Place the vegetables in the casserole and allow them to fry gently for a few moments to absorb the fat. Add sufficient wine or cider just to cover the vegetables and bring to a simmer.

Replace the meat in the casserole setting it on top of the vegetables. Add the bay leaf and cover with a lid. Place in the centre of a very moderate oven (160°C., 325°F., Gas Mark 3) and cook for 2–2½ hours.

When the meat is cooked, lift from the pan and keep hot. Strain off the liquor, skim and make it up to 4 dl (¾ pint) with stock or water. Add the cornflour blended with the water and stir until boiling. Check seasoning with salt and pepper and serve as gravy.
Serves 6

Note Don't waste the vegetables. Purée with 6 dl (1 pint) stock in a blender to make soup.

Duckling with sweet and sour pineapple

Duckling makes a good dinner party choice when the messy carving or cutting up can be done in the kitchen. Here the pieces of duck are served in a piquant pineapple sauce which goes well with the rich flavour of the duck flesh.

2 oven-ready ducklings, about 2–2.25 kg/4½–5 lb	salt

for the sauce:

1 340-g/12-oz can pineapple chunks	1 tablespoon soy sauce
4 tablespoons vinegar	¼ level teaspoon salt
75 g/3 oz soft brown sugar	2 level tablespoons cornflour

Wipe the ducklings and rub a little salt into the skin. Prick the surface all over with the prongs of a fork and place the ducklings in a roasting tin. Add 2 tablespoons cold water – no fat. Set the tin in the centre of a moderate oven (180°C., 350°F., Gas Mark 4) and roast, allowing 25 minutes per 0.5 kg (1lb). Simmer the giblets in water for 30 minutes, then strain to make stock.

Meanwhile prepare the sauce. Drain the pineapple from the can and reserve the syrup. Make the syrup up to 3 dl (½ pint) with the duck stock – or use water. Add the vinegar, sugar, soy sauce and salt. Measure the cornflour into a saucepan. Moisten with a little of the liquid, then add the remainder. Place the pan over moderate heat and cook, stirring all the time, until the mixture has thickened and is boiling. Add the pineapple pieces and draw off the heat.

Carve the cooked duck in portions and arrange in a hot dish. Pour over the sweet and sour sauce and serve.
Serves 8

Chicken curry

The best curried dishes are made with fresh meat, not leftovers. Slow oven cooking encourages this sauce to give lots of flavour to the chicken joints.

4 chicken joints seasoned flour	25 g/1 oz butter for frying

for the curry sauce:

40 g/1½ oz butter
1 small onion, finely chopped
½ cooking apple, diced
2–4 level tablespoons curry powder
6 dl/1 pint chicken stock
small bay leaf
1 tablespoon mango chutney or
  apricot jam

1 tablespoon brown sugar
juice of ½ lemon
½ level teaspoon salt
1 level tablespoon cornflour
  blended with 2 tablespoons cold
  water

Trim the chicken joints and toss in seasoned flour. Melt the butter in a frying pan, add the chicken joints and fry to brown on both sides. Lift the joints from the pan and place in a casserole. Set aside while preparing the curry sauce.

Melt the butter in a saucepan and add the onion and diced apple. Cook gently for a few minutes until the onion is soft. Stir in the curry powder and cook for a further few moments, then stir in the stock and bring up to the boil. Add the bay leaf, chutney or apricot jam, sugar, lemon juice and salt. Bring up to the boil, then draw off the heat and pour over the chicken joints in the casserole. Cover with a lid, place in the centre of a moderate oven (180°C., 350°F., Gas Mark 4) and cook for 1 hour, or until the chicken is tender.

Lift the chicken joints from the casserole on to a serving dish. Stir the blended cornflour and water into the curry sauce remaining in the casserole. Stir over the heat until the sauce has thickened and is boiling. Draw off the heat and strain the sauce over the chicken. Serve with plain boiled rice and the usual curry accompaniments.
Serves 4

Game pie

Use tender young game and lean steak in game pie so that the cooking time can be completed within the 1½ hours. Grouse, venison, pigeon or a mixture of game could also be used.

1 plump pheasant
1 onion
salt and freshly milled pepper
4 tablespoons red wine
225 g/8 oz lean steak
3–4 rashers lean bacon
seasoned flour

25 g/1 oz dripping or white
  cooking fat
100 g/4 oz mushrooms
pinch dried herbs
225 g/8 oz puff or flaky pastry
egg for glazing

Cut the flesh from the pheasant, removing as much bone as possible. Place the wings and backbone in a saucepan. Add half the onion and a seasoning of salt and pepper. Add cold water to cover the carcass and bring to the boil. Skim and simmer gently for 1 hour. Strain and then boil rapidly to reduce and concentrate the game stock to about 3 dl (½ pint). Meanwhile cut the game flesh into neat pieces. Place in a shallow dish and add the remaining half onion, finely chopped. Season with salt and pepper and add the red wine. Leave to marinate until ready to use.

Cut the steak into strips, trim and chop the bacon rashers. Toss the steak in seasoned flour and add to the hot fat in a frying pan. Fry gently until browned. Lift the steak from the pan and place in a 1-litre (1½-pint) pie dish along with the chopped bacon, trimmed mushrooms and the pieces of game drained from the marinade. Add the herbs.

To the hot fat in the frying pan add about 1 level tablespoon of the seasoned flour. Stir over gentle heat until the flour has absorbed the fat and cooked to a good brown colour. Carefully stir in the reserved game stock and the strained marinade. Bring to the boil and simmer, stirring well to make a good gravy. Check for seasoning and then strain into the pie dish.

Roll out the pastry and cut a top for the pie. Use the trimmings to line the greased pie dish rim. Damp the pastry rim and cover with the pastry top. Knock up the pie edges and brush the whole pie with lightly mixed egg. Make a hole in the centre and arrange an attractive decoration cut from any remaining pastry pieces.

Put the pie to bake above centre in a hot oven (220°C., 425°F., Gas Mark 7) for 30 minutes. Then lower the oven heat to moderate (180°C., 350°F., Gas Mark 4) and bake for a further hour. Cover the pie top with greased paper or foil if it begins to brown too much. Serve hot.
Serves 4-6

Partridge casserole

Use older birds for casseroling and have them plucked and drawn. Towards the end of the year there is usually plenty of game available for this kind of recipe.

3 partridges	a scant litre/1½ pints stock
100 g/4 oz streaky bacon rashers	25 g/1 oz dripping or vegetable fat
225 g/8 oz button onions	1 small onion
225 g/8 oz button mushrooms	1 heaped tablespoon flour
bouquet garni	salt and pepper
1.5 dl/¼ pint red wine	

Wipe over the partridges and set aside. Trim and dice the streaky
bacon and, reserving half, heat the remainder in a heavy flameproof
casserole until the fat runs. Add the partridges and brown all over.
Peel the button onions, leaving them whole. Trim the mushrooms,
leaving them whole, and reserve any stalks. Draw the casserole off
the heat and add the button onions, mushrooms and bouquet garni.
Pour over the red wine and 3 dl (½ pint) of the stock and cover with
a lid. Place in the centre of a very moderate oven (160°C., 325°F.,
Gas Mark 3) and cook for 2–2½ hours or until the birds are tender.

Meanwhile, heat the remaining bacon pieces in a saucepan along
with the dripping or vegetable fat. Finely chop the onion and add to
the pan. Cook gently until the onion is soft. Add the flour and
continue to cook gently until the mixture is a dark brown colour –
about 15 minutes. Gradually stir in the remaining stock and bring
up to the boil, stirring all the time to make a brown sauce. Add any
mushroom trimmings, lower the heat and allow to simmer for 30
minutes. If the sauce thickens during cooking time leave it until the
partridges are cooked and then thin the sauce with a little of the
liquid from the casserole.

When the partridges are cooked, strain off the liquid and remove the
bouquet garni. Lift the birds from the casserole, cool for a few
moments, then cut the birds in half, removing each breast and leg
section from the carcass. Replace these in the casserole with the
vegetables. Add any liquid necessary to the brown sauce and season
with salt and pepper. Strain the sauce over the birds, sprinkle with
chopped parsley and keep hot until ready to serve.
Serves 6

Roast parsnips

*One of our most useful winter vegetables is the parsnip. Parsnips can be
added to stews or served as a vegetable on their own. They are*

particularly good roasted and are usually very popular mixed with potatoes in the roasting pan.

675 g/1½ lb parsnips   50–75 g/2–3 oz hot dripping
seasoned flour

Peel the parsnips and cut up into sticks about 5 cm (2 in) long. Place in a saucepan, cover with cold salted water and bring up to the boil. Simmer gently for 5 minutes, then draw off the heat and drain. Return them to the hot saucepan and dry for a moment over the heat. Toss in a little seasoned flour to coat all over.

Add to the hot dripping around the joint, or place in a separate roasting tin with the hot dripping. Turn them in the dripping to coat all over. Place in a moderately hot oven (190°C., 375°F., Gas Mark 5), or set above the roast; bake for 45 minutes. Turn and baste once or twice until golden and tender.
Serves 4

Deep-fried onion rings

Crisp onion rings make a marvellous garnish for grilled or fried steak or pork chops. Use the large Spanish onions to get the best rings.

2 large onions   seasoned flour
1 egg white

Peel the onions leaving them whole and cut across into thin slices. Separate into rings and chill in iced water for about 20 minutes so that they are nice and crisp.

Drain the onion rings and pat dry. Beat the egg white with a fork, just enough to break up the white but not to make it frothy. Spear the onion rings on a fork and dip first in the egg white and then in seasoned flour. Shake away any excess coating and deep-fry the rings in hot fat for 1–2 minutes or until crisp and pale golden. Drain and serve at once.
Serves 4

Baked potatoes with salt

Potatoes are just right now for baking in their jackets. Choose potatoes that go soft and floury. Roll them in kitchen salt before baking – salt brings out the flavour and keeps the skins crisp.

4 large even-sized potatoes   **butter**
coarse kitchen salt

Scrub the potatoes well and while still damp roll in kitchen salt. Set in a baking or roasting tin – this is easiest for four or more potatoes. Place in a moderate oven (180°C., 350°F., Gas Mark 4) and bake for 1½–1¾ hours. When cooked the potatoes will feel quite soft when the sides are gently pressed.

Make a crossways slit on the top of each one using a sharp knife. Hold the potato in a cloth and squeeze gently to force the potato open and push the middle up. Top with a pat of butter and serve.
Serves 4

Sweetcorn fritters

Serve sweetcorn fritters as an accompaniment to grilled or fried chicken, or with bacon for breakfast.

100 g/4 oz plain flour   salt and freshly milled pepper
1 large egg   50 g/2 oz butter
1.25 dl/¼ pint milk   1 tablespoon oil
1 312-g/11-oz can creamed-style
  sweetcorn

Sift the flour into a mixing basin and make a well in the centre. Add the egg and gradually stir in the milk, gradually drawing in the flour from around the sides of the basin. Beat to make a smooth batter. Stir in the sweetcorn and season with salt and pepper to taste.

Heat the butter and oil in a frying pan and when hot add tablespoons of the corn fritter batter. Cook until golden brown on the underside, then turn each fritter and fry to brown the second side. Fry fritters a few at a time, keeping the prepared ones hot, uncovered so they remain crisp.
Makes 12 fritters

Rosy salad

For salads buy beetroot that are already cooked and only the skin needs to be removed. The bright juices from the beetroot flesh which so annoyingly stain other ingredients are used to advantage in this recipe, for they colour the whole salad a pretty pink.

1 medium-sized cooked beetroot
2–3 stalks celery
225 g/8 oz hard dessert apples

4 tablespoons oil and vinegar
dressing

Skin the beetroot and cut into neat, small dice. Slice the celery stalks thinly and peel, core and dice the apples. Mix all together with the dressing until the apple and celery take on a delicate pink colour from the beetroot. Pile in a dish and serve. You can add a border of watercress sprigs, endive or chicory if you like.

Serves 4

Fresh cranberry pie

The bright red cranberries that begin to appear in the shops from now until Christmas make a delicious pie. Pick over the fruit removing the stalks and any soft berries before using them.

175 g/6 oz sweet shortcrust pastry

milk to glaze

for the filling:

1.5 dl/¼ pint water
175 g/6 oz soft brown sugar
225 g/8 oz fresh cranberries

1 rounded teaspoon cornflour
25 g/1 oz butter

Divide the pastry in half and on a lightly floured working surface roll one piece out to a circle 2.5 cm (1 in) larger all round than a buttered 20- to 23-cm (8- to 9-in) shallow pie plate. Line with the pastry and set aside while preparing the filling.

Measure the water and sugar into a saucepan and stir over moderate heat until the sugar has dissolved. Bring up to the boil and add the cranberries. Simmer gently, stirring occasionally, for about 10 minutes until the skins have popped and the berries are tender. Draw off the heat. Blend the cornflour to a smooth paste with 1 tablespoon water, stir into the fruit and bring back to the boil, stirring until thickened. Draw the pan off the heat, stir in the butter and leave to cool.

Pour the cranberry filling into the lined pie shell. Roll out the remaining pastry and cover the pie. Seal the edges together and trim. Brush with milk and place the pie above centre in a hot oven (220°C., 425°F., Gas Mark 7) and bake for 30 minutes. Serve hot with fresh cream.

Serves 6

Baked cranberries and bananas

Sometimes the most unlikely fruits turn out to be very compatible, like this sharp-flavoured and colourful mixture of cooked cranberries with bananas.

175 g/6 oz castor sugar
1.5 dl/¼ pint water
225 g/8 oz fresh cranberries

6 firm ripe bananas
25 g/1 oz melted butter
pinch salt

Measure the sugar and water into a medium-sized saucepan. Stir over low heat to dissolve the sugar. Wash the cranberries, remove any soft berries and stalks. Add the berries to the pan and bring up to the boil. Reduce the heat and simmer for about 10 minutes until the berries are quite soft. Draw off the heat.

Peel the bananas and slice lengthways. Place in a shallow baking dish, brush with the melted butter and sprinkle with salt. Pour over the cranberries. Place in the centre of a moderate oven (180°C., 350°F., Gas Mark 4) and cook for 15 minutes or until the bananas are soft. Serve warm with single cream.
Serves 6

Apple snow

The famous Bramley's Seedlings appear much later in the apple season. Remember that these very acid apples tend to 'fluff and fall' during cooking and because of this are best used for purées and in desserts where puréed apples are required.

675 g/1½ lb cooking apples
3 tablespoons water
2 pieces thinly pared lemon rind
100 g/4 oz castor sugar

few drops green food colouring
 (optional)
3 egg whites

Peel and core the apples and slice into a saucepan. Add the water and pared lemon rind. Cover and simmer gently until tender – about 15 minutes. Draw off the heat, remove the pieces of lemon rind and add the sugar. Make a smooth purée by rubbing the mixture through a sieve into a large mixing basin. Add a few drops of green colouring if you like – it improves the appearance of the finished dessert. Set the purée aside until cold.

Whip the egg whites until stiff and fold into the apple purée. Whisk again until the mixture becomes thick and light. Pour into a dish and chill until ready to serve.

Serves 4-6

Pear and grape compote

Pears are plentiful and so are grapes. Combine them to make this fruit compote, one that goes well with vanilla ice cream.

4 firm dessert pears	juice of 1 lemon
175 g/6 oz castor sugar	225 g/8 oz green grapes
1.5 dl/¼ pint water	

Peel and halve the pears, then using a teaspoon scoop out the cores. Measure the sugar and water into a saucepan and stir over low heat to dissolve the sugar. Add the lemon juice and bring up to the boil. Add the pear halves, cover with a lid and simmer gently for 10–15 minutes or until the pears are tender.

Lift the pears from the pan and place in a serving dish. Add the washed, halved and deseeded grapes and pour over the syrup. Cool, then chill until ready to serve.

Serves 4

Oranges in Cointreau

Keep a large bowl of these in the refrigerator ready chilled. They make a quick dessert and are particularly delicious with vanilla ice cream.

6 oranges	juice of ½ lemon
175 g/6 oz castor sugar	1–2 tablespoons Cointreau
1.5 dl/¼ pint water	

Mark the peel of the oranges into quarters with a sharp knife. Put the oranges together in a large basin and cover them with boiling water. Allow to stand for 5 minutes, then drain and peel away the skins. Using this method both the outer peel and the inner white pith will come away from the fruit. If any white pith remains, simply scrape it away with a knife. Slice the oranges thinly, remove any pips and place the slices in a serving dish.

Measure the sugar and water into a saucepan. Stir over low heat until the sugar has dissolved. Bring to the boil and simmer for 2–3 minutes. Draw off the heat, add the lemon juice and allow to cool for 5 minutes.

Add the Cointreau and pour the hot syrup over the fruit. Cool then chill in the refrigerator until required.

Serves 6

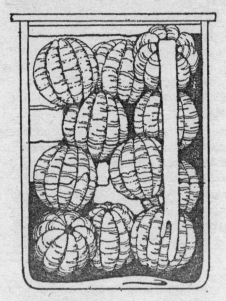

Coffee layer cake

This is a coffee cake with a soft moist texture and a particularly easy-to-make fudge icing that sets firm. Use the light golden soft brown sugar in the cake mixture in preference to the Barbados type.

100 g/4 oz self-raising flour	100 g/4 oz soft brown sugar
pinch salt	2 large/standard eggs
100 g/4 oz butter	2 teaspoons coffee essence

for the fudge icing:

175 g/6 oz icing sugar	2 tablespoons water
40 g/1½ oz butter	1 teaspoon coffee essence
50 g/2 oz castor sugar	

Sift the self-raising flour and salt on to a square of greaseproof paper and set aside. Cream the butter and soft brown sugar until light.

Lightly mix the eggs and coffee essence and beat into the creamed mixture a little at a time, adding some of the sifted flour along with the last few additions of egg. Using a metal spoon fold in the remaining flour. Spoon the mixture into two greased and lined 18-cm (7-in) sponge sandwich tins and spread level. Place above centre in a moderate oven (180°C., 350°F., Gas Mark 4) and bake for 20–25 minutes. Allow the cake layers to cool.

Meanwhile sieve the icing sugar into a bowl. Measure the butter, castor sugar, water and coffee essence into a saucepan. Set the pan over the heat and stir until the butter has melted and the mixture is almost boiling. Pour at once into the icing sugar and stir with a wooden spoon until smooth. At this stage the icing is quite thin. Set aside to cool and thicken.

For a coating fudge icing use the mixture when thick enough to coat the back of a spoon generously. For a thick fudge icing leave the mixture until quite cold and then beat with a wooden spoon to a fudge consistency. Use a little of the icing to sandwich the cake layers and spread the remainder on top of the cake. Set aside until quite firm before serving.

Makes one 18-cm (7-in) layer cake

Cherry cake

To prevent cherries sinking in a cake the outer sugary coating that surrounds them must be removed. A little cream of tartar sifted with the dry ingredients toughens the flour; this also helps to keep the cherries in place.

225 g/8 oz plain flour
2 level teaspoons baking powder
¼ level teaspoon cream of tartar
100 g/4 oz glacé cherries

175 g/6 oz butter
175 g/6 oz castor sugar
3 large eggs
½ teaspoon vanilla essence

Sift the flour, baking powder, cream of tartar and salt on to a square of greaseproof paper and set aside. Rinse the cherries in warm water to remove the sugary coating. Cut in quarters, then pat dry in a clean cloth or absorbent kitchen paper. Place the cherries in a basin and add 2 tablespoons of the sifted flour. Toss the cherries to coat them well and set aside.

Cream the butter and sugar together until light. Mix the eggs and vanilla essence, then gradually beat into the creamed butter and sugar. Beat each addition of egg in well before adding the next. Add a little of the sifted flour along with the last few additions. Using a metal spoon fold in the remaining sifted flour, then fold in the cherries.

Spoon the mixture into a 20-cm (8-in) round deep cake tin which has been greased and lined with greaseproof paper. Place in the centre of a moderate oven (180°C., 350°F., Gas Mark 4) and bake for 1 hour. Then reduce the heat to 160°C., 325°F., Gas Mark 3, for a final 30 minutes. Cool in the tin for 30 minutes before turning out. Leave until quite cold before cutting.

Makes one 20-cm (8-in) cake

Cake-making

The temperature of ingredients is important when you mix a cake. Fat which is chilled will not cream easily. Cold eggs will quickly curdle when added to the creamed fat and sugar, and the cake will lose in lightness and good texture.

Bring fat and eggs required out of the refrigerator or cold larder some time in advance. While preparing the other ingredients, fill the mixing bowl to be used with warm water and put the eggs in to warm up. By the time everything else is ready the eggs will be at just the right temperature for cracking and whisking and the bowl will be pleasantly warm when the fat and sugar are put in for creaming.

Oven and tins should be ready. Prepare the cake tins, set the oven at the correct temperature and make sure the shelves are at the right height. Small cakes and sandwich cakes may be baked on the second or third shelf from the top, but large cakes need the centre for even baking.

Keep ready-cut paper liners for tins in a kitchen drawer. Use *squares of paper* for round sandwich tins – cut several at a time. As long as two-thirds of the base of a round tin is covered, the cake will turn out easily.

Any additional ingredients such as fruit, nuts, cherries or peel should be prepared ready for use. Fruit should be cleaned, dried and picked over, and glacé cherries or fruits and candied peel well rinsed to remove the sugary coating, dried and cut up. Nuts should be blanched and chopped.

Using an electric mixer An electric mixer can take much of the effort out of cake-making. But machines vary in size so always read the instructions carefully, noting in particular any limitations regarding quantities to use at any one time. Only the larger, more powerful machines will be able to cope with the heavier fruit cake quantities.

Avoid taking fat straight from the refrigerator. Butter, margarine or cooking fat used must be at room temperature. Blend until soft before adding the sugar.

Use low speed to start with and increase to medium speed. Usually 3–4 minutes is sufficient for creaming fat and sugar.

Reduce the speed to add the lightly mixed eggs. Add eggs a little at a time, blending well before the next addition.

Fold in flour and added fruit *by hand*. Stop the machine, remove the beaters and fold in using a metal spoon. Even the lowest speed on an electric mixer is inclined to over-mix at this stage.

Traditional Christmas cake

Butter makes rich cakes keep moist much longer. Use it to make your Christmas cakes, and any other cakes that are intended to be kept for some time to mature.

275 g/10 oz plain flour
1 level teaspoon mixed spice
1 level teaspoon salt
225 g/8 oz butter
225 g/8 oz soft brown sugar
4 large eggs
1 tablespoon black treacle
½ teaspoon vanilla essence
225 g/8 oz currants

225 g/8 oz sultanas
225 g/8 oz seedless raisins
100 g/4 oz chopped candied peel
100 g/4 oz glacé cherries, washed and quartered
50 g/2 oz blanched almonds, chopped
2 tablespoons brandy or milk to mix

Sieve together the flour, spice and salt and set aside. Cream together the butter and sugar until very soft and light. Lightly mix the eggs, treacle and vanilla essence together, then gradually beat into the creamed mixture a little at a time. Add some of the flour along with the last few additions of egg. Add 1–2 tablespoons of the sieved flour to the prepared fruit and mix well. Using a metal spoon, fold in first the remaining sieved flour, then the fruit mixture and the brandy or milk.

Spoon the mixture into a greased and lined 20-cm (8-in) round deep cake tin and hollow out the centre slightly. Place on the shelf below the centre of a pre-heated slow oven (150°C., 300°F., Gas Mark 2) and bake for $1\frac{1}{2}$ hours. Then lower the heat to very slow (140°C., 275°F., Gas Mark 1) and bake for a further $2\frac{1}{2}$ hours. Allow the baked cake to cool in the tin before turning out, wrapping and storing.

Makes one 20-cm (8-in) cake

Small Christmas pudding

Smaller families or people living on their own may find this recipe for a single Christmas pudding very useful. Pour over a little rum or brandy before storing to give extra flavour.

50 g/2 oz self-raising flour
$\frac{1}{4}$ level teaspoon mixed spice
pinch salt
25 g/1 oz (or 3 rounded tablespoons) fresh white breadcrumbs
40 g/$1\frac{1}{2}$ oz shredded beef suet
175 g/6 oz mixed dried fruit
25 g/1 oz chopped mixed peel

$\frac{1}{2}$ apple, peeled and coarsely grated
50 g/2 oz soft brown sugar
finely grated rind and juice of $\frac{1}{2}$ lemon
1 small egg
1 teaspoon treacle
1 tablespoon milk

Sieve the flour, mixed spice and salt into a mixing basin. Add the breadcrumbs, suet, dried fruit, mixed peel, grated apple and sugar and mix well. Stir in the grated lemon rind and strained juice, lightly mixed egg, treacle and enough milk to mix to a medium-soft consistency.

Spoon into a well-buttered 0.5-litre (1-pint) pudding basin. Cover with buttered double thickness greaseproof paper, buttered side inwards, fold in a pleat to allow the pudding to rise and tie securely. Steam gently for 3 hours.

Allow the pudding to cool, remove the damp papers and pour over a tablespoon of rum or brandy. Re-cover with fresh ungreased paper, tie securely and store.

On Christmas morning, re-cover with buttered paper and steam briskly for 2 hours.

Makes one 450-g (1-lb) pudding to serve 4

Rich Christmas pudding

Some cooks like to make the Christmas puddings every two years, which is sensible enough when one considers the work involved in their preparation. This recipe makes two lovely puddings, one of which will keep perfectly until the next Christmas.

100 g/4 oz self-raising flour	225 g/8 oz seedless raisins
pinch salt	225 g/8 oz currants
1 level teaspoon mixed spice	225 g/8 oz sultanas
½ level teaspoon ground cinnamon	100 g/4 oz chopped mixed peel
¼ level teaspoon ground nutmeg	100 g/4 oz prunes, soaked
225 g/8 oz shredded beef suet	2 tablespoons black treacle
225 g/8 oz fresh white breadcrumbs	3–4 tablespoons rum (optional)
grated rind and juice of 1 lemon	3 eggs
350 g/12 oz soft brown sugar	2.5 dl/½ pint stout, brown ale or
50 g/2 oz blanched almonds,	milk
chopped	

Sieve the flour, salt and spices into a large mixing basin. Add the suet, breadcrumbs, grated lemon rind, brown sugar, blanched and chopped almonds, raisins, currants, sultanas and chopped mixed peel. Remove the stones from the soaked but uncooked prunes, chop finely and add to the mixture. Mix thoroughly and make a well in the centre.

Warm the treacle a little to make it thin and runny. Draw the pan off the heat and add the rum and the strained juice of the lemon. Beat the eggs well and stir into the treacle-rum mixture. Pour the liquid from the saucepan and the stout or milk into the centre of the dry ingredients. With a large spoon that will get to the bottom of the bowl, stir all the ingredients together until they are moist and very well mixed. Cover the basin with a cloth and leave until the next day.

Stir up the mixture, and if it seems at all dry add a little milk. At this stage add any small charms wrapped neatly in greaseproof paper. Prepare one 2-pint pudding basin and one 1½-pint basin (see note) by greasing thoroughly with butter. Fill to within 2½ cm (1 in) of the top with the pudding mixture. Cover with double-thickness greaseproof paper, fold in a pleat to allow the pudding to rise and tie securely with string. Place each pudding in a large saucepan on an upturned saucer with boiling water to come a third of the way up the basin. Cover and steam gently for 5–6 hours. Refill the pans with boiling water when necessary.

When the puddings are cool, remove the damp paper and replace with a layer of fresh ungreased paper. Tie securely and store in a cool but airy place until required. Do not cover airtight or mould may develop.

On Christmas morning, re-cover with fresh buttered greaseproof paper and foil. Steam briskly for 2 hours. Remember that the second steaming always makes the pudding darker.
Makes one 2-lb pudding to serve 6 and one 1½-lb pudding to serve 4 (see note)

Note Instead of using a 2-pint and a 1½-pint basin you could use two equal-sized 1-litre basins and make two equal puddings each to serve 5–6. (See p. 331 for accompanying sauces.)

Using the freezer in November

Freezing winter vegetables
Use main-crop winter vegetables in the preparation of casseroles and soups and freeze ready for serving. With the exception of Brussels sprouts, winter vegetables are not really suited for the freezer. Bags of mixed vegetables ready for making soups or stews can be handy, but for short-term storage only.

Celery This vegetable cannot be used raw after freezing but is ideal for serving as a vegetable or for use as a flavouring agent. Wash well, trim hearts down to a neat size and cut stalks in 2.5-cm (1-in) pieces. Blanch hearts for 5 minutes and pieces for 3 minutes. Pack in polythene. Serve hearts as a vegetable and use pieces in soups and stews.

Leeks Cut away green tops and roots and wash well. Blanch in boiling water for 1 minute, then pack in polythene. Use in soups and casseroles.

Onions Small button onions are seasonal and useful for casseroles. Cut a slice from the top and base of each one. Place in a basin and cover with boiling water. Allow to stand for 5 minutes then drain and slip off the skins. Blanch for 4 minutes, then drain and cool. Freeze in single layers on a tray – place inside polythene to prevent odour spreading. Tip onions into a bag when frozen, tied closed.

Chopped onions for cooking can be blanched for 2 minutes. Chill then open freeze and tip into polythene bags for storage. Use in soups and stews.

Brussels sprouts Pick firm small heads. Trim and blanch for 3–4 minutes according to size. Pack in polythene.

December

The highlight of *December* is of course Christmas with all the careful preparation and planning. There are the traditional dishes to plan as well and the stuffings and special sauces to make. Select some of the fine beef and pork for main meals and weekend roasts and order your turkey well in advance if you want one for Christmas.

Remember that root vegetables store better if they are unscrubbed and for winter salads choose celery, beetroot, chicory and crisp cabbage. Imported oranges, satsumas, figs and cranberries can cheer up desserts and let polished apples, pears, grapes, nuts and bananas crown the fruit basket on the Christmas table.

Vichyssoise

Because it is always served cold, vichyssoise is a soup that one might associate with summer months only. But it should be made in winter and spring while leeks are still in season. Use the white part of the leeks only so that the soup is very creamy in colour, and add a little finely chopped mint or chives about 10 minutes before serving, stirring it in so that the flavour is absorbed.

275 g/10 oz white part of leeks	salt and freshly milled pepper
1 small onion	1.5 dl/¼ pint single cream
25 g/1 oz butter	chopped chives
450 g/1 lb potatoes	
a generous litre/2 pints chicken stock	

Wash the leeks and shred very finely. Peel and finely chop the onion. Melt the butter in a saucepan, add the leek and onion and sauté very gently, without allowing them to brown, for about 5 minutes.

Peel and slice the potatoes and add to the pan. Toss in the butter, then stir in the stock and a seasoning of salt and pepper. Bring just to the boil, then cover and simmer gently for 30 minutes.

Blend the vegetables and liquid to a purée in a blender and allow to cool. Check the seasoning and make sure that the consistency is that of flowing cream, not too thick. Stir in the cream and chill until required. Add chives and serve.
Serves 6

Salad of pears with cream cheese

Many fruits go well with the milder flavour of cream or cottage cheese and pears are no exception. Choose ripe, juicy pears for this recipe; they make an attractive first course prepared in this way.

3 ripe pears
175 g/6 oz fresh cream cheese
1–2 tablespoons double cream

salt and freshly milled pepper
lettuce leaves

for the dressing:

salt and freshly milled pepper
pinch sugar

juice of 1 ½ lemon
4 tablespoons olive oil

Peel the pears and slice in half lengthways. Scoop out the cores with a teaspoon and rub the pears over with the cut side of a lemon to prevent them from becoming dark.

Blend the cream cheese and soften by adding a little cream. Season with salt and pepper and spoon into the cavity in each pear half. Arrange on crisp lettuce leaves.

Mix the seasoning, sugar and lemon juice for the dressing. Add the oil and shake or whisk well to make an oil and vinegar dressing, using lemon juice instead of vinegar. Spoon over the pears and serve.

Serves 6

Hare pâté

Cutting the raw flesh from game for pâté mixture is a task most cooks hate. In this recipe the meat is cooked and then pounded with the flavouring ingredients. This is really a potted hare, if one were to be honest about the title, but it has the texture and flavour of a delicious pâté. Order your hare in advance so that the butcher can prepare it when he's not busy.

1 hare, skinned and cut in pieces
vinegar (see method)
1 onion
2 carrots
1 small clove garlic
bay leaf

salt and few peppercorns
175 g/6 oz butter
grated rind of ½ lemon
freshly milled pepper
pinch ground nutmeg
1–2 tablespoons dry sherry

Wipe the pieces of hare with a damp cloth and place in a large basin. Add cold water and about 1.5 dl (¼ pint) vinegar to cover the pieces.

Leave for several hours or overnight during which time the vinegar draws the blood and makes the hare meat less rich. Drain and pat the pieces dry.

Place the hare pieces in a good-sized saucepan. Peel and slice the onion. Add to the pan with the scraped and sliced carrots, the peeled and cut-up clove of garlic and the bay leaf. Add cold water to cover the hare, then add a good seasoning of salt and a few peppercorns. Bring slowly to the boil, then lower the heat and allow to simmer gently for about 3½–4 hours or until the flesh is quite tender and coming away from the bones.

Lift the hare pieces from the pan and leave until cool enough to handle. Remove the flesh from the bones and mince the hare flesh into a basin. Melt 100 g (4 oz) of the butter with the grated lemon rind over low heat. Add to the minced hare and beat well with a wooden spoon, add a few tablespoons of hare stock from the pan and beat well to get a firm well-blended mixture. Season with salt and pepper to taste and a pinch of nutmeg and beat in the sherry to taste.

Spoon the mixture into a pâté dish or white china soufflé dish and spread level. Melt the remaining butter and pour over the surface. Decorate with the bay leaf rescued from the hare stock and chill for several hours. Serve with hot toast or French bread.
Serves 6–8

Party dips

Party dips should be well flavoured. They should also be fairly soft in consistency, so that biscuits or crisps dipped into the mixture do not break up and leave the dip looking unattractive. The most simple dips are those using a mixture of soured cream and dried soup powder. They are made in a jiffy and are surprisingly tasty.

Onion dip
Mix together 6 dl (1 pint, 4 cartons) soured cream and 1 packet French onion soup powder. Leave to stand for 3–4 hours before serving so that the pieces of onion soften and the flavour matures.

Leek dip
Mix together 6 dl (1 pint, 4 cartons) soured cream and 1 packet leek soup powder. Allow to stand for 3–4 hours before serving.

Spoon the dips into a serving bowl. Surround with potato crisps or salty biscuits or a few carrot sticks.

Chicken and rice soup

Prepare this soup when there is a turkey or chicken carcass available with which to make a good well-flavoured stock.

40 g/1½ oz butter	bay leaf
1 large onion	salt and freshly milled pepper
50 g/2 oz long-grain rice	3 dl/½ pint milk
a scant litre/1½ pints chicken or turkey stock	1 level tablespoon flour

Melt the butter in a large saucepan over low heat. Peel and chop the onion and add to the pan. Cover and fry gently until tender but not browned. Stir in the rice, then the chicken stock and add the bay leaf. Bring up to a fast boil, stir well and then lower the heat. Cover with a lid and simmer gently for about 30 minutes. Check seasoning with salt and pepper. Measure the milk into a small basin, sieve the flour on to it and mix thoroughly using a whisk. Add to the soup and stir until boiling and thickened, remove the bay leaf and serve.
Serves 4-6

Smoked haddock with poached egg

Smoked haddock cutlets are the smaller inshore fish which have been split, boned and smoked whole. They are tender, very tasty and completely free of bones. This is a typically Scottish way of preparing them and could be served for breakfast or high tea.

4 small smoked haddock cutlets	40 g/1½ oz butter
milk (see method)	4 eggs

Trim the fish and place in a large frying pan. Add sufficient milk to cover and add the butter in small pieces.

Place the pan over gentle heat and simmer for 5–7 minutes to heat the fish through. Lift the fish from the pan and keep hot. Crack the eggs one at a time first into a teacup then tip into the hot milk in the frying pan. Add all four eggs and poach gently in the hot milk until just set. Top each haddock with a poached egg and serve.
Serves 4

Buckling-stuffed eggs

Smoked buckling pâté makes a tasty filling for eggs. These are an ideal accompaniment to salads and cold meat for a supper party.

1 large buckling	freshly milled black pepper
100 g/4 oz butter (see method)	12 hard-boiled eggs
1 tablespoon lemon juice	2–4 tablespoons cream

Remove the skin and bones from the buckling. Pound the flesh with a wooden spoon and beat in the softened butter. Alternatively flake the buckling flesh into the glass container of an electric blender. Add the melted butter, cover and blend to a purée. Beat the lemon juice and plenty of freshly milled pepper into the mixture. Leave covered until ready to use.

Slice the eggs in half and tip out the yolks. Sieve the yolks and beat into the buckling mixture. Stir in sufficient cream to give a piping consistency. Pipe or spoon the buckling mixture into the egg whites. Garnish with watercress and serve with brown bread and butter.
Makes 24 egg halves

The Christmas stock pot Specially good soups can be made with packets or condensed soups using turkey stock instead of water. Use it in home-made soups too.

Into a really large saucepan put the broken-up carcass of the bird, along with any bones from the meat, ham skin, bacon rinds or giblets. Add a large onion stuck with a clove, a large carrot scrubbed and cut in half, 1–2 stalks celery, a small bay leaf and a few parsley stalks.

Add cold water to cover and a level teaspoon of salt for every generous litre (2 pints) of water used. Bring to the boil for 2 minutes only. Then skim carefully and reduce the heat to a gentle simmer – if stock boils it goes cloudy. Leave to cook for 3–4 hours, strain carefully and use.

Whisky rarebit

This recipe makes no claims to traditional origins, but the whisky gives the mixture a good flavour and the egg added makes the rarebit puff up under the heat of the grill. It makes a delicious snack to serve on its own or with a salad.

25 g/1 oz butter
175 g/6 oz Cheddar cheese, grated
1 tablespoon whisky
dash made mustard

1 egg
salt and freshly milled pepper
4 slices hot toast

Melt the butter in a saucepan. Add the cheese, whisky, mustard and
a seasoning of salt and pepper. Stir over low heat until the cheese has
melted and the mixture is smooth. Remove from the heat and stir in
the egg yolk. Add the stiffly beaten egg white and fold evenly
through the mixture.

Have the hot toast ready and arrange the slices in the grill pan.
Spoon some of the mixture on to each slice of toast and spread
evenly. Place under a hot grill and the rarebit mixture will puff up
and brown beautifully. Serve at once.
Serves 4

Wine Camembert

*If you like the flavour of Camembert, here's a cheese mixture that you
would enjoy. It makes an attractive addition to a cheese tray and is a
good way of using up a Camembert that is just a little too ripe.*

1 ripe Camembert
dry white wine (see method)

100 g/4 oz butter
25 g/1 oz fresh white breadcrumbs

Using a knife, scrape away the white rind on the cheese. Place the
whole Camembert in a basin and cover with white wine – about
1.5 dl ($\frac{1}{4}$ pint). Set aside for 12 hours or overnight.

Drain off the wine and reserve. Cream the butter until soft then add
the Camembert cheese and beat the two together until smooth and
creamy. Beat in 1–2 tablespoons of the wine to make a smooth but
not too soft mixture.

Turn the mixture into a well-oiled mould, such as a 15-cm (6-in)
cake tin, lined with a circle of greaseproof paper, and chill in the
refrigerator until firm. Turn out and coat all over with the
breadcrumbs. Serve with a garnish of green grapes or watercress
and with cheese biscuits, of course.
Serves 8

Potted meat

This mixture is ideal for sandwich fillings or as a spread for toast. It makes good use of any leftover bits from a cold roast. Make the same mixture with bits of cold turkey.

225 g/8 oz cold roast chicken or beef
100 g/4 oz bacon rashers
50 g/2 oz butter

salt and freshly milled pepper
pinch ground mace
dash Worcestershire sauce

Pick over the pieces of chicken and discard any skin or bones. Trim the bacon rashers and fry until crisp. Pass the chicken meat and bacon twice through the mincer into a mixing basin. Add the butter, a seasoning of salt and pepper, the mace and Worcestershire sauce. Beat thoroughly to mix well and pack into a small pot. Cover with a lid or a little extra melted butter and store in the refrigerator. Use as required.
Serves 4

Moussaka

Moussaka can be made in advance and left ready for reheating, which makes it a good recipe to prepare for a party. A rich and substantial dish; for most people a green salad is quite sufficient as an accompaniment.

900 g/2 lb aubergines
kitchen cooking salt
6–8 tablespoons oil
2 large onions
450 g/1 lb lean lamb, minced

1 level teaspoon salt
freshly milled pepper
2 teaspoons concentrated tomato purée
1.5 dl/¼ pint red wine

for the topping:
25 g/1 oz butter
25 g/1 oz flour
3 dl/½ pint milk

salt and freshly milled pepper
1 egg

Leave the aubergines unpeeled and slice them. Sprinkle with cooking salt and leave in a colander for about 1 hour to draw the juices, with a plate pressed down on top. Rinse in cold water and pat dry. Fry the aubergine slices in plenty of oil in a large frying pan. Turn to brown them on both sides before removing them from the pan.

Peel and slice the onions and fry in about 2 tablespoons oil until soft.
Add the minced lamb and cook gently to brown the meat. Stir in the
salt, a seasoning of pepper, the tomato purée and the wine. Bring to
a simmer, cover with a lid and cook gently for 20–25 minutes.

Arrange layers of meat mixture and aubergines in an earthenware
ovenproof dish, ending with a layer of aubergines. Set aside while
preparing the topping.

Melt the butter over low heat and stir in the flour. Cook gently for a
few minutes, then gradually stir in the milk. Bring up to the boil,
beating well to get a smooth sauce. Season with salt and pepper and
simmer for 1–2 minutes. Draw off the heat and beat in the egg – the
addition of egg helps to form a topping that remains on the surface
of the moussaka.

Pour the topping over the moussaka. Place in the centre of a
moderately hot oven (190°C., 375°F., Gas Mark 5) and cook for
45 minutes–1 hour when the top should be golden brown. Serve hot
or cold with salad.
Serves 6

Roast leg of pork

*A whole leg of pork weighs something in the region of 5.2 kg (12 lb) and
makes a handsome roast for a special party. For very large joints like
this the time allowed per 450 g (1 lb) is reduced from the amount normally
allowed because of the size of the joint. So check the weight with your
butcher so that you can calculate the cooking time accurately.*

1 leg of pork	caraway seeds (optional)
cooking salt	50–75 g/2–3 oz white cooking fat

Make sure the rind has been scored sufficiently; not only does this
give the joint an attractive appearance but it makes the carving of
the meat very much easier. Rub the rind all over with cooking salt;
you may like to rub in a few caraway seeds along with the salt – it
gives the roast a delicious flavour.

Set the joint in the largest roasting tin you have. Add the cooking
fat and set in a hot oven (220°C., 425°F., Gas Mark 7) for the first
20 minutes of the cooking time. Then lower the heat to moderate
(180°C., 350°F., Gas Mark 4) and roast, allowing a total cooking
time of 25 minutes per 450 g (1 lb) and 25 minutes extra. Do not

baste during roasting. Raise the heat back to hot for the last 25 minutes of the cooking time to crisp the crackling.

Serve the pork cold for a buffet supper with crisp coleslaw salad or serve it hot with cooked *red cabbage with apple* (see page 269).
Serves 25

Roast turkey

Check the weight of your turkey so that the cooking time may be calculated accurately. Place the stuffed and trussed bird in a roasting tin. Spread the breast liberally with butter or bacon fat and cover it with a sheet of foil or a piece of muslin. You can baste the bird through the muslin during cooking and the bird browns beautifully without drying up – a good method if you intend to serve the turkey cold for a buffet supper.
Some people prefer to slow roast the turkey while others prefer the traditional method of starting the bird off in a hot oven.

For the traditional method
Roast in a hot oven (220°C., 425°F., Gas Mark 7) for the first 30 minutes. Then reduce the heat for a small turkey to moderate (180°C., 350°F., Gas Mark 4) and for a large turkey to very moderate (160°C., 325°F., Gas Mark 3) for the remainder of the time.
3.5 to 4.5 kg/8 to 10 lb 3–3$\frac{1}{2}$ hours
4.5 to 6 kg/10 to 14 lb 3$\frac{1}{2}$–4 hours
6 to 8 kg/14 to 18 lb 4–4$\frac{1}{2}$ hours
8 to 9 kg/18 to 20 lb 4$\frac{1}{2}$–5 hours

For the slow roasting method
Set the bird in a very moderate oven (160°C., 325°F., Gas Mark 3) from the start. Allow an extra hour's cooking time or calculate the time allowing 25 minutes per 0.5 kg (1 lb) up to 5.5 kg (12 lb) in weight and 20 minutes per 0.5 kg (1 lb) for a turkey over 5.5 kg (12 lb). Large birds are excellent cooked by this method which keeps them succulent and juicy. Increase the heat in the oven for the last 20–30 minutes and baste the bird with butter, after removing the covering, to get a rich brown colour.

Making the gravy

The best gravy is made in the roasting tin after straining off the fat. Retain all the brown bits from the bird. Add a generous 6 dl (1 pint) giblet stock. Stir briskly over the heat for several minutes. Season to taste and strain into a hot gravy boat. If you like a thicker gravy add 1 level dessertspoon cornflour blended with ½ teacup water, stock or port wine. Stir until boiling to cook the starch in the cornflour. Pour into a hot gravy boat.

Roast potatoes

These are always crisper and more golden if cooked in a separate roasting tin. Peel the potatoes, cut up if large and blanch in boiling water for 4–5 minutes. Drain. Dust lightly with seasoned flour and put into a roasting tin with 50–75 g (2–3 oz) melted cooking fat. Cook near the top of the oven for 1 hour, turning once or twice. If slow roasting the turkey you may need to turn the heat up towards the end of the roasting time to ensure that the potatoes are crisp and golden brown.

Chipolata sausages and bacon rolls

These accompaniments may be grilled separately or cooked around the bird. Fix bacon rolls on skewers before cooking to keep the neat shape. Sausages will take about 20 minutes and bacon 8–10 minutes.

Stuffing for the turkey

Traditional forcemeat

225 g/8 oz fresh white breadcrumbs
4 heaped tablespoons chopped parsley
¼ teaspoon dried thyme
½ teaspoon dried mixed herbs
1 teaspoon salt

freshly milled pepper
finely grated rind of 1 lemon
100 g/4 oz butter
2 eggs
juice of ½ lemon

Measure the breadcrumbs, parsley, thyme, mixed herbs, salt and a seasoning of pepper into a basin. Melt the butter and using a fork stir into the crumb mixture. Lightly mix the eggs and lemon juice and stir in sufficient to bind the ingredients together and make a moist but not wet stuffing.

To stuff the breast of a 4.5- to 5.5-kg (10- to 12-lb) oven-ready turkey

Chestnut stuffing

Instead of fresh chestnuts you can use 675 g (1½ lb) dried chestnuts soaked overnight in cold water and then simmered in stock or milk, following the recipe as if they were freshly peeled chestnuts. Otherwise use a 425-g (15-oz) can unsweetened chestnut purée and omit the initial stages of peeling, cooking and sieving the chestnuts.

900 g/2 lb fresh chestnuts	1 egg
milk or stock (see method)	50 g/2 oz melted butter
100 g/4 oz fresh white breadcrumbs	2 tablespoons milk
grated rind of ½ lemon	salt and freshly milled pepper

Slit the skins on the flat side of the chestnuts. Place in boiling water and simmer for 10 minutes. Drain and remove the outer skins. Replace the chestnuts in the boiling water and simmer for 10 minutes. Drain and remove the inner skins. Replace the chestnuts in the pan and cover with milk or stock. Simmer for 20 minutes until tender. Drain the nuts and rub through a coarse sieve to make a purée.

Put the chestnut purée in a basin and add the breadcrumbs, grated lemon rind, mixed egg, melted butter, milk and seasoning. Mix all the ingredients well to blend.
Sufficient for the body of a 4.5- to 5.5-kg (10- to 12-lb) oven-ready turkey

Savoury sausagemeat stuffing

225 g/8 oz streaky bacon	900 g/2 lb pork sausagemeat
1 large onion	1 teaspoon powdered sage
15 g/½ oz butter	

Trim the bacon and chop into small strips. Peel and chop the onion. Fry the bacon and onion in the melted butter until tender but not brown. Add to the sausagemeat along with the powdered sage and mix well.
Sufficient for the body of a 4.5- to 5.5-kg (10- to 12-lb) turkey

Veal scallopine

Veal in a red wine sauce is perfect for serving with rice. The rice grains will be tender and fluffy if you follow this easy method of cooking.

4 veal escalopes (see method)	225 g/8 oz button mushrooms,
seasoned flour	trimmed and sliced
50 g/2 oz butter	1.5 dl/¼ pint red wine

for the oven-cooked rice

| 225 g/8 oz long-grain rice | 6 dl/1 pint boiling water |
| 1 level teaspoon salt | 25 g/1 oz grated Parmesan cheese |

Ask the butcher to beat the escalopes flat. Dip each one on both sides in seasoned flour. Melt the butter in a large frying pan, add the veal and fry gently in the hot butter to brown on both sides. Lower the heat and add the mushrooms. Cook gently for 2–3 minutes, then add the wine. Cover with a lid and simmer for 20 minutes.

While the veal is cooking measure the rice into a buttered casserole. Add the salt and stir in the boiling water. Cover the casserole with a lid and place in the centre of a moderately hot oven (200°C., 400°F., Gas Mark 6) and bake for 30 minutes. During cooking the rice will absorb all the liquid and become soft and dry. When the rice is cooked fluff up with a fork.

Transfer the cooked veal and mushrooms from the pan to a hot serving dish. Boil the wine remaining in the pan rapidly to reduce and concentrate the flavour, then pour over the meat.

Sprinkle the warmed cooked rice with Parmesan cheese and serve with the veal.
Serves 4

Boiled and baked gammon

Nowadays there is no need to soak gammon joints overnight. Most cooks find it sufficient to put the joint straight into the pan with cold water to cover and then to change the cooking water for fresh cold water as soon as it comes to the boil.

1 piece corner gammon, about
 1–1.25 kg/2½–3 lb

for the honey glaze:

| 2 tablespoons honey | juice of 1 lemon |
| 50 g/2 oz soft brown sugar | 1 teaspoon made mustard |

Place the gammon skin side downwards in a saucepan and cover with cold water. Bring up to the boil, drain off the cooking water and re-cover with fresh cold water. Bring to the boil again, lower the heat to a simmer and cover with a lid. Cook gently, allowing 30 minutes per 450 g (1 lb). Then lift the gammon from the pan and when cool enough to handle strip the rind from the joint with a sharp knife.

Blend together the honey, sugar, lemon juice and mustard. Score the fat in a criss-cross fashion and set in a roasting tin. Smear the fat all over with the honey and sugar mixture. Add 2 tablespoons water to the roasting tin so that any glaze that drips down does not caramelize on to the hot tin.

Place in the centre of a moderately hot oven (200°C., 400°F., Gas Mark 6) and flash bake for 15 minutes so that the surface becomes shiny and brown. Remove from the heat and leave until quite cold. Serve sliced.
Serves 6

Brussels sprouts with chestnuts

A traditional accompaniment to the roast turkey but quite a lot of work to prepare. You can peel and skin the chestnuts the day before or use dried chestnuts, soaking them overnight in cold water.

675–900 g/1½–2 lb Brussels sprouts   stock (see method)
350–450 g/12 oz–1 lb chestnuts   50 g/2 oz butter

Trim the sprouts, removing any damaged outer leaves, and make an incision in the stalk. Set aside to soak in salt water while preparing the chestnuts.

Using a sharp knife, make a small incision in each chestnut. Cover with cold water, bring to the boil and simmer for 10 minutes. Drain and then peel away both outer and inner skins. Replace the peeled chestnuts in the saucepan, cover with stock, bring up to the boil, simmer gently for 20 minutes until the chestnuts are tender, then drain.

Meanwhile cook the sprouts separately in boiling salted water for 15 minutes until tender. Drain. Replace the hot saucepan over the heat with the butter added. When the butter is melted, add both the sprouts and chestnuts. Toss well and serve.
Serves 6

Cabbage salad

Winter salads are really no more difficult to make than summer ones; it is just a question of using different raw ingredients. Crisp cabbage with crunchy peanuts added has lots of flavour and texture and makes a lovely salad to serve with cold turkey, ham or chicken.

225 g/8 oz shredded cabbage (see method)
2 dessert apples
6 dried apricots, cut in slivers and soaked for several hours in the juice of 1 orange

2 tablespoons salted peanuts
4–6 tablespoons oil and vinegar dressing

Cabbage needs careful preparation to get really fine shreds. About a quarter of a head should provide 225 g (8 oz) shredded cabbage. Choose a firm cabbage. Quarter it and cut away the stalk. Press the cut side firmly on a chopping board and shred across the leaves very thinly with a sharp knife. For a really crisp salad, soak the shredded cabbage in a bowl of iced water for about 1 hour. Drain through a colander and pat dry.

Peel, core and quarter the apples, then cut in dice. Combine the shredded cabbage, apricot slivers, diced apples and peanuts. Toss in oil and vinegar dressing and serve.
Serves 4

Gratin à la dauphinoise

A good choice for a party, this recipe needs very little attention, looks good and can be served from the baking dish. Gratin à la dauphinoise goes well with any roast.

675 g/1½ lb potatoes
1 clove garlic
50 g/2 oz butter
salt and freshly milled pepper

1 egg
3 dl/½ pint single cream or milk and cream

Peel the potatoes, cut them into very thin slices and pat dry in a cloth. One of those vegetable slicers – sometimes called a 'mandolin slicer' – is really very useful when preparing the potatoes for this dish. Crush the clove of garlic and rub round the inside of an earthenware baking dish. Generously butter the dish with about half the butter.

Arrange rows of potato slices in the dish, seasoning each layer with salt. Whisk the egg with a seasoning of salt and pepper and whisk in the cream or milk and cream. Pour over the potato slices, lifting them gently so the egg mixture runs to the base of the dish. Dot the surface of the potatoes with the remaining butter.

Place above centre in a moderately hot oven (190°C., 375°F., Gas Mark 5) and bake for 1 hour. Test the potatoes with a knife; if they feel tender they are ready to serve. The top should be crisp and brown, so pass under a hot grill for a few moments if necessary before serving.

Serves 6

Curry rice salad

A curry-flavoured rice salad with apples, raisins and almonds goes well with leftover turkey, cold ham or pork. Use it to liven up a platter of cold meats for Boxing Day lunch.

100 g/4 oz long-grain rice	1 sharp-flavoured dessert apple
1 tablespoon oil	2 teaspoons mango chutney
1 small onion	2 tablespoons seedless raisins
1 level teaspoon curry powder	25 g/1 oz toasted flaked almonds
4–5 tablespoons oil and vinegar dressing	

Cook the rice in boiling salted water for 8–10 minutes or until tender. Meanwhile heat the oil in a second saucepan and add the finely chopped onion. Cover and cook gently for about 5 minutes until the onion is tender but not brown. Add the curry powder, fry gently for a moment and then draw off the heat.

Drain the cooked rice and turn into the saucepan with the onion and curry powder. Toss well to flavour the rice, then turn the contents of the pan into a basin. To the hot mixture, add 2–3 tablespoons of the oil and vinegar dressing. Toss to glaze the rice grains and leave until cold.

Peel, core and dice the apple. Add to the salad along with the mango chutney, raisins, toasted flaked almonds and the remainder of the dressing. Mix well and serve.

Serves 4-6

Haggis

If you buy a haggis to celebrate the New Year here's what to do with it. Place the haggis in a saucepan and cover with tepid water. Bring slowly to the boil, cover with a lid and simmer very slowly for about 45 minutes, depending on the size. Drain and serve hot, with plenty of mashed swedes seasoned with salt and pepper and creamed potato. Traditionally you should drink whisky with haggis.

Waldorf salad

Celery combines happily with most salad vegetables and with fruit and nuts too. Waldorf salad is always popular; the crisp crunchy texture and fresh flavour goes well with most cold meats. A good choice for a buffet supper salad.

4 firm dessert apples
3 stalks celery
40–50 g/1½–2 oz shelled walnuts
2 tablespoons mayonnaise

2 tablespoons lightly whipped
 cream
squeeze of lemon juice

Wipe the apples and leave on the peel if it is a pretty red colour.
Quarter and core the apples and cut into neat dice. Shred the
celery and coarsely chop the walnuts.

Mix together the mayonnaise and lightly whipped cream to make a
very light dressing and sharpen with a squeeze of lemon juice.
Combine at once with the prepared apples to prevent discolouration
of the apple pieces. Mix in the shredded celery and leave in a cool
place until ready to serve. Just before serving, mix in the coarsely
chopped walnuts.

Serves 4

Wine jelly

*A pretty alternative method of serving this dessert would be to omit the
grapes and cream from the recipe. Serve the grapes sugared in small
clusters around the outside of the moulded jelly instead.*

3 dl/½ pint water
15 g/½ oz powdered gelatine
finely pared rind of 1 orange
finely pared rind of 1 lemon
175 g/6 oz castor sugar

3 dl/½ pint red wine
juice of 1 orange
juice of ½ lemon
225 g/8 oz fresh grapes
1.5 dl/¼ pint double cream

Measure out 3 tablespoons from the 3 dl (½ pint) of water into a
teacup and sprinkle in the gelatine. Set aside to soak while preparing
the remainder of the recipe.

Measure the remaining water into a saucepan. Add the orange and
lemon rinds and the sugar, bring up to the boil, then lower the heat
and allow to simmer gently for 10 minutes. Draw off the heat and
add the cake of soaked gelatine. Stir until dissolved; the heat of the
pan should be sufficient to do this. Add the wine and orange and
lemon juice, then strain and set aside until the mixture is beginning
to thicken and set.

Meanwhile peel and deseed the grapes. Reserve a few for decoration.
Add the grapes to the thick jelly and pour it into a glass serving dish.
Set aside until set firm. Lightly whip the cream and spoon over the

top of the jelly, decorate with the reserved grapes and chill until ready to serve.

Serves 6

Upside-down trifle

Here's a novel idea for a Christmas dessert – a trifle made in a mould, with gelatine added to set the custard and turned out so that the pretty sponge cake and fruit base is uppermost.

6 dl/1 pint prepared lime or lemon
  jelly
1 banana
1 Chinese gooseberry

100 g/4 oz green grapes
1 packet of 4 trifle sponge cakes
raspberry jam

for the custard:

4 dl/¾ pint milk
3 tablespoons cold water
15 g/½ oz powdered gelatine
4 egg yolks

50 g/2 oz castor sugar
2 tablespoons sherry
1.5 dl/¼ pint double cream

Select a cake tin or shallow mould, preferably 20 cm (8 in) in diameter and of not less than 1-litre (1½-pint) capacity. A 20-cm (8-in) cake tin would do, but you can find some excellent shallow moulds that have come over from the Continent in many of the cookware shops.

Prepare the jelly first and allow to cool. Slice the banana, peel and slice the Chinese gooseberry to reveal its beautiful green flesh, and halve and deseed the grapes. Sandwich the trifle sponge cakes with raspberry jam and cut into chunky pieces. Pour a little of the jelly into the base of the mould and allow to set. Then arrange the fruit and the sponge cakes (dipping each piece of sponge cake in a little jelly first) attractively over the base. Spoon a little more jelly and chill to fix the decoration in place. Then spoon in the remaining jelly and chill until set firm before adding the custard layer.

Measure the milk for the custard into a saucepan and set over low heat, allowing it to become quite hot. Measure the water into a teacup, sprinkle in the gelatine and set aside to soak for 5 minutes. Crack the egg yolks into a basin, add the sugar and, using a wooden spoon, stir the mixture until creamy and light. Gradually stir in the hot milk, blend well and then return the mixture to the saucepan. Add the soaked gelatine and stir over low heat just long enough to dissolve the gelatine. Draw off the heat, strain into a basin, stir in the sherry and allow to cool.

When the mixture is cold and shows signs of setting, lightly whip the cream and fold gently but evenly into the custard. Pour at once into the mould over the jelly and fruit layer. Chill until set firm.

When ready to serve, loosen round the top edges of the mould with a knife. Dip in hot water (as hot as the hand can bear) for a few seconds. Then invert on to a plate. Serve with cream.
Serves 6-8

Flambéed bananas with rum

The fresh cream served with these bananas provides a delicious contrast to the hot newly cooked fruit; it also helps to cool them down. For best results, choose bananas that are slightly under-ripe; they should be a little green at the stalk end.

6 bananas
juice of ½ lemon and a little grated
  lemon rind
50 g/2 oz soft brown sugar
pinch ground cloves

pinch ground nutmeg
¼ level teaspoon ground cinnamon
50 g/2 oz butter
4 tablespoons rum

Peel the bananas and cut in half lengthways. Place cut side down in a well-buttered fireproof baking dish and sprinkle with the lemon juice. Blend the sugar and spices and sprinkle over the bananas.

Dot with the butter and place under a hot grill for about 5 minutes, or until the bananas are golden and soft and the sugar has melted. Baste the bananas occasionally with the juices in the dish.

Warm the rum in a saucepan with a little lemon rind. Flame and pour over the bananas. The flame will burn for about 1 minute. Serve at once with double cream.
Serves 6

Orange syllabub

Syllabub never fails to be a success as a dinner party dessert and it is very easy to make. This mixture is rich and portions should be small. Serve with soft sponge fingers.

| 2 small oranges | 50 g/2 oz castor sugar |
| ½ lemon | 3 dl/½ pint double cream |

Finely grate the rind from 1 orange into a mixing basin. Add the strained juice from both the oranges and the lemon. Add the sugar and stir until dissolved. Add the cream and whisk until the mixture is thick. Pour the mixture into individual glasses. Decorate with a little grated rind from the remaining orange peel. Chill until ready to serve.
Serves 6

Christmas pudding sauces

The crowning touch for Christmas Day's plum pudding is the sauce, rich with a flavouring of fruit or spirits. (See p. 307 for Rich Christmas pudding recipe.)

St. Clement's sauce
If the cold hard sauces are not to your taste here's a hot sauce for you. Orange and lemon give the mixture a good flavour and lovely colour.

100 g/4 oz butter	1 rounded teaspoon cornflour
100 g/4 oz castor sugar	finely grated rind and juice of
juice of 1 orange	1 lemon

Measure the butter and sugar into a saucepan and cream together until light. Set the pan over low heat and bring slowly up to the boil. Stir in the orange juice and cornflour blended together and the lemon rind and juice. Reheat until thickened and boiling. Draw the pan off the heat and serve warm.
Serves 6

Brandy butter
One miniature bottle contains just the right amount of brandy for this recipe; a little finely grated orange rind added gives the mixture a really lovely flavour.

| 175 g/6 oz unsalted butter | 2 tablespoons brandy |
| 225 g/8 oz sieved icing sugar | |

Cream the butter until soft, then gradually beat in the icing sugar. Beat in the brandy very thoroughly. Pile roughly into a serving dish and chill well before serving.
Serves 8

Rum butter

Any leftover rum butter makes a delicious filling for baked apples.

175 g/6 oz unsalted butter
175 g/6 oz soft brown sugar
little grated lemon rind

1 teaspoon lemon juice
pinch cinnamon
3–4 tablespoons rum

Cream the butter and sugar until soft, then mix in the lemon rind and juice and cinnamon and beat thoroughly. Beat in the rum gradually and chill until firm.
Serves 8

Mince pies

The unusual pastry adds to the attraction of these delicious mince pies. They can be baked 1–2 days before serving and should be stored in an airtight tin.

275 g/10 oz plain flour
25 g/1 oz ground almonds
175 g/6 oz butter
75 g/3 oz castor sugar

finely grated rind of ½ lemon
1 egg yolk
3 tablespoons milk

for the filling:
450 g/1 lb mincemeat
1–2 tablespoons brandy

icing sugar (see method)

Sift the flour into a mixing basin and add the ground almonds. Add the butter, cut in small pieces, and rub into the mixture evenly. Add the sugar and grated lemon rind. Lightly mix the egg yolk and milk and stir into the dry ingredients. Mix to a fairly firm dough, turn out on to a lightly floured board and knead until smooth. Chill for 30 minutes before using.

Roll out the pastry on a lightly floured working surface and using a floured plain or fluted cutter stamp out 48 circles of pastry. Place 24 of these in lightly greased tartlet tins – prepared in batches if necessary. Mix the mincemeat with the brandy and place a teaspoonful of the mixture in the centre of each pastry circle. Take care not to overfill the pies. Damp the edges of the pastry and cover each one with a pastry top. Seal the edges and snip two slits in the top of each with a pair of scissors. Place in the centre of a moderately hot oven (200°C., 400°F., Gas Mark 6) and bake for

15–20 minutes or until golden brown. Dust with icing sugar and serve hot.

Makes 2 dozen

Shortbread

A small proportion of rice flour is used along with the flour to give the shortbread a crisp sandy texture. The amount used varies according to personal taste.

100 g/4 oz plain flour
50 g/2 oz rice flour

100 g/4 oz butter
50 g/2 oz castor sugar

Sift the flour and rice flour on to a clean pastry board. Cream the butter and sugar and add to the flour mixture. Using the fingers work the blended butter into the flour. At first the mixture will become crumbly, but continue rubbing in until the mixture forms a shortbread dough. Roll the dough out or press into a mould – see below.

Set the shortbread in the centre of a very moderate oven (160°C., 325°F., Gas Mark 3) and bake fingers and petticoat tails for 25–30 minutes and the moulded shortbread for 45–50 minutes. Cool and store in an airtight tin so that the shortbread remains crisp.

To make shortbread fingers Roll the shortbread out to a long strip about 0.5 cm ($\frac{1}{4}$ in) thick. Crimp the edges with floured fingers and prick the surface all over with a fork. Cut into fingers with a knife and place on a buttered baking tray.

Makes about 1$\frac{1}{2}$ dozen

To use a wooden shortbread mould Dust the shortbread mould thoroughly with flour. Using floured fingertips press the shortbread into the mould. Turn out on to a buttered baking tray and lift the mould away.

Makes one shortbread mould

To make petticoat tails Roll the dough out to a circle about 0.5 cm ($\frac{1}{4}$ in) thick. Crimp the edges with floured fingers and prick all over with a fork. Cut into triangles and arrange on a buttered baking tray.

Makes 1–1$\frac{1}{2}$ dozen petticoat tails

Tablet

Practice makes perfect where tablet is concerned. Care should be given to the graining of the mixture. If too highly grained the tablet may set in the pan and will not pour flat in the tin. If not grained sufficiently, the tablet will be coarse and sticky.

450 g/1 lb granulated sugar
50 g/2 oz butter
1 rounded tablespoon golden syrup

1.5 dl/¼ pint thin cream or milk
½ teaspoon vanilla essence

Measure the sugar, butter, syrup and cream or milk into a saucepan. Set over low heat and stir to dissolve the sugar. Bring up to the boil and cook, stirring frequently, until the mixture shows a temperature of 118°C. (245°F.) on a sugar thermometer, or until a little spooned into a saucer of cold water forms a soft ball of putty-like consistency. Draw the pan off the heat and allow the bubbles to subside.

Add the vanilla essence and using a wooden spoon beat the mixture until it becomes creamy in consistency. This is the most difficult part and is called 'graining' the mixture. When ready not only does the mixture visibly thicken to a creamy texture, but it begins to sound gritty in the pan and it also loses its shine. Pour at once into a buttered 18-cm (7-in) shallow square pan or one of similar size. When firm mark in squares and when quite cold turn out and break in pieces.

Makes 550 g (1¼ lb)

Mulled cider

A cold winter evening is just the time to serve a hot, heartening cider punch, rich with spices and decorated with fruit. Remember that for mulls a still cider is preferable to a sparkling type.

2 small eating apples
6 cloves
a generous litre/1 quart cider
1 10-cm/4-in stick cinnamon

2 level teaspoons ground ginger
50 g/2 oz soft brown sugar
1.5 dl/¼ pint water
1 small orange

Core the apples and run a knife tip round the centre of each apple just to break the skin. Stick two cloves in the side of each apple and bake in a moderate oven (180°C., 350°F., Gas Mark 4) for 20 minutes.

Meanwhile heat the cider gently in a saucepan – it must not be allowed to boil. Put the remaining 2 cloves, the cinnamon stick broken into 4 pieces, the ginger, sugar and water into a separate saucepan and stir over the heat until the sugar has dissolved. Bring to the boil and simmer gently for 5 minutes. Remove from the heat.

Transfer the baked apples to the punch bowl and add the orange cut in slices. Strain in the spiced water and then pour in the hot cider. Serve at once.
Serves 10-12

Flambéed desserts

Simple flambéed desserts are easy and dramatic to serve. Fruit is usually the main ingredient and a brandy or liqueur that complements the flavour is used to flame the dish.

When preparing any flambéed recipe it is always necessary to release the alcohol by warming the spirit over heat for a moment. When a match is put to it, the spirit instantly bursts into flames. Shake the pan gently so that the flames spread all over the ingredients.

Cook for a moment longer after the flames have died, so that the spirit loses its rawness and the sauce remaining tastes smooth and mellow.

Mulled wine

Choose inexpensive vin ordinaire *for mulling. This is a marvellous way of making wine go further, besides providing a cheering drink. Take care not to allow your mull to boil – this evaporates the alcohol and spoils the flavour – nor to stand too long after preparation when the spices tend to become too concentrated.*

225 g/8 oz castor sugar	1 small stick cinnamon
3 dl/½ pint water	1 lemon
2 bottles red wine	4–6 cloves

Measure the sugar and water into a saucepan. Stir over low heat to dissolve the sugar and then bring up to the boil. Add the red wine, cinnamon stick and the lemon stuck with the cloves. Reheat gently until the mull is pleasantly hot, then draw off the heat. Cover and leave to infuse for 10 minutes.

Pour the mull into a large punch bowl, remove the stick of cinnamon

but leave the lemon to float in the wine. Alternatively ladle the mull straight into glasses from the pan.
Makes 12–16 glasses

Non-alcoholic fruit cup

Consideration on the part of the hostess means having at least one non-alcoholic drink among the others at a party. This fruit cup looks pretty served in a tall glass jug and it tastes good too.

2 lemons
100 g/4 oz castor sugar
6 dl/1 pint boiling water

1 539-ml/19-fl oz can orange juice
6 dl/1 pint ginger ale or ginger beer
slices of orange

Wash the lemons, halve, squeeze out the juice and reserve it. Put the lemon halves in a bowl, add the sugar and the boiling water. Stir to dissolve the sugar and set aside until quite cold.

Strain into a tall jug. Add the reserved lemon juice and the orange juice. Chill until ready to serve. Then stir in the ginger ale or beer and add a few orange slices to garnish.
Serves 10–12

Coffee-making

Good coffee is something everybody should be able to make. The two simple methods of preparing coffee are to use either jug or saucepan.

To make coffee in a jug Select an earthenware, china or enamel jug. Heat it thoroughly with boiling water, pour this away and put in 2 heaped tablespoons (40 g, 1½ oz) coffee for each 6 dl (1 pint) water. Have the water briskly but freshly boiling and pour it at once on to the grounds. Stir well, then cover and leave the coffee to infuse for 4 minutes. Pass a cold spoon through the top of the coffee to settle the grounds. Then strain through a nylon (never metal) strainer into a hot jug.

To make coffee in a saucepan Bring the required amount of water to a brisk boil in an enamel or stainless steel saucepan. Stir in the measured coffee. Leave over gentle heat until the coffee rises up in the pan, then draw off the heat. Cover and leave to infuse for 4 minutes. When infused, strain through a nylon sieve into a heated coffee pot and serve.

Generally speaking, coffee with a mild character and a light roast is best for breakfast, whereas a medium roast giving a slightly stronger coffee is a good choice for mid-morning. For after dinner, coffee with a strong character and a dark or continental roast would be the one to serve.

The fineness of the grounds depends on the method used for making the coffee. For the jug or saucepan method use a coarse or medium ground; finely ground coffee is difficult to strain. For percolators a medium-ground coffee is recommended and for the filter type of coffee maker a fine-ground coffee should be used.

Using the freezer in December

It's never too soon to start planning ahead. Your freezer makes it possible to reduce the last-minute food preparation for Christmas. For most families Christmas means a turkey. If this is the case buy a frozen oven-ready bird, the size you want, well before Christmas.

When planning your work timetable remember that large birds take some time to thaw completely and turkeys must be completely thawed before cooking. Leave the bird in its polythene bag in a cold larder and allow to thaw slowly. Remove the giblets as soon as the bird becomes pliable. Up to 5.5 kg (12 lb) a turkey requires 30 hours to thaw, for a 5.5- to 8-kg (12- to 18-lb) bird allow 48 hours. Prepare and freeze stuffings with sausagemeat or bacon not more than 2 weeks in advance; those using breadcrumbs or chestnuts can be made up to 4 weeks in advance. Trim and roll up bacon rashers, impale on skewers and freeze with the sausages – about a week beforehand.

Early in December weigh and prepare the vegetables you will require. Peel and cut up potatoes for roasting; blanch in boiling water for 5 minutes then drain, cool and freeze in polythene bags. For a change croquette or duchesse potatoes can be prepared ready for cooking. Freeze uncovered until firm then pack in polythene or rigid containers. *Red cabbage with apple* (see page 269) goes very well with turkey, and can be served instead of one of the traditional green vegetables. It can be reheated in the oven, saving space on the cooker top. About a week in advance you can prepare Brussels sprouts and pack without blanching – for short-term storage blanching is not necessary.

Make *mince pies* (see page 332) and freeze unbaked. The best method is to mould them in the mince pie tins. Set unbaked in the freezer, uncovered, until firm, then remove from the tins and repack in boxes or polythene bags for storage. To serve, simply take out the number of pies required and replace in the original tins. Allow to thaw for 1–2 hours or overnight in the refrigerator and bake as usual. Store not more than 1 month. Make *brandy butter* (see page 331), spoon into a covered container or box and freeze. Thaw later in the refrigerator.

Short-term storage can be given to recipes like *hare pâté* (see page 313) and *moussaka* (see page 318) prepared in advance for party entertaining. Freeze in a foil container with a lid to seal airtight. Grapefruit segments can be cut and frozen in polythene boxes with sugar. Use for fruit salads or as a first course.

Freezing leftovers to serve another day

When you have carved enough turkey meat for the Christmas meal, allow the bird to become quite cold, then carve the surplus meat as soon as possible. Interleave large slices of meat with thin polythene or waxed paper and overwrap in foil. Cut small pieces of meat into cubes and slivers ready to use later for pancake fillings, fricassées and risotto. Tiny scraps can be chopped for filling sandwiches or vol-au-vent cases.

Seasonal charts

Seasonal vegetable chart

Many vegetables, such as potatoes and carrots, are available from one source or another all the year round. The seasonal vegetables are those which can add variety to your menus so use them as much as possible.

	Jan	Feb	Mar	Apr	May	June	July	Aug	Sept	Oct	Nov	Dec	
Artichoke, globe	✱		✱	✱	✱	✱							Boil, then serve with melted butter for a starter.
Artichoke, Jerusalem		✱	✱								✱	✱	Blanch and roast around the joint. Make a delicious soup. Dip in batter and deep-fry. Boil and pour over well-seasoned white sauce.
Asparagus					✱	✱							Serve hot with melted butter or cold with oil and vinegar dressing. Excellent for first courses. Cut up and use in a quiche for a supper dish.
Beans, broad						✱	✱	✱					Short season, serve tender young beans. Pod beans and cook; serve in melted butter.
Beans, French						✱	✱	✱	✱				Top and tail, cook lightly, and serve with melted butter.

Vegetable	Serving suggestions
Beans, runner	Slice, boil, serve with melted butter. Salt or freeze young beans for later in the year.
Broccoli	One of the nicest vegetables; serve with melted butter or hollandaise sauce.
Celery	Serve crisp raw celery with cheese after a meal. Celery hearts can be braised. Make soup and serve sprinkled with cheese.
Chicory	Use fresh in salads. Boil, then wrap in ham slices and serve with cheese sauce. Boil, cool, then flour and fry in butter.
Corn on the cob	Short season; serve plain boiled with melted butter and salt.
Courgettes	Slice, blanch, and fry in butter with parsley and garlic added. Use with other vegetables in casseroles. Make soup, serve cold.
Leeks	Use leeks a lot – shredded in salad; in soups and casseroles; poached and served in white sauce; cold with oil and vinegar dressing.
Marrow	Make soup. Stuff and bake it. Blanch and cook in a casserole with butter; pour over well-seasoned white sauce.

341

	Jan	Feb	Mar	Apr	May	June	July	Aug	Sept	Oct	Nov	Dec	
Parsnips	★	★	★	★					★	★	★	★	Parboil and roast round a joint. Boil and serve with melted butter. Add to stews.
Peas, garden						★	★	★					Serve with mint; cook with lettuce and spring onions and serve à la française.
Red cabbage										★	★	★	Serve shredded raw in salads. Excellent cooked slowly in a casserole with onions and plenty of apples; serve with rich foods – pork, goose, duck, or gammon.
Spinach			★	★	★	★	★	★	★	★	★	★	Use as vegetable or for soup. Use to fill quiche with cottage cheese; serve with eggs.
Sprouts, Brussels	★	★	★							★	★	★	Serve plain boiled with butter or with chestnuts. Towards end of season 'blown' varieties can be puréed, or made into soup.

Oranges and apples can be bought throughout the year. Seasonal fruits can add more variety and interest to your cooking, so make good use of them.

	Jan	Feb	Mar	Apr	May	June	July	Aug	Sept	Oct	Nov	Dec	
Apricots					✱	✱	✱						The first apricots in are firm and hard. Bake them in a slow oven with brown sugar and honey, serve with cream. Serve stewed with ice cream; use in tarts, pies, crumble.
Blackberries								✱	✱	✱			Use in mousse or pie with apples. Make blackberry fool or blackberry sauce.
Cherries						✱	✱						Best served fresh for dessert. Use in pies or fruit salad.
Cranberries	✱										✱	✱	Use for sauces or stuffings; also make marvellous pies.
Currants, red, black						✱	✱	✱					Blackcurrants freeze well. Make into pies or use in summer compote or summer pudding. Both types make good ice cream.
Damsons									✱	✱			Serve stewed with cream. Use for pies or crumble. Pickle for use with cold meats.

	Jan	Feb	Mar	Apr	May	June	July	Aug	Sept	Oct	Nov	Dec	
Gooseberries					★	★	★						First in are the hard green ones; use for jams and jellies, gooseberry pie, crumble, mousse, or cobbler. Later dessert varieties can be served raw.
Greengages							★	★					Short season. Stew or bake with brown sugar and lemon juice, serve hot or cold with ice cream.
Loganberries							★						Very short season. Serve fresh with sugar and cream.
Peaches								★	★				Serve fresh with cream, or skinned and sliced in sugar syrup with brandy added. Pickle peaches for Christmas.
Pears								★	★	★	★	★	Picked in autumn and sold from store through to the beginning of the year when imported varieties take over. Serve fresh with Camembert cheese; poached with lemon; cooked in red wine; hot with sugar and cream; in open flans; in fruit salad.
Plums								★	★				Bottle or freeze plums for later in the year. Serve in plum pie, cobbler, crumble, fruit salad.

Fruit										Notes
Raspberries				★	★	★				Serve fresh with sugar and cream. Use for pies, summer fruit compote, fruit salad. They freeze well.
Rhubarb	★	★	★	★	★					Delicate pink sticks of forced rhubarb appear early in the year. By April garden rhubarb appears. Use both in pies and crumble, or stew with orange juice added.
Strawberries					★	★				Serve fresh with sugar and orange juice or cream. Add to fruit salad or hot fruit compote. Serve in raspberry purée; make sauce for ice cream.

Seasonal poultry and game chart

	Jan	Feb	Mar	Apr	May	June	July	Aug	Sept	Oct	Nov	Dec	
Chicken	★	★	★	★	★	★	★	★	★	★	★	★	Poussins are best from March to July. Roast whole birds. Oven-bake chicken joints with tarragon and serve in cream sauce or casserole in barbecue sauce. Grill or fry young birds particularly spring chickens and very small poussins when they are nice served with almonds.
Duck	★	★	★	★	★	★	★	★	★	★	★	★	Young duckling best from March to July. Flesh is rich so serve with apple sauce, orange salad or red cabbage with apple. Boned and stuffed birds are excellent for parties. Use duck flesh for pâté too.
Goose	★	★	★							★	★	★	Roast goose is good with apple and prune or raisin stuffing, or stuffed with chestnuts. Good cold with Cumberland sauce.
Rabbit	★	★								★	★	★	Tame rabbit has tender flesh rather like chicken. Use in casseroles; especially good with prunes added. Flesh also good in pâté.

	C1	C2	C3	C4	C5	C6	C7	C8	C9	C10	C11	C12	Notes
Turkey	★	★							★	★	★	★	Makes a good cold roast for a buffet party. Try with a lemon and parsley stuffing. Sliced fresh turkey breasts can be egg-and-breadcrumbed and fried. Use cold cooked turkey in mousses.
Grouse	★	★	★	★	★								Roast young birds. Older ones can be casseroled.
Hare	★	★	★	★							★		Joints can be casseroled traditionally in red wine but also nice in beer with prunes. Use haremeat for pâté. Roast the saddle when it is delicious with soured cream stirred into the gravy.
Partridge	★	★	★	★								★	For a gourmet dish serve roast partridge with hot wild rice. Braise or casserole older birds.
Pheasant	★	★	★									★	Roast. Older birds are best casseroled when they are good with apples and cream. Pheasant also makes good pâté.

	Jan	Feb	Mar	Apr	May	June	July	Aug	Sept	Oct	Nov	Dec	
Wild duck	✱	✱							✱	✱	✱	✱	To remove fishy flavour put hot water, salt and sliced onion in a pan. Baste the birds with this for some minutes while in oven. Then pour liquid away and roast in usual way. Serve with orange salad. Casserole older birds – good with wine and olives.
Venison							✱	✱	✱	✱	✱	✱	Roast, when delicious served with quince or rowan jelly. Braise joints, which are good with poivrade sauce, or it can be casseroled. Use venison in pâté too.

Seasonal fish chart

Most fish can be bought all year round but there are some months when they are of better quality and more plentiful than others and it is these that are shown.

	Jan	Feb	Mar	Apr	May	June	July	Aug	Sept	Oct	Nov	Dec	
Brill				★	★	★	★	★					A flat fish like turbot but smaller in size. Poach whole in a court bouillon and serve like turbot. Or cook fillets according to your favourite recipe for sole.
Carp	★	★	★			★	★	★	★	★	★	★	Soak in salt water before cooking. Then poach in court bouillon and serve with horseradish sauce. Or stuff and bake.
Cod										★	★	★	Bake steaks of cod with parsley and lemon stuffing, or coat pieces of cod fillets in batter and deep-fry. Use cooked flesh in made-up dishes like fish pie.
Crab					★	★	★	★					Fresh cooked crab is delicious in salads or sandwiches. Crab meat also makes a delicious quiche for supper parties.
Crayfish				★	★	★	★	★	★				Flesh similar to lobster but crayfish have no claws. Serve cooked and cold for salads.

	Jan	Feb	Mar	Apr	May	June	July	Aug	Sept	Oct	Nov	Dec	
Dab									★	★			A small fish which is ideal for cooking whole. Very good grilled with parsley butter. Treat as plaice.
Haddock	★	★			★	★	★	★	★	★	★	★	Poach or grill cutlets. Or poach haddock fillet and serve with butter sauce. Use cooked flesh in made-up dishes. Smoked haddock makes delicious soup, kedgeree and lovely cold mousse.
Hake	★	★	★				★	★	★	★	★	★	Grill cutlets and serve with cheese topping. Or poach fillets and serve with anchovy sauce. Use flesh in made-up dishes. Treat like cod.
Halibut	★	★	★				★	★	★	★	★	★	Grill steaks and serve with butter or poach steaks and serve with beurre blanc sauce. Has firm flesh which is very good cold – delicious with mayonnaise or in salads.
Herring	★	★	★		★	★	★	★	★	★	★	★	Grill with mustard butter inside. Or bone and coat with oatmeal before frying. Also very nice soused to make roll-mops for summer salad suppers.

										Notes
Lobster			★	★	★	★	★	★			Delicious flesh, use cooked and cold in salads. Also excellent with curry mayonnaise. Or hot in Newburg sauce or for Lobster Thermidor.
Mackerel						★	★	★			Whole mackerel can be grilled. Also good poached in wine and served cold. Mackerel fillets can be fried and then served with gooseberry sauce. Also good soused.
Mullet			★	★	★	★	★				Red mullet is plentiful in summer – grill or bake in butter paper envelopes. Grey mullet is best in autumn – can be grilled or stuffed and baked.
Mussels	★	★	★	★					★	★	Best in winter months. Steam and serve with wine sauce or stuff open shells with garlic butter and serve hot. Also lovely for soups. Excellent egg-and-breadcrumbed, deep-fried and served with tartare sauce.
Oysters	★	★	★	★				★	★	★	Eat raw with lemon and brown bread and butter. Can also be egg-and-breadcrumbed and shallow-fried.
Pike	★	★	★	★	★				★	★	Can be stuffed and baked whole or cut in steaks and grilled or fried. Cooked flesh is used as ingredient for quenelles.

	Jan	Feb	Mar	Apr	May	June	July	Aug	Sept	Oct	Nov	Dec	
Plaice	★	★	★	★	★	★	★	★	★	★	★	★	Egg-and-breadcrumb fillets and fry in butter. Or poach in wine and serve in sauce.
Salmon		★	★	★	★	★	★	★					Bake large cuts wrapped in buttered foil or poach in court bouillon and serve hot with hollandaise sauce. Also good cold with mayonnaise. Use cooked salmon pieces in potted salmon or in salmon quiche.
Salmon trout			★	★	★	★	★	★					Also called seatrout. Small fish can be grilled. Bake larger ones wrapped in buttered foil. Serve hot or cold with mayonnaise.
Scallops	★	★	★								★	★	Poach in wine and serve in sauce using shells as containers. Can also be egg-and-breadcrumbed and fried, when they are good with chilled anchovy butter.
Skate	★	★	★							★	★	★	Poach pieces in court bouillon and serve with capers or black butter. Skate has firm flesh that is also delicious in cold salads.
Sole	★	★	★		★	★	★	★	★	★	★	★	Grill whole fish on the bone and serve with parsley butter. Fillets can be fried 'meunière' or poached and served with various sauces. Cut into small pieces, sole is delicious egg-and-breadcrumbed and fried for 'goujons'.

Fish										
Sprats	★	★						★	★	Nice deep-fried. Can also be grilled.
Trout		★	★	★	★	★	★			Flour whole fish and fry in butter and serve with browned almonds. Or poach in wine with tarragon and serve in cream sauce. If very fresh, trout can be poached and served 'au bleu'.
Turbot			★	★	★	★	★			Very delicious white flesh. Grill or fry turbot steaks. Or poach and serve with hollandaise sauce.
Whitebait				★	★	★	★			Flour and deep-fry. Serve with lemon and brown bread and butter.

Index